User Studies for Digital Library Development

User Studies for Digital Library Development

Edited by

Milena Dobreva, Andy O'Dwyer
and Pierluigi Feliciati

facet publishing

Published by Facet Publishing,
7 Ridgmount Street, London WC1E 7AE
www.facetpublishing.co.uk

Facet Publishing is wholly owned by CILIP: the Chartered Institute of Library and Information Professionals.

British Library Cataloguing in Publication Data
A catalogue record for this book is available from the British Library.

ISBN 978-1-85604-765-4
First published 2012

Mixed Sources
Product group from well-managed forests and other controlled sources
www.fsc.org Cert no. SA-COC-1565
© 1996 Forest Stewardship Council

Text printed on FSC accredited material.

Typeset from editors' files in 10/14pt Palatino and Frutiger by Flagholme Publishing Services.
Printed and made in Great Britain by MPG Books Group, UK.

Contents

Preface

Once upon a time the behaviour of people in relation to information involved a highly complex and interacting set of possible information sources. Studies dealt with how students searched library shelves, how people searched card catalogues, how abstracting services were used and how journals were purchased, how offprints were collected, stored and used and a myriad other phenomena. The academic scholar had to find time in his or her schedule (easier then than now!) to work in the library, scanning the latest issues of a core set of journals, identifying papers of interest, photocopying them, or recording the details on 5" x 3" cards or, in my case for a few years, edge-notched cards. In fields outside academia, the process appeared to be less systematic: there was considerable reliance upon the knowledge of work colleagues and on organizational documentation and procedure manuals. Many organizations lacked any form of information service and those working in the organization were very much on their own in trying to find information of relevance to their work, to the development of a new product or to marketing in a new area or exporting to a new country. Banks, chambers of commerce, public reference libraries and company legal advisers were the routes to information, and the process of finding exactly what one needed was time consuming and often frustrating. Writing about this now feels almost like trying to recall the neolithic era of information management!

It is quite amazing how much has changed in such a relatively short space of time, although anyone under the age of about 40 is unlikely to have much recollection of the earlier situation. The emergence of the digital world has been more gradual than many suppose, beginning with the early work on computer-based information retrieval in the 1960s and the emergence of online databases such as Dialog and MEDLINE in the 1970s – the 'internet revolution' did not begin in 1993 with the development of the Mosaic browser, but it certainly received a significant push. Since then, the growth of the world wide web has been staggering: in 1995, according to Internet

World Statistics, there were 16 million users, representing 0.4% of the world's population; by December 2011 there were 2,267 million users, or almost one third of the world's population.

This growth has had its impact on human information behaviour: today, for most academic work and for the greater part of organizational work in business and industry, information is digital. In many companies, for example, the 'special library' has disappeared, its functions replaced by information systems, with the former library staff employed to man helpdesks and to assist in the organization and maintenance of the corporate intranet.

The term 'digital library' now signifies almost any collection of digital documents of one kind or another. We have 'born digital' texts in the form of word-processed documents and spreadsheets in business organizations, collections of which are regarded as 'digital libraries'; collections of images of manuscripts – 'digital libraries'; collections of images of art objects – 'digital libraries'; and so on, and on. The world of digital libraries is as diverse as the world of physical libraries, perhaps even more so.

This diversity and the very nature of digital collections raises challenges for the exploration of human information behaviour; challenges that motivated the editors and that are addressed by the contributors to this volume. The editors note that they wished to achieve 'a book which would present this area in a more holistic manner, thus helping readers to make more informed decisions about user-related issues in the digital library context'.

They seek to achieve this goal by combining theoretical studies with case-based investigations. Thus, Elaine Toms presents an interesting review of models of information behaviour in the context of digital libraries, and Giannis Tsakonas explores the differences between user behaviour studies and the evaluation of digital libraries. Toms concludes that perhaps we have too many models of behaviour and not enough research that leads to system design: a conclusion with which I would concur. Tsakonas, as one might expect, finds the user in all aspects of digital library design, development and evaluation, but notes that other factors than user satisfaction enter into the evaluation process – there are, for example, significant technological issues to be dealt with.

These theoretical papers – and, of course, there are more – are followed by a set of chapters dealing with research methods. Here, the focus of my interest is on the new techniques that arise out of the very nature of the digital library, such as log analysis and eye tracking, both of which offer the means to explore behaviour at what we might call the micro-level. Panos Balatsoukas deals with eye tracking, which is essentially about the user's interaction with the screen display and is clearly concerned with usability. Eye-tracking studies are less about the digital objects in the library collection and more about the means devised to access those objects from the screen display. Deep log analysis is covered by David Nicholas and David Clark: they note that this mode of analysis records what people actually do in using a digital library site, and does so in an unobtrusive fashion, 'without bothering the user one bit'. Given the information user's increasing dislike of intrusive research methods, especially questionnaires, this is a great advantage. The authors, however, also point out the disadvantages of the technique, including the vast amount of data produced, the difficulty of interpreting the data and the difficulty of identifying individual users – although, from a privacy perspective, this might be considered an advantage!

The case studies explore different research methods in the context of different digital domains and Susan Hazan, writing on museums, raises the interesting question 'So where has the wonder gone; and how can online environments possibly deliver the aura of the original object and replace the embodied physical experience of the encounter with the real object in the gallery?'.

She notes that this mirrors the debate over 'real' books and e-books, and I can't imagine a time when all we have are e-museums. Physical museums have undergone an amazing transformation in recent years, with exhibits one can touch, games for children involving the exhibits and so forth. Some of this is transformable into the digital world, but not everything.

The editors of this collection have set themselves a challenging task and I think that they have largely accomplished it. The chapters presented here will enable anyone interested in 'user studies' in the digital world to get a grasp of the research issues and appropriate research methods enabling them either to embark upon an investigation or, at the very least, understand the products of research.

T. D. Wilson
Visiting Professor, University of Borås, Sweden

Acknowledgements

This book is quite a complex project in terms of scope and number of contributors. We would like to particularly thank all authors for their enthusiasm and commitment.

We would like also to thank all our colleagues, who were supportive of our work and thus helped to develop our competences on the topic. Multiple projects in which we took part provided rich and diverse experiences – the list would be too long to appear here but, nevertheless, working with different stakeholders – JISC, EDL Foundation, the European Commission, the Scottish Funding Council, AIB and with users of different kinds: intermediaries, end-users, school children, professionals from different communities – helped us to appreciate the complexity of various points of view on user studies.

Three recent events – EVA 2010 in Jerusalem; the 6th International Conference of the South-Eastern European Digitisation Initiative (SEEDI 2011) held in Zagreb in May 2011; and ELAG 2011 in Prague in May 2011 – all of which invited us to deliver workshops on user studies, were very helpful and reassuring on the timeliness of this book. Targeted at different professional communities, these events showed how huge is the interest in this topic across the information sectors.

We would also like to thank the team at Facet, especially Helen Carley and Sarah Busby, for their guidance and outstanding support.

Spending time on putting the book together meant a lot of support from the people closest to us. Milena would like to particularly thank Emilia, Tatiana-Alexandra and Ian.

Milena, Andy and Pierluigi

Abbreviations

5S	Streams, Structures, Spaces, Scenarios, Societies
AoI	areas of interest
API	Application Programming Interface
App	application
AXSNet	Archival eXcellence in Information Seeking Studies Network
BBC	British Broadcasting Corporation
CASPAR	Cultural Artistic and Scientific knowledge for Preservation, Access and Retrieval
CASSM	Concept-based Analysis of Surface and Structural Misfits
CC0	Creative Commons Zero
CCDS	Consultative Committee for Space Data Systems
CDLR	Centre for Digital Library Research at University of Strathclyde
CERIF	Common European Research Information Format
CeRLIM	Centre for Research in Libraries, Information and Media, Manchester Metropolitan University
CIBER	Centre for Information Behaviour and the Evaluation of Research
CILIP	Chartered Institute of Library and Information Professionals
CLIR	Cross-Language Information Retrieval
CMYK	Cyan, Magenta, Yellow, blacK
DAFFODIL	Distributed Agents for User-Friendly Access of Digital Libraries
DEA	Data Exchange Agreement
DEVise	Data Exploration and Visualization
DiSCmap	Digitisation in Special Collections: mapping, assessment and prioritisation
DL	Digital Library

DLRM	Digital Library Reference Model
DP	digital preservation
DVD	digital versatile disc
DWE	Digital Work Environment
EBLIP	Evidence Based Library and Information Practice
EC	European Commission
EIAO	European Internet Accessibility Observatory
E-LIS	e-prints in library and information science
EU	European Union
FE	front end
GIS	Geographical Information System
GPS	Global Positioning System
HATII	Humanities Advanced Technology & Information Institute, University of Glasgow
HCI	human–computer interaction
HEI	UK Higher Education Institution
ICA	International Council on Archives
IFLA	International Federation of Library Associations
IMI-BAS	Institute of Mathematics and Informatics – Bulgarian Academy of Science
IP	Internet Protocol
IPR	intellectual property rights
IR	information retrieval
ISBN	International Standard Bibliographic Number
ISSN	International Standard Serials Number
ISP	Internet Service Provider
IT	information technology
ITF	Interaction Triptych Framework
JISC	Joint Information Systems Committee
KEEP	Keeping Emulation Environments Portable
LIS	library and information science
LOC	Library of Congress
MARC	MAchine Readable Cataloging
MINERVA	Ministerial Network for Valorising Activities in Digitisation
MLIA	Multi-Lingual Information Access
MLIR	Multi-Lingual Information Retrieval
NE	Normative Evaluation
NLA	National Library of Australia

OAI	Open Archives Initiative
OAIS	Open Archival Information Systems Reference Model
OCLC	Online Computer Library Centre
OCRIS	Online Catalogue and Repository Interoperability Study
OER	Open Educational Resources
OPAC	Online Public Access Catalogue
OS	operating system
PATHS	Personalised Access to Cultural Heritage Spaces
PC	personal computer
PLANETS	Preservation and Long-term Access through Networked Services
POCOS	Preservation Of Complex Objects Symposia
PPOC	Prints and Photographs Online Catalog
PSQG	Public Service Quality Group
RCAHMS	Royal Commission on the Ancient and Historical Monuments of Scotland
RDF	Resource Description Framework
REVEAL THIS	REtrieval of VidEo And Language for The Home user in an Information Society
RIN	Research Information Network
SAM	Self Assessment Manikin
SCONUL	Society of College, National and University Libraries
SE	summative evaluation
SHAMAN	Sustaining Heritage Access through Multivalent ArchiviNg
TEL	The European Library
TIME	Task, Information model, Manipulation of materials, Ergonomics
UCL	University College London
UK	United Kingdom
UNESCO	United Nations Educational, Scientific and Cultural Organization
URL	Uniform Resource Locator
UTS	University of Technology, Sydney (Australia)
UX	User eXperience
VLE	Virtual Learning Environment
W3C	World Wide Web Consortium
ZVDD	Zentrales Verzeichnis Digitalisierter Drucke

Glossary

5S model – a formal framework which explores the content and functionality of a digital library defining five conceptual building blocks: Streams, Structures, Spaces, Scenarios, and Societies.

Accessibility – the degree to which a product, device, service or environment is available to as many people as possible. For digital environments, it is also the capability of computer systems to supply services and to provide information that can be availed of, without discrimination, by those who need assistive technologies or special configurations because of some disability.

Actor – an entity in software or system design (either real or notional and either a system component or a human being) represented graphically (usually through use of a modelling language) in high-level documents and deployed symbolically in imagined usage scenarios and use cases to aid understanding of user roles, requirements and needs during design, testing and potentially evaluation. See also **usage scenario** and **use case**.

Archival intelligence – 1) knowledge of archival theory, practices and procedures; 2) strategies for reducing uncertainty and ambiguity when unstructured problems and ill-defined solutions are the norm; 3) intellective skills, or the ability to understand the connection between representations of documents, activities and processes and the actual object or process being represented.

Artefactual literacy – the practice of criticism and analysis that reads texts as objects and objects as texts.

Berrypicking – a metaphor to represent how users search for information. A person constantly changes his/her search terms in response to the results returned from the information retrieval system. See also **information-seeking behaviour**.

Bit-stream preservation – preservation of the bit stream (the basic sequences of binary digits) that comprises a digital resource. See also **digital preservation**.

Bottom-up – a design philosophy common in software and system design. An approach to a problem that begins with a detailed analysis and definition of low-level units or sub-systems, progressing upwards to the highest conceptual level and incorporating those smaller units into an over-arching framework or top-level system. See also **top-down**.

Business model – the rationale of how an organization creates, delivers and captures value.

CC0 – the most open tool that Creative Commons offers, where the rights holder permanently hands over all copyright and (if applicable) database rights to descriptive metadata, granting the data public domain status. See also **Creative Commons**.

Cognitive load – the increase in the processing ability of the working memory that takes place during problem solving and decision making.

Common European Research Information Format (CERIF) – an EU Recommendation to member states intended to facilitate data exchange and the resolution of schema differences between heterogeneous distributed databases.

Creative Commons – a suite of licences designed to encourage sharing and reuse of digital materials. Licences may allow reuse or reuse with remixing, they may allow or prohibit reusing material for commercial purposes and sometimes they stipulate that any derived must be shared on a 'Share-Alike' basis and thus licensed for remix.

Cyber-bullying – the process of bullying online; it may manifest in different ways, such as flaming (the sending of large numbers of targeted abusive e-mails), attempts to damage reputation (through comments, through tagging of an individual in inappropriate content or images), etc.

Data migration – moving data from one system into another (which often involves converting from one format into another) – usually as part of a long-term preservation strategy. This helps to ensure that data remains intelligible by locating it within up-to-date system environments. Changes to technology or standards can be accommodated and reflected through successful migration as opposed to modifying the environment (system) in which the data is stored. See also **bit-stream preservation**.

Digital Library Reference Model – conceptual model developed by

DELOS network of excellence exploring six major concepts within the digital library universe: Content, Functionality, User, Architecture, Policy and Quality.

Digital preservation – the act of ensuring that digital items are kept intact, intelligible (to machine and/or human users) and usable over the long term. See also **bit-stream preservation**.

Digital preservation community – an identified group of potential consumers who should be able to understand a particular set of preserved information.

Distributed ingest – method whereby ingest processes are handled by a decentralized set of interacting computer systems; for example, a network or grid of machines. Generally used when large datasets are to be ingested. See also **ingest**.

Dublin Core – a metadata format standard (ISO 15836, NISO Standard Z39.85-2007) that defines metadata elements used to describe and provide access to online materials.

Empirical study – the process of developing systematized knowledge gained from observations that are formulated to support insights and generalizations about the phenomena under study.

Ergonomics – the study of designing equipment and devices that fit the human body, its movements and its cognitive abilities.

Eye tracking – the process of recording and analysing human eye movement behaviour in order to investigate the mechanisms that underpin the operation of the human mind when a decision to look at any point is made.

Faceted search – a search that may be explored through multiple routes or facets. For instance, the ability to browse around the author, publication year, keyword, subject heading or similar from any given catalogue record. Many catalogues enable faceted search or discovery through visual metaphors – a map of keywords related to the currently viewed item, for instance.

Focus group – a group selected for its relevance to an evaluation and that is engaged by a trained facilitator in a series of discussions designed for sharing insights, ideas and observations on a topic of concern.

Fonds – the whole of the records, regardless of form or medium, organically created and/or accumulated and used by a particular person, family, or corporate body in the course of that creator's activities and functions (International Council on Archives, 2000).

Formative evaluation – evaluation methods used to determine how to improve an object (e.g. a system) while it is still being developed.

Gaze-plot – a graphical representation of a scan-path showing the order in which eye movements occurred in a specific area of interest.

Heat-map – a graphical representation of users' visual behaviour where the frequency and length of fixations are represented by the use of colours.

Human–computer interaction – the study, planning and design of the interaction between people (users) and computers.

Illustrative statistics – used to summarize data in a similar manner to descriptive statistics. Summarizing data in a graph can be more meaningful to the reader than merely reporting descriptive statistics in a table. In a graph the main features of the data and any patterns can be clearly seen. Illustrative statistics can also facilitate statistical judgement.

Information retrieval – the theories and techniques used for the retrieval of relevant information from large-scale databases, digital libraries or the web.

Information-seeking behaviour – human behaviour in relation to sources and channels of information, including both active and passive information-seeking, and information use, or the micro-level of behaviour employed by the searcher in interacting with information systems of all kinds, be it between the seeker and the system, or the pure method of creating and following up on a search.

Ingest – the OAIS entity that contains the services and functions which allow transfer of digital content into an archive for the purpose of long-term preservation; the term is also used to describe the process of submitting content for deposit into digital repositories.

Institutional repository – a software system (generally a database and user interface) used to store, manage and disseminate digital publications, other objects and their metadata. Mainly used by educational institutions or information-centred institutions such as publishers, government agencies or research groups.

Interaction Triptych Framework – a model focused on the interaction between the main constituents of a digital library, namely user, content and system. It proposed a user-centred evaluation model based on the users' views of the system and the content attributes as they interact with these constituents.

Interoperability – this refers to how well two or more systems work together to achieve a common goal: direct processing by one auto-mated system or sub-system, of data provided by another. This will usually be assisted by the use of standards and standard protocols.

MAchine-Readable Cataloguing (MARC) – standardized data formats (including UKMARC, UNIMARC, MARC21, MARCXML) for the representation and communication of bibliographic and related information in machine-readable form. MARC emerged from a Library of Congress-led initiative.

Meaningful usability – furthering the methods by which usability is addressed by closely considering how usability relates to goals, processes and ambitions, for example, task completion, ease of learning or the actual practices and workflows of an individual or organization.

Metadata – term used for two fundamentally different concepts: 'data about data' (descriptive metadata); and 'data about the containers of data' (structural and administrative metadata).

Metadata extraction – the processes (sometimes automated) whereby a computer system or program extracts bibliographic, descriptive or technical information (i.e. metadata) relating to, or embedded in, a digital object.

Multilevel description – archival descriptions that are related to one another in a part-to-whole relationship and that need complete identification of both the parts and the comprehensive whole in multiple descriptive records. Multilevel finding aids provide descriptions for fonds, or series, files and items. See also **fonds**.

Online Public Access Catalogue – generally the main library catalogue that may be searched or browsed online. In some cases the OPAC may be presented as part of an institutional or library website.

Open Archival Information Systems Reference Model – an international standard model defining the elements required for a long-term, persistent digital archive.

Open Archives Initiative Protocol for Metadata Harvesting – a protocol created to facilitate discovery of resources distributed in many repositories or locations.

Performance – in business, defined as the accomplishment of a given task measured against preset known standards of accuracy, completeness, cost, and speed. In the **Interaction Triptych Framework** performance is one of the evaluation metrics, corresponding to the interaction between system and content.

Persona – a fictional character with all the characteristics of a system or service user.

Preservation system – a system that manages the processes of digital preservation, ensuring that content is preserved and accessible (to varying extents) over the long term.

Rationalization biases – an attempt made by the researcher or a participant in order to explain or justify an observed behaviour. Often these attempts are biased by personal views or theories and do not necessarily describe the true meaning of the observed behaviour.

Real-time interaction – an interaction (e.g. performing some activity or taking a measurement) that takes place along a strictly sequential 'real-world' (and limited) time line.

Referring site – a website that provides a clickable means to allow visitors to access another site without manually typing a URL into a web browser.

Requirements capture – a standard part of most software and system design methodologies, this involves consultation with those commissioning and potentially using the entity being designed, to determine what they require and need to have in the system.

Saccades – rapid eye movements that take place between fixations and last no more than 100 milliseconds.

Scan-path – a map of participants' eye movements based on the collection of individual fixations and saccades.

Scenario – see **usage scenario**

Serendipity – the process of making unexpected discoveries by accident.

Smartboard – a hybrid of a projector, projector screen and virtual whiteboard (with pens that act like mouse pointers) that allows the display, interaction with and annotation of materials such as lecture notes, websites, etc.

Social informatics – a transdisciplinary field of study of the design, uses and consequences of information technologies that takes into account their interaction with institutional and cultural contexts.

Summative evaluation – the evaluation of a completed product or service that is already in use. See also **formative evaluation**.

Tag cloud – a visual technique to represent the tags used in a particular catalogue record, blog, website, or similar text.

Top-down – a design philosophy common in software and system design. A hierarchical approach that progresses from the modelling and conceptualization of a single, large basic unit (or an undetailed overview), progressing downwards to multiple, smaller sub-units, each of which becomes sequentially more detailed and refined until the entire specification is detailed enough to validate the model. See also **bottom-up**.

Triangulation – the use of multiple sources and methods to gather and compare similar information.

Usability – the extent to which an object, system or other item is easy to use for those working with it, in the field of **human–computer interaction**. See also **meaningful usability**.

Usage scenario – describes a real-world example of how one or more people or organizations interact with a system, detailing the steps, events and actions that occur during the interaction. Usage scenarios can be very detailed or reasonably high level, describing critical actions but not indicating how they are performed. Often a usage scenario incorporates or elaborates on a use case or set of use cases. See also **use case** and **actor**.

Use case – a short, high-level functional description of system requirements. A use case should consist of, at minimum, a verb and a noun and may include a subject or context if critical to understanding. A fully developed use case describes the steps involved in the completion of a use case by a user. See also **requirements capture**, **usage scenario** and **actor**.

Usefulness – the quality of having utility (in itself the measure of the happiness or satisfaction gained from a service) and, especially, practical worth or applicability. In the **Interaction Triptych Framework** it is one of the metrics categories, corresponding to the interaction between user and content.

User-centred design – a design philosophy and process in which the needs, wants and limitations of the end-users of a product are given extensive attention at each stage of the design process. User-centred design requires designers not only to analyse and foresee how users are likely to use a product, but also to test the validity of their assumptions with regard to user behaviour in real-world tests with actual users.

User community (or user group) – a community is a tight formation of members that share common ground in a variety of real or abstract areas. In OAIS model, a system must determine, either by itself or in conjunction with other parties, which communities should become the designated community (see **Open Archival Information Systems Reference Model**) and should therefore be able to understand the information provided. For a digital library, all users interacting with content are part of the user community.

User experience – how a person feels about using a product, system or service. User experience highlights the experiential, affective, meaningful and valuable aspects of human–computer interaction and product ownership, but it also includes a person's perceptions of the practical aspects such as utility, ease of use and efficiency of the system.

User interface – the system by which people (users) interact with a machine. The user interface includes hardware (physical) and software (logical) components.

User satisfaction – a user state determined by the influences of many factors, like the elements or characteristics of the system, the users or the task situation.

Widget – a tool allowing content from one website or data source to be embedded in another. Commonly used widgets include the Facebook 'Like' button or Flickr slideshow widgets.

CHAPTER 1

Introduction: user studies for digital library development

Milena Dobreva, Andy O'Dwyer
and Pierluigi Feliciati

Why did we put together this book?

We share a passion for understanding users in the digital library (DL) context and believe that user studies is an exciting area. In the last decade we have been involved in a wide range of user studies across the DL domain, exploiting various research methods to investigate fascinating and important topics with multiple focal points. Studying issues as diverse as individual information needs, the learning styles of people with specific disabilities, cross-sectoral user-driven priorities on a national scale, and user response to Europeana – the European Commission's showcase DL – we were faced with the challenge of choosing the most appropriate methods for overall study design, data gathering and analysis, and the presentation of our findings.

Is there a gap in user studies?

Although major reference models developed in the DL domain such as the Digital Library Reference Model (DLRM) (Athanasopoulos et al., 2010) and Streams, Structures, Spaces, Scenarios, Societies (5S) (Gonçalves et al., 2004) incorporate the concept of users, they explore this only from a certain perspective. In the case of DLRM, users are one of its six 'domain concepts', while in the 5S model they are viewed in relation to Scenarios and Societies; but in both cases they are positioned mostly as clusters or as simplified homogeneous groups. More work is needed on how exactly knowledge about different users and types of user can help the process of development of a DL. Adding clarity to our understanding of users within DL models could help to identify gaps in our knowledge and establish a new research agenda for the user studies domain. Do such gaps exist? Surprisingly, yes – if we take as an example the work on digitization across different information sectors. It is quite alarming that:

we are currently witnessing a paradox: major institutions from the cultural heritage sector clearly emphasize the place of user evaluation and feedback in digitization-related policies. But in reality, decisions about aspects of digitization that impact [on] users are frequently taken without direct user involvement.

(Dobreva et al., 2011)

An additional alarming fact is that not only are real people – the intended users of DLs – rarely consulted, but also they are not addressed in detail in state-of-the-art DL research. A recent study of research topics on DLs (Nguyen and Chowdhury, 2011) constructed a knowledge map of 15 core DL research topics and 210 subtopics, based on an analysis of the papers presented in 37 editions of three major first-tier international conferences. User studies appear with only four subtopics – user feedback evaluation, information needs, user models and user communities. Does this mean that we already know all about users?

Even the recent strategic outcome of the Comité des Sages – the EU reflection group making recommendations on bringing Europe's cultural heritage online – entitled *The New Renaissance*, mentions users mainly in the context of better accessibility. One expects to find more focus in a document entitled *The New Renaissance* on how the substantial work that continues to make Europe's cultural heritage available online changes the perspectives and involvement of real people – after all, a Renaissance is not a merely technological change but a change in human perception and participation. In this strategic document the most detailed recommendation relevant to users appears under the heading 'Technical issues' and is related to sustainability:

Research & Development initiatives with a strong reference to practical user needs have to be supported on national and European level to constantly monitor the technological environment and to enhance preservation solutions. In addition, further research into solutions for handling large volumes of dynamic data is necessary.

(The New Renaissance, 2011, 30)

Of course the needs of users in relation to preservation must be addressed; yet it is legitimate to ask how much we know about user issues related to the numerous other aspects of digital culture, and to DLs in particular. Or, to summarize, there are several burning questions related to users in the DL context:

- Why do the developers of resources for users often neglect to consult them during the development stages?
- Why do models in DLs not address in sufficient depth the concept of users and its interaction with other key concepts?
- Do users seem too predictable and obvious to be addressed properly?
- Why do technological issues still enjoy more attention than the human side of DLs? Are DLs now seen primarily as *only* about the technology?

User studies: myth and reality

These were questions that each of us – the editors of this volume – wished to see answered. As our professional paths started to cross more and more frequently, we started to discuss our personal experiences, and quickly realized that we would each have loved to be able to learn about this domain from a book – a book that would present this area in a more holistic manner, thus helping readers to make more informed decisions about user-related issues in the DL context. As nobody else seemed to be writing such a book, we decided that we would put it together, and we invited colleagues whom we knew for their excellent work in this domain to share their experiences in what we believe is the first book to focus on user studies for DL development.

We have taken great care to address multiple issues and to provide a rich set of case studies which both serve as reality checks and give the reader a practical feeling not just of what works but why and how. We hope also to have provided evidence to demolish several myths and misconceptions about the value of user studies:

- *'We know our users'* – in many cases people who start working on a specific DL are convinced that they know enough about their users already and do not need to bother with any further study. While this might seem somewhat justified in the 'brick' memory institutions (in relation to traditional offline services), it is certainly not true in the case of 'click' resources – where the user base is potentially very wide. Indeed, studying users is, we maintain, always essential in order to stay relevant to them and responsive.
- *'If we build it they will come'* – a philosophy that can be observed in projects in the digital domain where the major effort is directed towards digitization and/or online services, but without making sure that there will be an interest in the resource. Further, many such development

teams assume that providing 'good' and reliable content and functionality is the only realm aim – mirroring the gatekeeper thinking (this is the most valuable we have and we are ready to share it) and supply-driven logic.

- *'Users use similar devices and have similar abilities'* – in contrast with the funding motivations of the world wide web, developers of DLs sometimes neglect to ensure that all users should have access to content and services, regardless of any special information needs or disabilities and independently of the technology used and of the context in which they act; in that sense, accessibility seems to be a prerequisite for efficient DLs, and, even if we don't address the related issues in this book, we are convinced that this should not be forgotten.
- *'The Digital McDonald's'* – this is apparent when the developers of a resource believe that several standard options will meet the expectations and needs of any user – akin to choosing from the options on a unified menu. As any of us who are vegetarians or fans of world cuisine know, people are more complex than that!
- *'User studies is the same as evaluation'* – in fact, user studies and evaluation are different activities, and while evaluation can (and often does) involve users, users can be involved before a product is designed and during development.
- *'Quality means innovation'* is another common attitude when the effort of a project is primarily targeted to introducing the newest gadgets and technologies without really understanding how to support users better.

How to read this book

Our book has five major parts: the first sets up the general scene, the second looks at user study methods and their use, the third explores specific DL issues and the fourth highlights applications of user studies across the information sectors. The final part summarizes how user studies can be used in the DL projects lifecycle.

The chapters are self-contained and can be consulted on their own, but those readers who would like to form a deeper and consistent understanding on the area, issues and methods should try to read through the material sequentially. For readers who have been involved in user studies themselves, or have come across issues in this domain, starting with Part 1 will provide the necessary more general overview of where user studies in DL fit. However, for the novice reader, we would suggest starting with the chapters in Part 2 and then moving to Part 1, which taps into adjacent information science fields.

Readers will find that the styles of various chapters, contributed by 27 authors – from Australia, Canada, Denmark, Germany, Greece, Israel, Italy, the Netherlands, Switzerland, the UK and the USA – differ. Our aim has been to bring together points of view from different professional communities and, more particularly, of practitioners as well as of researchers, and we are particularly pleased to see that different voices can be 'heard' in our book. For a reader with only basic knowledge of the library and information sectors some chapters may seem overly specialized. However, as well as showing the depth and complexity of the domain, these chapters can usefully be returned to as the general reader develops their skills and experiences over time.

The first part of this collection, 'Setting the scene', presents the methodological underpinning of areas that help to contextualize user studies. Elaine Toms introduces the wider area of information behaviour studies and how such studies help better to address the users of DLs. Sudatta Chowdhury outlines an important trend of user-centric studies with examples from the DL domain. Petar Mihaylov looks at general design issues and how they can be accommodated better in DLs, while Giannis Tsakonas considers the convergences and differences between user studies and the evaluation of DLs in general.

Part 2, 'Methods explained and illustrated', presents specific methods for user studies as they are applied in the DL context. A traditional classification of user studies methods is into two groups – qualitative and quantitative. Qualitative methods are all methods which give a range of insights into users' opinions about a product (a DL in our case), while quantitative methods seek to provide quantifiable data – which, depending on the study methodology, might cover a complete user population (e.g. deep log analysis) or might be generalizable to a larger population (e.g. a questionnaire that sets up numbers of participants to be representative for a particular sample). Qualitative methods (focus groups, in-depth interviews, diary analysis and ethnographic studies) help to provide an idea of the perspective of the target user community; this is done most often through immersion in a particular task or situation. The immersion can be designed specifically for the study – in the case of focus groups, for example; but in some cases the researcher is observing normal daily activities – as in the case of ethnographic studies. Qualitative methods (depending on the skills of the researchers) can help to obtain very rich, detailed data about the participants' perspectives. While quantitative methods most typically help to answer 'how many?' questions, qualitative methods can be of great help to answer 'why?' questions.

Table 1.1 presents an overview of the existing methods according to the type of involvement of users and the size of user population. Some methods, like interviews, eye tracking, focus groups, ethnographic studies and questionnaires, involve users directly and there is some form of communication between the researcher and the users taking part in the study. Another group of methods are based on the analysis of the behaviour of users and do not necessarily involve the users – in some cases, such as deep log analysis, this indeed is impossible!

Summative methods are a relatively new development, but have a particular place in the DL domain. Their aim is either to suggest generalized models that represent users (such as personalization models, or personas), or to tap into expert knowledge about the user behaviours of large user communities, using the experts' predictions as to which user behaviours will be most typical in a particular situation.

Each chapter in this part of the book includes a case study of recent user study research – most studies reflect projects from the last 1–6 years. The range of methods that we address include focus groups and questionnaires, presented by Jillian Griffiths; expert evaluation, addressed by Claus-Peter Klas; deep log analysis, by David Nicholas and David Clark; eye-tracking studies, introduced by Panos Balatsoukas; and personas by Katja Guldbæk Rasmussen and Gitte Petersen.

Many of the case studies use mixed methods, i.e. they combine two or more methods as an instrument to gather a richer set of observations on different user-related viewpoints. The third part of the book, entitled 'User

Table 1.1 *User study methods*			
Method	Size of user population involved		
	Individual users	User samples (small to mid-size groups)	Entire population (huge groups)
Summative	Personalization and recommender models	Use scenarios and use cases ➲ Chapter 2	**Personas** ➲ Chapter 10 **Expert evaluation** ➲ Chapter 7
Indirect observation	Diaries Personal log analysis	Mid-size log analysis	**Deep log analysis** ➲ Chapter 8
Direct observation	**In-depth interview** ➲ Chapter 6 **Eye tracking** ➲ Chapter 9	**Focus groups** ➲ Chapter 6 Ethnographic studies	**Web questionnaires** ➲ Chapter 6

studies in the digital library universe: what else needs to be considered?' aims to provide the reader with a more detailed understanding of the range of issues that can be addressed by user studies in the DL domain. It addresses such issues as dealing with multilingual resources (presented by Paul Clough), studies of children – the future DL users (by Ian Ruthven, Monica Landoni and Andreas Lingnau), social media (by Jeffery Guin), digital preservation (by Kathleen Menzies and Duncan Birrell), the shift to mobile devices (by Lina Petrakieva), the specific issues in resource discovery for researchers working with special collections (by Zsuzsanna Varga), and the educational applications of social media (by Nicola Osborne).

Part 4, 'User studies across the cultural heritage sector', highlights how user studies are applied in different settings and makes a bridge of the 'brick' and 'click' issues in the context of different types of institutions; it looks at libraries (presented by Derek Law), archives (by Wendy Duff), museums (by Susan Hazan), audiovisual collections (by Andy O'Dwyer) and digitized art collections (by Leo Konstantelos). Harry Verwayen and Martijn Arnoldus then explore the new area of open metadata and what it actually means for cultural heritage institutions and aggregators who need to make new decisions on matters that have impact on the end-users.

The concluding summary chapter puts various elements together and gives an idea of what studies can be helpful at various stages of DL work, including front-end-user involvement, normative and summative evaluation and direct engagement.

Finally, the book refers to a wide range of sources. They cannot be considered as a complete bibliography of user-related research, but would be a good starting-point for any curious reader who would like to explore more on this topic.

What you will not find in this book

First of all, we should warn readers that this is not a handbook. Our final chapter provides some guidance on how to select an appropriate user-related method according to the aims of a particular study, but we do not provide step-by-step guidance or sample protocols for the different study types discussed – nor do we explain how to process data from different types of studies. Our aim was not to introduce methods from the social sciences domain such as questionnaires or focus groups in detail: rather than explaining different methodologies and their foundations, we focus on how these are used in relation to current DL practice.

Who contributed to the book

We were extremely happy to work with many authors who paved the way in this domain. They share not only theoretical thoughts; they have lived through all the pains of doing truly pioneering work. Putting a book together with 27 contributors is a great challenge, but our authors were extremely committed – to the extent that Lina Petrakieva, author of the chapter on mobile technologies, edited her whole chapter on a mobile phone!

Martijn Arnoldus specializes in the creative industries, particularly copyright and open content issues, and works for Knowledgeland in Amsterdam. He has been pivotal in the majority of Knowledgeland's projects on the creative economy since 2005. Martijn's current work is around creative industry policy and entrepreneurship, ranging from requests for strategic advice, to copyright problems, to business models for creative entrepreneurs. As a senior consultant on open content licences, Martijn is a member of the Creative Commons Netherlands project team. Martijn has a social geography background and before joining Knowledgeland he worked at the University of Amsterdam and the Technical University of Delft as a researcher.

Panos Balatsoukas is a researcher focused on information retrieval and the user-centred design and evaluation of information systems. He holds a PhD in Information Science and an MSc in Knowledge Management from Loughborough University, UK. His bachelor studies were also focused on Information Science and completed in the Department of Library Science and Information Systems of the Alexander Technological Institute of Thessaloniki, Greece. Recently, he completed two years of post-doctoral research in the Department of Computer and Information Sciences, University of Strathclyde in Glasgow.

Duncan Birrell was formerly a researcher at the Centre for Digital Library Research (CDLR) at the University of Strathclyde, UK, where he specialized in the user-led evaluation of DLs, digital archives and online cultural heritage resources for the arts and humanities. His research there included such projects as DiSCmap (Digitisation of Special Collections: mapping, assessment, prioritisation), funded by the Joint Information Systems Committee (JISC); the User and Functional Testing of *Europeana Version 1.0* and SHAMAN (Sustaining Heritage Access through Multivalent ArchiviNg). He currently works in the Cataloguing and Metadata department of Strathclyde University's Andersonian Library. He has research interests in user studies, academic and digital libraries, methodologies for the digital humanities and the future of archives.

Sudatta Chowdhury is a Lecturer at the University of Technology (UTS), Sydney. She got her MPhil degree from the University of Sheffield and her PhD from the University of Strathclyde, UK. She has been involved in teaching and research for more than a decade, and has worked in different parts of the world, including Africa, Singapore and the UK. Before joining UTS, she was involved in two UK Higher Education Academy projects and two European projects, RevealThis and SHAMAN. Her publication track record includes over 50 papers in peer-reviewed journals and international conferences and five books. Her research interests include information seeking and retrieval, especially in the context of the web, DLs and social networking.

David Clark has worked at the interface of publishing and computation for 40 years: as bookseller, data analyst, publisher, software developer and information manager. He has a PhD in Computer Science from the University of Warwick, UK. David is a director of CIBER Research Ltd and is the world's leading expert in deep log analysis and is currently analysing the logs of Europeana and many leading publishers.

Paul Clough is a Senior Lecturer in Information Retrieval (IR) in the Information School at the University of Sheffield, UK. He is an active member of the IR community and his research has studied areas such as multilingual information access, geographical IR, evaluation and image retrieval. He has written over 80 peer-reviewed conference and journal papers and is co-author of the book *Multilingual Information Access: from theory to practice*, published in 2012 by Springer.

Milena Dobreva is a Senior Lecturer in Library, Information and Archive Studies at the University of Malta. She was the principal investigator of EC, JISC and UNESCO funded projects in the areas of user experiences, digitization and digital preservation and is a regular project evaluator for the EC. In 1990–2007 she worked at the Bulgarian Academy of Sciences, where she earned her PhD in Informatics and served as the founding head of the first Digitisation Centre in Bulgaria. Milena was also a chair of the Bulgarian national committee of the UNESCO Memory of the World programme. In 2007–11 she worked for the University of Glasgow and the University of Strathclyde. Milena was awarded an honorary medal for her contribution to the development of the relationship between Bulgaria and UNESCO (2006) and an Academic Award for young researchers (Bulgarian Academy of Sciences, 1998).

Wendy M. Duff is a professor at the University of Toronto's School of

Information. She is currently the Director of the Digital Curation Institute and teaches archives and records management, with a focus on access to archival materials. She is a founding member of AXSNet, an evolving international team of researchers interested in facilitating access to primary materials. Her current research focuses on archival users, access to archival material, digital curation and the convergence of libraries, archives and museums.

Pierluigi Feliciati is currently the ICT and information systems co-ordinator and Senior Researcher on Information Science (ING-INF/05) at the University of Macerata, Italy. Previously he co-ordinated the National Archives information system within the Italian Ministry of Culture. He is an Assistant Professor of Information Science Applications to Cultural Heritage and Digital Humanities at the University of Macerata, and teaches regularly in the Digital Archives Management and Preservation Masters Programme and in the International Masters in Digital Libraries (DILL). His research interests, since his involvement in the MINERVA European working groups on cultural web quality, are focused on the quality of web applications, the management of cultural heritage digital repositories, and evaluation methods for DL users' behaviour and satisfaction. He was the technical co-ordinator of the Europeana Local Project for Italy, and he is a member of the board of AIDA – Italian Association for Advanced Documentation – and of the Scientific Board of the Italian Central Institute for Archives.

Jillian R. Griffiths is a qualified information professional with experience in the fields of information behaviour and user experience (UX) of information systems in various contexts. Jill initially joined the Centre for Research in Libraries, Information and Media, CeRLIM, at Manchester Metropolitan University, UK, in 2000, where she worked on a wide range of projects including, for example, The Publication and Dissemination Behaviour of Researchers and the Influence of Research Assessment (funded by RIN and JISC), DiSCmap (funded by RIN and JISC), DEvISE funded by the Library & Information Commission), the European Internet Accessibility Observatory, EIAO (EC funded) and user evaluations of the MOSAIC and PERTAINS demonstrator services. She became a Lecturer in Information Studies in 2009 and recently joined MDR Partners as Consultant for the EC-funded PATHS project.

Jeffery K. Guin has more than 15 years' experience in writing, branding, design and communications management. In 2001 he began working with the US National Park Service's preservation technology research centre. There he initiated one of the first strategic campaigns using social media in the field of cultural heritage. Since 2006, he has coached individuals and organizations in the use of social media technologies to create and grow vibrant communities that promote heritage resources. This effort has included development of his personal website, Voices of the Past, which was chosen by Alltop.com as a 'Best of the Best' blog in the social media category.

Katja Guldbæk Rasmussen is web usability consultant at The Royal Library in Copenhagen. She has worked with internet-based communication within the library sector since 1998 and since 2006 has increasingly focused on web usability and the usability of online information and communication. Katja has broad experience in usability test methods and has served as a testing consultant at both national and European levels.

Susan Hazan is Curator of New Media and Head of the Internet Office at the Israel Museum, Jerusalem (since 1992), identifying and implementing electronic architectures for the gallery, online and mobile platforms and outreach programmes. Her Masters and PhD at Goldsmiths College, University of London, in Media and Communications focused on electronic architectures in the contemporary museum. Susan has been recognized for her numerous publications on new media in education, art, museums and cultural heritage, and is currently investigating social networks, innovative platforms for disseminating the virtual museum, and DLs in the context of cultural heritage. Susan is a renowned visiting lecturer in the UK, Hong Kong and Israel.

Claus-Peter Klas has a doctorate in Computer Science from the University of Duisburg-Essen. In 2008 he became the chair of multimedia and internet applications at the FernUniversität (distance-teaching university) in Hagen, Germany. His research focuses on information retrieval, information systems, databases, DLs and long-term preservation architectures in GRID/Cloud environments. Claus-Peter has worked in several national and EC-funded projects, including EuroSearch (A Federation of European Search Engines) and Eurogatherer (Personalised Information Gathering System), DAFFODIL (Distributed Agents for User-Friendly Access of Digital Libraries), DELOS (Network of Excellence on Digital Libraries), and is currently involved in the projects European Film Gateway, SHAMAN and Smart Vortex. His track record includes around 40 publications.

Leo Konstantelos is a Research Fellow at the University of Portsmouth and the Principal Investigator for the POCOS (Preservation Of Complex Objects Symposia) project at HATII, University of Glasgow. At Portsmouth, Leo works on the KEEP (Keeping Emulation Environments Portable) project, where he investigates knowledge-base structures for emulation environments. At Glasgow, his research explores concepts relating to the preservation of complex objects, focusing primarily on the digital arts. Leo has previously worked for a number of UK- and EU-funded projects, including PLANETS, SHAMAN, IVES and the Digital Preservation Console. Leo has a BSc in Management of Tourism and Cultural Resources, an MSc in Information Technology and a PhD in Humanities Computing.

Monica Landoni has been a senior researcher at the faculty of Informatics at the University of Lugano in Switzerland since January 2007. She has been a Lecturer in the Department of Computer and Information Sciences, University of Strathclyde, Glasgow, since December 1997. She was awarded a PhD from the University of Strathclyde in November 1997 for her thesis 'The Visual Book System: a study of the use of visual rhetoric in the design of electronic books'. Previously, she was a Research Fellow at Strathclyde University and a Grant Holder at the Joint Research Centre, Ispra, Italy. Monica's research interests are in the broad areas of human–computer interaction, DLs and interactive information retrieval. In particular, she has been actively exploring how e-books should be designed and evaluated, by focusing on different readers and reading types. Monica has also been proposing and evaluating novel interfaces for interactive information retrieval systems including web IR.

Derek Law MA, DUniv, FCLIP, FIInfSc, FKC, FLA, FRSE is an Emeritus Professor; he is chair of the JISC Advance Board, has worked in several British universities and has published and spoken at conferences extensively. He is a regular project evaluator for the EU. Most of his work has been to do with the development of networked resources in higher education and the creation of national information policy. A committed internationalist, he has been involved in projects and research in over 40 countries. He was awarded the Barnard Prize for contributions to Medical Informatics in 1993, Fellowship of the Royal Society of Edinburgh in 1999, an honorary degree by the Sorbonne in 2000, the IFLA medal in 2003, Honorary Fellowship of CILIP in 2004 and was an OCLC Distinguished Scholar in 2006.

Andreas Lingnau studied mathematics and computer science at the Gerhard Mercator University in Duisburg, Germany. From 1999 to 2005 he worked at the Institute for Computer Science and Interactive Systems at the University of Duisburg-Essen. His main focus has been on computer-supported learning in the classroom and technology-enhanced learning. He gained his PhD in this area (2005). He has also worked at the Knowledge Media Research Center in Tübingen, Germany; as a scientific co-ordinator of the LMMP project Learner Supporting Multimedia Platform for Pupils with Cognitive Disabilities he was responsible for the development of the software

Learning Chest, a learning environment for pupils with cognitive disabilities and learning difficulties. In September 2009 he joined the University of Strathclyde in the project PuppyIR, which aims to provide new search interfaces for children by using innovative hardware such as tabletop devices.

Kathleen Menzies is a PhD student in the Information and Communications Department at Manchester Metropolitan University, UK. Her PhD topic will seek to discern, measure and model the attitudes of academics across disciplines to new media/social media in relation to 'traditional media', scholarly research lifecycles and the wider socio-political and philosophical environments. She worked as a Researcher in the University of Strathclyde, Glasgow, where she contributed to the EU-funded SHAMAN project and to a number of DL projects, many of which have involved user studies and engagement with professionals and/or end-users. These include DiSCmap (Digitisation of Special Collections: mapping, assessment, prioritisation) and OCRIS (the Online Catalogue and Repository Interoperability Study).

Petar Mihaylov gained his MSc in Product Design and worked as a professional graphic designer for more than four years, during which time he gained a substantial insight into the main problems surrounding the display and the perception of various visual stimuli. Further, he explored different aspects of human perception, which led him to pursue a PhD in Visual Sciences (2011). His basic research interest is in in-depth understanding in the processes of human perception.

David Nicholas is a Director of CIBER Research Ltd. Previously he was Director of the Department of Information Studies, University College London, and Head of the Department of Information Science, City University London. His prime interest is in evaluating behaviour in the virtual space, especially that of the Google generation. His work was featured in the BBC's 'Virtual Revolution' television programme. Currently, he is researching the impact of social media on the research process.

Andy O'Dwyer is a Technologist/Project Manager at the BBC, working on digitization and access to audiovisual collections. He is active on a number of EU collaborative projects to bring archives online for public and academic use. As a member of the Television Studies Commission of the International Federation of Television Archives (FIAT) he promotes new techniques in linking audiovisual material with the education sector. He is a member of the European Television History Network, and a contributing author of the book *A European Television History*.

Nicola Osborne is the Social Media Officer for EDINA, a JISC-appointed national data centre based at the University of Edinburgh. Nicola acts as an evangelist for new technologies, advising projects, services and colleagues on current social media tools, practice and opportunities, and contributing to organizational strategy in these areas.

Gitte Petersen holds an MA in language, literature and art. She has 15 years of experience working with online content, user experience and usability testing at The Royal Library of Denmark. She was Work Package Lead in the EuropeanaConnect project, with responsibility for user involvement and new access channels. Over the years, she has been involved in many cross-sectoral projects and networks within the domain of the Danish Ministry of Culture.

Lina Petrakieva teaches at Glasgow Caledonian University, UK. Her research interests were initially concentrated on computational linguistics, to which she was first introduced at age 15. After graduating with her MSc in IT and being continuously involved in research in computation linguistics, information retrieval, parsing and disambiguation Lina moved on to do a PhD in Machine Learning and Pattern Recognition. All of these different areas have one thing in common – the vision of how one day people will be able to use natural language and intuitive interfaces to achieve better human–computer interaction. After approaching the problem from the human side and realizing that humans are very difficult to change, Lina concentrated on looking for ways to change the technology and the ways humans work with it.

Ian Ruthven is a Professor of Information Seeking and Retrieval at the University of Strathclyde, UK. His research is centred on the development of effective and usable information access systems and is aimed at uncovering how people think about the process of searching, how information access systems could be designed differently to provide better support for searchers and how we can evaluate new types of information access system. He has carried out funded research projects on developing interactive information systems for children, cognitive decision-making processes in web retrieval and the information-seeking behaviour of marginalized groups. He received a PhD in Computer Science from the University of Glasgow, an MSc in Cognitive Science from the University of Birmingham and a BSc (Hons) in Computing Science from the University of Glasgow.

Elaine G. Toms is Chair of Information Science at the Information School, University of Sheffield, UK. She previously held appointments at Dalhousie University and the University of Toronto in Canada and to date has been the only Canadian information scientist to hold a Canada Research Chair. Her research focus lies at the intersection of human–computer interaction with content-rich systems and information retrieval, as well as in the evaluation of various types of information systems. She organized the first DL workshop in Canada at the University of Toronto in 1999. She remains an ardent supporter of technology designed for people and is working towards next-generation information appliances (nGAIAs) – information tools that deliver information and not objects.

Giannis Tsakonas holds a BSc in Librarianship and a PhD in Information Science from the Department of Archives and Library Sciences, Ionian University, Corfu, Greece. He is a member of the User Support Department of the Library and Information Centre, University of Patras, Greece, and a post-doctoral researcher in the Database and Information Systems Research Group, Ionian University, Greece. He has been actively involved in national and European projects, such as the DELOS Network, the Hybrid Libraries project for the exploration of mobile devices in knowledge and memory institutions and the CARARE project. He has participated in the design and management of repositories and museum information systems. He is also a member of the Executive Board of E-LIS, the international subject repository on librarianship and information science. His research interests include DL development in information contexts, such as the fields of academia and museums; user-centred DL evaluation; information behaviour; aspects of information services integration; and visual communication.

Zsuzsanna Varga is the Keeper of the Hungarian Collection at Oxford University Libraries and has recently completed the project *East Looks West: East European Travel Writing in the Electronic Domain* with UCL. She holds a PhD in English Literature and a MSc in Library and Information Studies. Her research interests lie at the intersection of humanities and the digital domain. Her previous projects have included the bibliography of Scottish literature in translation, the bibliography of Hungarian literature in English translation, and the web representation of Glasgow University Library's Novel Collection. She is very keen on exploring the potential of digital libraries and collections for research and teaching purposes.

Harry Verwayen is the Director for Business Development at Europeana. His main focus is the design and implementation of new business models and strategies that will support Europeana to fulfil its mission as a driver of innovation in the cultural heritage sector. Prior to this position, Harry worked at the Amsterdam-based think-tank Knowledgeland, where he was responsible for innovation and positioning of the project Images for the

Future. He has over 10 years of experience in the academic publishing industry in various positions, including sales, business and product development, and worked for Kluwer Academic Publishing, Springer and IDC. Harry holds a MA in History from Leiden University and a certificate from Nyenrode Business University.

Many cultural heritage professionals are involved in digital projects these days, and they inevitably face a wide range of issues related to users: from understanding their needs and expectations to finding efficient ways of enhancing their engagement. Understanding the users is also closely related to the measurement of the impact and value of digital resources – because the value, which seems an abstract metric, actually becomes quite tangible when projected onto real people and how they see a digital resource. We hope that this book will help all such specialists to get a better idea of how to understand their users better. The book will also be helpful for students taking library, information science and archival courses.

References

Athanasopoulos, G., et al. (2010) *The Digital Library Reference Model*, http://bscw.research-infrastructures.eu/pub/bscw.cgi/d167719/D3.2a%20The% 20Digital%20Library%20Reference%20Model.pdf.

Bignell J. and Fickers, A. (eds) (2008) *A European Television History*, Wiley-Blackwell.

DiSCmap (2009) *Digitisation in Special Collections: mapping, assessment, prioritisation*, report and appendices, www.jisc.ac.uk/whatwedo/programmes/digitisation/reports/discmap.aspx.

Dobreva, M., O'Dwyer, A. and Konstantelos, L. (2011) User Needs in Digitization. In Hughes, L. (ed.), *Evaluating and Measuring the Value, Use and Impact of Digital Collections*, Facet, 73–84.

Gonçalves, M. A., Fox, E. A., Watson, L. T. and Kipp, N. A. (2004) Streams, Structures, Spaces, Scenarios, Societies (5S): a formal model for digital libraries, *ACM Transactions on Information Systems*, **22** (2), 270–312.

Nguyen, H. S. and Chowdhury, G. (2011) Digital Library Research (1990–2010): a knowledge map of core topics and subtopics. In Crestani, F. and Rauber, A. (eds), *Digital Libraries: For Cultural Heritage, Knowledge Dissemination, and Future Creation. Proceedings of the International Conference on Asia-Pacific Digital Libraries (ICADL2011), Beijing 24–28 October*, LNCS vol. 7008, Springer Berlin/Heidelberg, 367–1.

The New Renaissance (2011) *The New Renaissance: report of the Comité des Sages. Reflection group on bringing Europe's cultural heritage online,* http://ec.europa.eu/information_society/activities/digital_libraries/doc/refgroup/ final_report_cds.pdf.

PART 1

Setting the scene

CHAPTER 2

Models that inform digital library design

Elaine G. Toms

Introduction

The development of any interactive system is predicated on the understanding of user requirements that include both the context in which the system will be used and the user community who will use it. In human–computer interaction and user-centred design, design usually entails the extraction of tasks, scenarios and personas that reflect the potential and intended use (see Chapters 3 and 4). A digital library (DL), a type of interactive system, provides 'a community of users with coherent access to a large, organized repository of information and knowledge' (Lynch and Garcia-Molina, 1995). Unlike design in other areas, the development of DLs seems to be considered an extension of the physical library and its early technologies, rather than a highly specialized application to service a particular task domain or community. As a result, DLs are often designed as generic applications, taking a one-size-fits-all approach, with little variation on the functionality required from one DL to the next.

DLs evolved from an information world with a long history of examining information needs and seeking, as well as the information searching and browsing of particular user groups. This has resulted in a plethora of models and frameworks to describe and understand the information environment in which a DL will exist. In this chapter, we will examine some of that fundamental work illustrating what fits and what falls short of being pertinent to the design of DLs. At the same time, we will intertwine fundamentals from other disciplines, illustrating both the foundations and the complexity of the DL design spectrum.

In the next section, we examine briefly the types of models that have emerged in information science. The second section discusses the range of models that inform the design of a DL, not all of which are from information science. The third section examines the challenges we face with our current intellectual foundations, required to support DL design.

Models from information science

Many of the information science models that have emerged over recent years start with the notion of information need, an acknowledgement that existing 'knowledge is inadequate to satisfy a goal' (Case, 2007, 5). They then integrate conceptual components that pertain primarily to sources of information, individual differences, roles, desired outcomes and motivation of the information user, as identified by Saracevic (1996) and Wilson (1999), among others. For the most part, these models are descriptive in nature, illustrating how needs emerge and trigger information-seeking activities, and identify influential elements.

Models developed in information science are typically considered to be of two varieties (Wilson, 1999), and are considered complementary (Beaulieu, 2000):

- information behaviour models that describe how needs emerge and trigger information-seeking activities, and ultimately add to information use
- information search models, which today would be called interactive information retrieval models, that describe the actions and activities undertaken by the searcher.

In general, information behaviour is a particularly troublesome concept, as it is defined and construed in many different ways; for simplicity, we will interpret it according to Case:

> Information behavior encompasses information seeking as well as the totality of other unintentional or passive behaviors (such as glimpsing or encountering information), as well as purposive behaviors that do not involve seeking such as actively avoiding information.
>
> (Case, 2007, 5)

Fundamentally, the core concept is information seeking, 'a conscious effort to acquire information in response to a need or gap in your knowledge' (Case, 2007, 5). Historically, this has been more about sources of information rather than about the user. Wilson (1999) would add information use to that definition, but how information is subsequently used is less frequently addressed (Choo 2002; Bartlett and Toms, 2005). The models that have resulted from information behaviour research and the consequential application of these models have the potential to provide the rich context in which particular types of DLs are intended to operate, and identify the purposes and functions that DLs could serve.

Information search models express the problem from a different viewpoint, focusing instead on the search behaviour, and reflect the situation closer to the level of user–system interactivity. Some, not all, are more similar to information behaviour models, providing high-level conceptual views of an information-use environment. In some instances information search models are considered a subset of information behaviour models, while in other cases they are considered independent.

In general, the models created to date in information science do not provide a holistic view of the process involved in user–system interactivity in DLs. They tend to stop short of enabling design requirements, as we will see. In the next section, we examine the range of models that apply to DLs, from the lowest layer of interactivity, to the context in which the DL will operate.

The pool of models that inform DL design

Figure 2.1 illustrates how existing models from multiple disciplines contribute to the DL design space, which is represented here as a set of

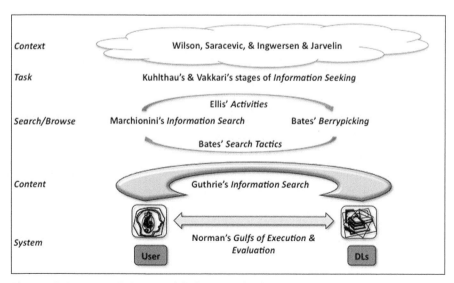

Figure 2.1 *How existing models from multiple disciplines contribute to the DL design space*

interconnected layers. This is not an exhaustive set; there are many other aspects that could be considered, from models of the user as an individual to document models. Instead, we take a user-centred, interaction design perspective, from the point when a user engages with a system to the context – the information-use environment – that the DL will support.

Overview

DLs, like any information-rich interactive system, work at multiple layers which address aspects beyond merely technological solutions. The user interface facilitates communication between the user and the system and, at this most generic layer, the activity that occurs is about user action and reaction, with the user evaluating and responding to the system. For this activity we borrow recommendations from human–computer interaction (see Chapter 4).

At the next layer the user is engaged with the content of the system, reading, interpreting and digesting the substance of the information object(s) displayed, regardless of whether these are audio, image (i.e. still or moving) or textual. For this we look primarily to education, cognitive science and psychology for primarily reader–text interaction models. At the next layer are task-specific interactions, some that relate to the search task, that is, the information seeking and retrieval, and some that relate to the formal work or pleasure task space, that is, the task environment that the DL will support. For DLs, these models come primarily from the domain of information behaviour (i.e. information needs and seeking) and information search models developed in information science. At the very top are the context or generic models that describe the view from 30,000 feet.

At the generic layer of user–system interaction

Starting from the bottom of the figure is the fundamental user–system interactivity that operates at the keystroke, mouse-click and touchscreen or other interaction technique level. Norman's (1986) 'Gulfs of Execution and Evaluation', operationalized as a seven-stage process for describing user–system interactivity, specifies a generic set of actions:

1 establish a goal
2 form an intention
3 specify the action sequence to fulfil the intention
4 execute the action

5 perceive the system state
6 interpret the system state
7 evaluate the system state.

This set of actions operates at the lowest level of user interaction, illustrating the cognitive gaps that users must navigate in order to communicate with a system. It can be applied to something as simple as cut and paste, as well as to higher cognitive levels such as entering a query or selecting from a results list. Except for models of particular aspects of human behaviour and cognition (e.g. how memory works), this is about as low a level of abstraction that useful models reach.

At the interaction with information-bearing objects layer

At the next layer is the interaction of user with content, during which the user is engaged in consuming and interpreting the text, although this could be also images or other forms of content. Models of reader–text interaction describe the complex process that occurs when a user processes what is viewed on the display and activates or integrates that information with existing knowledge. This is not just about the reading and comprehension process, but also about how the textual cues or landmarks (Heffron, Dillon and Mostafa, 1996) are used as perceived textual affordances (Toms, 2000), which are words or phrases that influence a user to stop reading or scanning and examine the text. For this we can look at a range of work primarily but not exclusively from psychology, from how people comprehend text (e.g., Colley, 1987; Kintsch and van Dijk, 1978; Meyer, 1984) to how people use cues (Gibson, 1977) and how people read an article (Dillon, 2004). Guthrie's Information Search Model (Guthrie, 1988; Dreher and Guthrie, 1990), unlike the information seeking and search models created in information science, examines the user–system activity at the level of content, identifying how the search is initiated and the information read, extracted, integrated and evaluated.

At the search and browse layer

Each of the models and processes discussed thus far examines the generic user–system interactivity that is elemental to working with information-rich systems. Beyond the reader–text (or other information object) interaction, Ellis's (1989) activities (which he called features of information seeking) and Bates's (1979) information search tactics come into play. Ellis identified eight activities in which users engage: starting, chaining, browsing, differentiating, monitoring, extracting, verifying and ending. It could be argued that each of these needs to be fully described and operationalized from a design perspective; each could technically become a tool that is deployed while a user is engaged in the process described by Guthrie.

Bates's (1979) information search tactics operate at a lower level of granularity; she defined:

- term tactics for modifying words or phrases within queries
- information structure tactics that suggest how to interlink among the various information objects
- query reformulation tactics for query modification
- monitoring tactics for managing and controlling the process.

Bates's tactics may be used within Ellis's activities or Guthrie's stages.

At this point we have reached the place where most DLs start, the concept of search and browse, which are the two modes of interaction present in information-rich systems: *search*, in which the goal-oriented seeking of information occurs, and *browse*, in which non-goal-based searching occurs (although the word 'browse' gets very confused, as there are many interpretations, such as non-goal-based search, and sometimes it is even equated with following links and navigating a page). Arguably, we should add serendipitous access as well. Search and browse tend to support two well-known cognitive science concepts: people *recognize* things more easily than they *recall* them. We sometimes think that search supports the recall function, and that browse supports recognition, but that depends on how one implements search and browse at the interface.

Often the description of the search process is attributed to Marchionini (1995) but it is a process that has been well articulated for quite some time, and has subsequently been 're-invented' many times (see Sutcliffe and Ennis (1998) and Shneiderman, Byrd and Croft (1998)). The process depicts search at a concrete level, including:

- identify information need
- understand problem
- select the appropriate system
- formulate a query
- execute a query
- examine results

- extract results
- reflect and continue until satisfied.

Every DL has overtly or by default implemented this process in some fashion.

Bates's (1989) berrypicking approach describes the browse process from a cognitive perspective. Although she specifically applied berrypicking to the changing nature of search and query as new information is found and interpreted, the concept, when divorced from the query, is analogical to foraging. Bates's dynamic approach to the information quest highlighted the shifting nature of user involvement with a system. At the same time, it provided the fodder for the development of Pirolli and Card's (1999) information foraging theory. The berrypicking concept supports an elemental ingredient in DL design – that not finding information is not just about the query. Along with the reader–text interaction discussed above, it clearly denotes the need for enriched user interfaces.

At the task layer

Perhaps asking the question 'what is the work task in a DL?' might seem too obvious. It is anything but. We tend to connect only the search and browse facilities and associated functions with DLs. But what should a DL for graduate students offer that is different from one for lawyers or one for patients? This is the information use case, which tends not to be systematically addressed in information science. But it is exactly the case that user-centred design would make prior to the development of any software application (for more information on user-centred design see Chapter 4).

That said, there have been some developments in information science that arguably fit into this category. The information-seeking process model devised by Kuhlthau (1991) and augmented by Vakkari (2001) is one of the few models that address the task that a system should support. While this robust model is best known for articulating the search process from a cognitive perspective, it also describes the course of action that students take in writing a term paper or proposal. Thus, it delineates the high-level steps that are taken in completion of a task, and that should be supported by a software application. Vakkari's augmentation enhanced the distinction between work task and search task and the overarching concept, information use; that is, there is a purpose to information search. It could be argued that the combined perspectives of Kuhlthau and Vakkari could (and should) inform the design of academic DLs, as the core task for most students is writing a paper or proposal. As Kuhlthau (2005) has pointed out, 'User-centered information systems call for a broad vision of users as people actively engaged in tasks rather than the narrow view of information searchers at the time of interface with the system' (p. 15).

Most DLs follow the traditional generic approach mentioned at the beginning. There are very few detailed examinations of a task environment for which DL support is needed. One of the few is Bartlett's (2004) in-depth description of how bioinformatics analysts do a functional analysis of a gene. After interviewing a group of those analysts, and observing the process they follow, she developed a detailed task analysis that included not only the tasks performed but also where and how data and information are used and interpreted and the sorts of tools needed within the process. The outcome of this work could be considered the requirements for a DL to support bioinformatics analysts. We need more of these enriched descriptions within specific task domains.

At the context layer

As suggested at the beginning, the bulk of the most highly cited research on information needs and seeking, and information search models operate at a high conceptual level. They define the scope and identify the core elements but are limited in their potential for use in design. At best they specify items that need to be included. Take, for example, one of the most cited, Wilson's (1999) model of information seeking, which identifies:

- the context
- the person in the context
- an activating mechanism or motivation for seeking information
- intervening variables that deal primarily with individual differences of the information seeker
- an activating mechanism which may be external, e.g. reward, or internal, e.g. satisfaction
- information-seeking behaviour that may be a type of search.

Similarly, Belkin's (1996) episodic and Saracevic's (1996) stratified models are simply about identifying the components at either side of the interface. Ingwersen and Järvelin's (2005) elegant but simple five-component model identifies the scope of the problem. All of these lack sufficient specificity to be used for design and, to be fair, were not created for that purpose.

Applying the information models to DLs

The models are not a design prescription as such; instead they provide a rich view of the complexity in the design of a DL. They also indicate the levels of abstraction that have to be accounted for in that design. In particular, they emphasize that DLs are neither just about access to some sort of repository, which is the systems approach, nor just a big picture view of the place of DLs in some sort of social milieu; they emphasize the need to stay focused on the user–system interactivity and provide an effective set of tools to support that process.

The challenge, thus, from a design perspective, is that many of the information-seeking and search models lack sufficient specificity for use in design, simply demarcating the territory. One of their most significant limitations is a lack of attention to task; when mentioned, it is but a single word or concept. Software applications are purposeful devices; they support or facilitate activities and perform functions from editing a document, creating a birthday card and crafting a chart, through to performing a statistical function and sending a Twitter feed. DLs are (or should be) more than search tools, as they are intended to service a community of users, and thus should be integrated into that particular use environment. In the student context, this may be helping to find a good topic for a term paper; for public servants, this may be identifying only the most pertinent and novel information on a particular issue that will inform new government policy. Neither group wants or needs the equivalent of information delivered at the end of a fire hose, e.g. 1 to 10 of 10,000,000 documents. At present, we fail to consider purposeful DLs built for a well-defined user community that has a well-defined set of tasks. Like their forebear, the lowly card catalogue, DLs mostly remain still about finding things.

Conclusions

As a community we have created a rich set of models that guide our research. It could be argued that we have too many models, and too many overlapping models. At the same time, we have seen many studies of the information behaviour of 'X', where X may be differing demographic groups perhaps based on age, gender or socio-economic status; many types of work domains, such as engineering, healthcare providers and lawyers; and many studies of ordinary citizens and the multiple roles they may play, from consumer to voter or patient (see Case, 2007 for examples). What we have failed to do is to extend that work to examine the needs of these specific groups for information support and use. For maximum research and development benefit, studies of information needs and seeking need to be extended so that systems requirements can be derived.

Many of the techniques used in capturing the information needs and seeking of various groups are also used in user-centred interface design (see Preece, Rogers and Sharp, 2002, for example). The problem may have arisen because historically it was all about finding the right information object; however, today we want to find the right information delivered in a humanly appropriate manner, and to do so we need to be aware of the most appropriate order and the best way for a user to digest it (Tague-Sutcliffe, 1995).

References

Bartlett, J. C. (2004) *Connecting Bioinformatics Analysis to Scientific Practice: an integrated information behaviour and task analysis approach*, Ph.D. dissertation, University of Toronto.

Bartlett, J. C. and Toms, E. G. (2005) Developing a Protocol for Bioinformatics Analysis: an integrated information behavior and task analysis approach, *Journal of the American Society for Information Science and Technology*, **56** (5), 469–82.

Bates, M. (1979) Information Search Tactics, *Journal of the American Society for Information Science*, **30** (4), 205–14.

Bates, M. (1989) The Design of Browsing and Berrypicking Techniques for the Online Search Interface, *Online Review*, **13** (5), 407–31.

Beaulieu, M. (2000) Interaction in Information Searching and Retrieval, *Journal of Documentation*, **56** (4), 431–9.

Belkin, N. J. (1996) Intelligent Information Retrieval: whose intelligence? In *ISI '96: Proceedings of the Fifth International Symposium for Information Science*, Konstanz: Universitaetsverlag Konstanz, 25–31.

Case, D. O. (2007) *Looking for Information*, 2nd edn, Academic Press.

Choo, C. W. (2002) *Information Management for the Intelligent Organization: the art of scanning the environment*, Information Today.

Colley, A. M. (1987) Text Comprehension. In Beech, J. R. and Colley, A. M. (eds), *Cognitive Approaches to Reading*, John Wiley, 113–38.

Dillon, A. (2004) *Designing Usable Electronic Text*, 2nd edn, CRC Press.

Dreher, M. J. and Guthrie, J. T. (1990) Cognitive Processes in Textbook Chapter Search Tasks, *Reading Research Quarterly*, **25** (4), 323–39.

Ellis, D. (1989) A Behavioural Approach to Information Retrieval Design, *Journal of Documentation*, **45** (3), 171–212.

Gibson, J. J. (1977) The Theory of Affordances. In Shaw, R. and Brandsford, J. (eds), *Perceiving, Acting and Knowing: toward an ecological psychology*, Lawrence Erlbaum, 67–82.

Guthrie, J. T. (1988) Locating Information in Documents: examination of a cognitive model, *Reading Research Quarterly*, **23**, 178–99.

Heffron, J. K., Dillon, A. and Mostafa, J. (1996) Landmarks in the World Wide Web: a preliminary study. In *ASIS '96: Proceedings of the 59th annual meeting of the American Society for Information Science, Baltimore, MD, October 21–24, 1996*, Information Today, 143–5.

Ingwersen, P. and Järvelin, K. (2005) *The Turn*, Springer.

Kintsch, W. and van Dijk, T. A. (1978) Toward a Model of Text Comprehension and Production, *Psychological Review*, **85** (5), 363–94.

Kuhlthau, C. C. (1991) Inside the Search Process: information seeking from the user's perspective, *Journal of the American Society for Information Science*, **42** (5), 361–71.

Kuhlthau, C. C. (2005) Accommodating the User's Information Search Process: challenges for information retrieval system designers, *Bulletin of the American Society for Information Science and Technology*, **25** (3), 12–16.

Lynch, C. and Garcia-Molina, H. (1995) *Interoperability, Scaling and the Digital Libraries Research Agenda: a report on the May 18-19, 1995 IITA Digital Libraries Workshop*, http://diglib.stanford.edu:8091/diglib/pub/reports/iita-dlw/main.html.

Marchionini, G. (1995) *Information Seeking in Electronic Environments*, Cambridge University Press.

Meyer, B. J.F. (1984) Text Dimensions and Cognitive Processing. In Mandl, H., Stein, N. L. and Trabasso, T. (eds), *Learning and Comprehension of Text*, Lawrence Erlbaum, 3–47.

Norman, D. A. (1986) Cognitive Engineering. In Norman, D. A. and Draper, S. W. (eds), *User Centered System Design: new perspectives on human–computer interaction*, Lawrence Erlbaum Associates, 31–61.

Pirolli, P. and Card, S. (1999) Information Foraging, *Psychological Review*, **106** (4), 643–75.

Preece, J., Rogers, Y. and Sharp, H. (2002) *Interaction Design: beyond human–computer interaction*, 2nd edn, Wiley.

Saracevic, T. (1996) Modeling Interaction in Information Retrieval (IR): a review and proposal. In Hardin, S. (ed.), *59th Annual Meeting of the American Society for*

Information Science, American Society for Information Science, 3–9.

Shneiderman, B., Byrd, D. and Croft, W. (1998) Sorting Out Searching: a user-interface framework for text searches, *Communications of the ACM,* **41** (4), 95–8.

Sutcliffe, A. and Ennis, M. (1998) Towards a Cognitive Theory of Information Retrieval, *Interacting with Computers,* **10**, 321–51.

Tague-Sutcliffe, J. (1995) *Measuring Information: an information services perspective,* Academic Press.

Toms, E. G. (2000) Understanding and Facilitating the Browsing of Electronic Text, *International Journal of Human-Computer Studies,* **52** (3), 423–52.

Vakkari, P. (2001) A Theory of Task-Based Information Retrieval Process: a summary and generalization of a longitudinal study, *Journal of Documentation,* **57** (1), 44–60.

Wilson, T. D. (1999) Models in Information Behaviour Research, *Journal of Documentation,* **55** (3), 249–70.

CHAPTER 3

User-centric studies

Sudatta Chowdhury

Introduction

As digital libraries (DLs) become a major source of information for many people, we need to understand better how people seek and retrieve information in digital environments. Information behaviour and information search models (see Chapter 2) help to contextualize the work on a particular DL within the larger area of use of digital resources. User-centric studies build on users' information needs and information-seeking behaviour and help in the formulation of specific requirements, and can be extremely helpful at different stages of DL development. These studies became popular in the late 20th century after decades of research that focused on better digital object representation or that was system-centric. User studies do not neglect the data models and technological developments, but place the focus on methods directly involving the users, with the rationale that this will help to develop systems that meet users' expectations and needs. User-centred design, according to Normore (2009), involves two approaches: user analysis in the early stages of a project, and usability research during the later stages. Through development of use cases and scenarios, user-centric methods become part of the important front-end activity for DL development. They also help to pinpoint any areas that need to be improved in terms of system design and services, and new usability features to help users perform information seeking in an effective and efficient manner. The usability of a DL relates primarily to its accessibility, i.e. how easily users can interact with the interface of the DL, how easily they can find useful information and how easily they can use the retrieved information. In general, if information can be accessed easily, then the DL will be used frequently and is likely to have a more noticeable impact and value for users.

This chapter discusses some major issues and research on user and usability studies in DLs. It then discusses four studies: Digital Work

Environment (DWE); REtrieval of VidEo And Language for The Home user in an Information Society (REVEAL THIS); evaluation of SCRAN, a Scottish DL for educational use with specific focus on 'value for money' for end-users; and the Europeana functionality study. These studies were done during the last decade and illustrate how specific situations require the specifics of the DL concerned to be addressed.

From user studies to usability studies

The utilization of DLs is measured by users' needs and satisfaction. Therefore, DL designers need to understand better what their users' needs are, so as to make DL services more useful. In this context, Beaulieu (2003) emphasizes:

> as more aspects of information seeking and richer information tasks are being developed in online environments, the boundaries between information seeking, searching and retrieval are breaking down. This is thus giving way to a more integrated approach and emergent interaction paradigm for user studies.
>
> (Beaulieu, 2003, 247)

Sumner (2005) highlights that understanding user needs is paramount in order to build innovative user interfaces and interaction mechanisms that can influence better use of DL resources, collections and services. By implication, therefore, a well-designed DL should have good usability features (Chowdhury, Landoni and Gibb, 2006).

The word 'usability' has a variety of definitions, but in one of the most comprehensive definitions of usability, that given in the ISO standard, emphasis is placed on users: 'the extent to which a product can be used by specified users to achieve specified goals with effectiveness, efficiency and satisfaction in a specified context of use' (ISO, 1998). Arguing that user requirements change from one search session to another, or even within a given search session, Bollen and Luce (2002) point out that usability factors such as user preferences and satisfaction tend to be highly transient and specific; for example, a user's search focus can shift from one scientific domain to another between, or even within, retrieval sessions. Therefore these authors recommend that research on usability factors needs to focus on the more stable characteristics of a given user community, such as 'the community's perspective on general document impact and the relationships between documents in a collection'.

Quite often, user-related studies, just like information-behaviour and search studies, are restricted to particular application domains. Many researchers have pointed out that users should be at the centre of the usability evaluation of DLs (Saracevic, 2004; Borgman, 2004; Chowdhury, Landoni and Gibb, 2006; Khoo et al., 2009; Chowdhury, 2010a; and Chowdhury and Chowdhury, 2011). The user-centric approach is strongly connected to the evaluation of DLs (see Chapter 5) because advanced definition of use cases, scenarios and any metrics relevant to the users helps in checking the performance of the DL after its development has been completed.

Usability in digital libraries: some recent research projects

User needs should not be studied in isolation, and both user-centric and context-based DL design (Chowdhury, 2010a) have been a major area of research in recent years. User-centric evaluations and usability studies of four DLs are discussed in the following sections.

The case studies show how, depending on the particular situation, different types of users' study approaches were taken. Details of all the methods of user involvement are not discussed here, since the idea is to illustrate how the nature of different DLs vis-à-vis study objectives requires different research methods and instruments to be adopted.

Case study 3.1: Digital Work Environment (DWE)

Users' information needs are usually triggered by the need to complete specific tasks. Current digital information systems, such as those accessed via DLs or the web, are not organized to match the various tasks that users perform. As a result, users often source information by trial and error, and browse from one web page to another or move from one information resource to another, in order to obtain the desired information. A DL called DWE was designed in 2000–4 to address these issues using a task-based approach (Meyyappan, Foo and Chowdhury, 2004). This approach provides an appropriate solution for organizing and grouping resources according to the tasks required to accomplish different types of scenarios (Meyyappan, Chowdhury and Foo, 2001). Users (academics and university students) were involved at various stages of development of DWE. A detailed user requirements analysis was carried out in order to make a list of the tasks that a typical academic user performs; these requirements were incorporated into the basic design requirements of DWE. The prototype was evaluated by involving student users and by creating specific tasks (Meyyappan, Foo and Chowdhury, 2004). For the majority of the tasks, participants took less time to identify the relevant information resources using the task-based approach over other approaches, i.e. subject category approach, alphabetical approach and a hybrid model combining the previously mentioned approaches. ▨

Case study 3.2: SCRAN DL evaluation

In a rare evaluation study of DLs where the primary focus was on the issue of 'value for money', Chowdhury, McMenemy and Poulter (2008) identified different categories of users of a DL:

1. the management and technical support team, who have a specific product design and functionalities for the SCRAN service to meet users' needs
2. the information intermediaries, who use the system on behalf of end-users and therefore have a good understanding of the users' skills, expectations and search behaviours
3. the end-users themselves, who use the DL in their day-to-day activities within their specific contexts.

The project team developed and used a series of data-collection methods and techniques for each category of users. Different data sets were collected through interviews with the management team, surveys of selected intermediaries and end-users, and deep log analysis. This research developed a detailed model for user-centric evaluation of DLs, which is reported in Chowdhury, McMenemy and Poulter (2008). ▨

Case study 3.3: REVEAL THIS (REtrieval of VidEo And Language for The Home user in an Information Society)

Users often find it difficult to determine which of the different available digital information channels can provide the required information in the most useful and efficient manner (Chowdhury and Landoni, 2006). In order to address the need for a service that can provide seamless access to a variety of multimedia and multilingual digital news information resources with appropriate personalization and facilities, an EC-funded project called REVEAL THIS was undertaken by a multidisciplinary research team from the UK, Greece, Austria, France and Belgium. The broad objective of this project was to design and develop an integrated infrastructure that would allow the user to capture, store, semantically index, categorize and retrieve multimedia (speech, text, image, video) and multilingual digital content across different sources – TV, radio, web, etc.

User-centric studies were carried out at two different levels. First, users were involved in focus groups (for this study method see Chapter 6) to identify their expectations and requirements in the context of an 'ideal' news aggregator service. A set of desirable features in an ideal news aggregator system was prepared as a result of this study and formed the basis of the design of the REVEAL THIS system (Chowdhury and Landoni, 2006). Such a system should provide users with search, retrieval, categorization, summarization and translation functionalities for multimedia content by means of automatically created semantic indices and links across media. REVEAL THIS addressed the needs of two groups – content providers and end-users. The system was seen as a tool to help *content providers* to add value to their content, restructure and repurpose it and offer personalized content to their subscribers; and to help *end-users* to gather, filter and categorize information collected from a wide variety of sources in accordance with their preferences. REVEAL THIS offered a pilot example of semantic enrichment of multilingual multimedia content where information on events, participants and topics was provided to the users.

After the prototype was designed, the performance of the system was measured against the set design objectives through a heuristic/expert evaluation (see Chapter 7 on expert evaluation) and then, to confirm the findings, a scenario-based user evaluation was conducted.

Case study 3.4: Europeana

Europeana is a DL for researchers, professionals and the public that provides a single access point to Europe's rich cultural heritage and links up to digitized content from memory institutions across Europe. A usability study of Europeana in 2009–10 (Dobreva and Chowdhury, 2010) focused on a number of areas, such as ease of use and intuitiveness; identification of young users' needs; increasing precision and reducing recall by improving the quality and consistency of metadata and improving search algorithms; users' expectations in relation to the resource coverage of different geographical areas; and similarities and differences in focus groups organized in different European countries.

Users' opinions were gathered through focus groups held in four countries

(Bulgaria, Italy, the Netherlands and the UK); in addition eye tracking was used to gather observations on user behaviour (see Chapter 9 for more on eye tracking).

Much of the feedback about Europeana that was received from users could be useful for other DLs. For example, users expected more digitized texts and wanted to be able to annotate and manipulate them; school students expected content to be downloadable and also wanted to be able to add their own content; users recommended improvements in the quality of the information about objects, i.e. the metadata records; they wanted more translation assistance in order to understand their results better; they also expected better classification of content. In relation to usability issues, users wanted to be able to see why a certain result appears and to understand how the ranking of results is made; they wanted to be able to refine their search within a results set; they expected greater precision in search results; and, more importantly, there was a call for more linking between items so as to show relationships, as well as for narratives that would contextualize the items (Dobreva and Chowdhury, 2010).

The user-centric study of Europeana provided a set of very valuable findings and recommendations that can be implemented to improve the Europeana DL, and that could also be helpful for other projects in the DL domain. ■

Conclusions

DLs differ significantly from one another in terms of their nature, content, target users and access mechanisms; it is difficult to measure the usability of such diverse DLs by means of one set of universally accepted tools and benchmarks (Chowdhury, Landoni and Gibb, 2006). As Chapter 2 in this collection argues, an in-depth understanding of users' information behaviour should underpin the design and delivery of information provision.

The case studies presented in this chapter have focused on studies made for different DLs during the last decade. They illustrate how user-centric studies can help to understand a particular DL situation – from testing a new approach (the novel task-based case in DWE) to trying to define the 'ideal service' (REVEAL THIS) to doing usability testing in order to better answer the needs of different user groups (SCRAN and Europeana). The case studies also clearly demonstrate that a range of methods exist that can be used to dig deeper into users' expectations and experiences. Readers will find more on these methods in Part 2 of this collection. One interesting feature of these studies is that, beyond answering questions about the specific DL, they also provided valuable sets of ideas for the larger DL community.

This corroborates the opinion of Bertot et al. (2006) that 'by enacting multi-method user-centric approaches to assessing digital libraries, researchers and practitioners can ensure that investments in digital libraries are returned through extensive use of resources by a community with diverse information seeking needs'.

Recent research emphasizes that users should be given an opportunity to comment on where services should be improved, so that their expectations can be better met, and, moreover, that DLs could try to improve their services through co-operation with their peers (Tammaro, 2008). A usable website should allow users to perform all the functions necessary to meet their information requirements with the minimum amount of time and effort (Chowdhury and Chowdhury, 2011).

In their review of the first decade of DL research, Chowdhury and Chowdhury (1999) noted that three major sets of issues are stumbling blocks to the development, implementation and successful use of DLs, viz. technical issues involving the appropriate network, hardware, software, standards, tools and techniques related to the different aspects of DLs; conversion issues related to digitization and related aspects; and economic, social and legal issues. Subsequently, two further sets of issues: design (e.g. architecture, interfaces and search tools) and usability (globalization, localization, language, cultural issues, content and human information behaviour) were added (Chowdhury, Landoni and Gibb, 2006), and most recently the environmental issue has also been added. Chowdhury (2010b) emphasizes that 'more research needs to be undertaken to study its (the environmental issue) impact on various stakeholders in the knowledge chain – on the knowledge creators and producers (publishers), on the knowledge consumers – users and downstream users ... and most importantly on the society as a whole' (p. 944). The question here is whether we have managed to address all the issues that were raised over a decade ago. We believe that, although there has been significant progress, more systematic research and more active cross-fertilization of research and development are still needed in the DL domain.

References

Beaulieu, M. (2003) Approaches to User-based Studies in Information Seeking and Retrieval: a Sheffield perspective, *Journal of Information Science*, **29** (4), 239–48.

Bertot, J. C., Snead, J. T., Jaeger, P. T. and McClure, C. R. (2006) Functionality,

Usability, and Accessibility. Iterative user-centered evaluation strategies for digital libraries, *Performance Measurement and Metrics*, **7** (1), 17–28.

Bollen, J. and Luce, R. (2002) Evaluation of Digital Library Impact and User Communities by Analysis of Usage Patterns, *D-Lib Magazine*, **8** (6), www.dlib.org/dlib/june02/bollen/06bollen.html.

Borgman, C. L. (2004) Evaluating the Uses of Digital Libraries. Paper presented at the DELOS Workshop on Evaluation of Digital Libraries, Padova, Italy, http://dlib.ionio.gr/wp7/WS2004_Borgman.pdf.

Chowdhury, G. G. (2010a) From Digital Libraries to Digital Preservation Research: the importance of users and context, *Journal of Documentation*, **66** (2), 207–23.

Chowdhury, G. G. (2010b) Carbon Footprint of the Knowledge Sector: what's the future?, *Journal of Documentation*, **66** (6), 934–46.

Chowdhury, G. G. and Chowdhury, S. (1999) Digital library research: issues and trends, *Journal of Documentation*, **55** (4), 409–48.

Chowdhury, G. G. and Chowdhury, S. (2011) *Information Users and Usability in the Digital Age*, Facet Publishing.

Chowdhury, S. and Landoni, M. (2006) News aggregator services: user expectations and experience, *Online Information Review*, **30** (2), 100–15.

Chowdhury, S., Landoni, M. and Gibb, F. (2006) Usability and Impact of Digital Libraries: a review, *Online Information Review*, **30** (6), 656–80.

Chowdhury, G., McMenemy, D. and Poulter, A. (2008) MEDLIS: Model for Evaluation of Digital Libraries and Information Services, *World Digital Libraries*, **1** (1), 35–46.

Dobreva, M. and Chowdhury, S. (2010) A User-Centric Evaluation of the Europeana Digital Library. In *The Role of Digital Libraries in a Time of Global Change, 12th International Conference on Asia-Pacific Digital Libraries, ICADL 2010, Gold Coast, Australia, 21–25 June 2010. LNCS 6102*, Springer, 148–57.

Europeana, www.europeana.eu/portal/.

ISO (1998) *Ergonomic Requirements for Office Work with Visual Display Terminals (VDTs); part II: guidance on usability*, ISO 9241-11:1998, Geneva, International Organization for Standardization.

Khoo, M., Buchanan, G. and Cunningham, S. J. (2009) Lightweight User-friendly Evaluation Knowledge for Digital Librarians, *D-Lib Magazine*, **15** (7/8), www.dlib.org/dlib/july09/khoo/07khoo.html.

Meyyappan, N., Chowdhury, G. G. and Foo, S. (2001) Use of a Digital Work Environment (DWE) Prototype to Create a User-centred University Digital Library, *Journal of Information Science*, **27** (4), 249–64.

Meyyappan, N., Foo, S. and Chowdhury, G. G. (2004) Design and Evaluation of a Task-based Digital Library for the Academic Community, *Journal of*

Documentation, **60** (4), 449–75.

Normore, L. F. (2009) Characterizing a Digital Library's Users: steps towards a nuanced view of the user, *Proceedings of the American Society for Information Science and Technology*, **45** (1), 1–7.

REVEAL THIS, http://sifnos.ilsp.gr/RevealThis.

Saracevic, T. (2004) Evaluation of Digital Libraries: an overview. DELOS Workshop on the Evaluation of Digital Libraries, http://dlib.ionio.gr/wp7/ws2004_Saracevic.pdf.

Sumner, T. (2005) Report on the Fifth ACM/IEEE Joint Conference on Digital Libraries – Cyberinfrastructure for Research and Education, *D-Lib Magazine*, **11** (7/8), www.dlib.org/dlib/july05/sumner/07sumner.html.

Tammaro, A. M. (2008) User Perceptions of Digital Libraries: a case study in Italy, *Performance Measurement and Metrics,* **9** (2), 130–7.

CHAPTER 4

Design issues and user needs

Petar Mihaylov

Introduction

The last decade has been marked by rapid developments in the accessibility and usability of online digital resources. Their number and popularity are rapidly increasing; however, digital libraries (DLs) still pay tribute to the perception stereotyping of the traditional library, and this does not always work in their favour; moreover, DLs present material across different sectors, and using metaphors only from the traditional library world does not always accommodate the needs of museums, galleries, archives and other institutions. The only way to further improve DLs is to revisit the requirements inherited from the traditional understanding and to update them to the technological developments and to combine this with the emerging deeper knowledge on human information behaviour. This chapter offers a short comparison of some traditional libraries and DLs.

Design issues and DLs

As highlighted in Chapter 2, DLs work at multiple layers, where the human–computer interaction is very complex. This has a strong influence on user design, which should facilitate communication between the user and the system, providing support for a range of information behaviours. Indeed, in 2002 Katy Börner and Chaomei Chen started their list of core challenges associated with the design of visual interfaces for DLs with this one:

> Research on any (visual) interface to DLs should be based on a detailed analysis of users, their information needs and their tasks.

> (Börner and Chen, 2002)

The DL design, however, has one more significant source to consult, and this is research in human–computer interaction, which has developed rapidly in the last decades. However, its advances are not embraced in the design of DLs, although the connection between usability and interface is long established. As early as 1999, Andrew Dillon suggested a qualitative framework for the usability evaluation of information resources, called TIME (Dillon, 1999), which included four elements: Task – what users want to do; Information model – what information structures best serve the intended use; Manipulation of materials – how users access the components of the document; and Ergonomics of visual displays – how these devices affect human perception of information (Dillon, 1999).

Research on the usability features of DLs has also underlined the role of the interface: G. Chowdhury suggested interface features in his detailed checklist of usability features for DLs (Chowdhury, 2004). Design is also a cultural phenomenon: the research of Duncker et al. (2000) showed that lack of understanding of the importance of colours, forms, symbols, metaphors and language for users coming from different cultural backgrounds can hinder the usability of DLs. Major work on interface design for DLs looks at novel visualization approaches that could improve the user experience (Ruecker et al., 2011).

Although the importance of connecting design to users' needs and the pivotal role of design in usability are clear, the design of DLs still follows ad hoc solutions rather than a set of generally accepted good practices. In the next section we will look at the inheritance of DLs from the analogue library world. Such an exercise is similar to an evaluation technique called Concept-based Analysis of Surface and Structural Misfits – CASSM (Connell, Green and Blandford, 2003). CASSM looks at the concepts that the user is working with, and those implemented within a digital system and manifested through its interface. The analysis aims to identify the similarity or dissimilarity between user and system concepts.

The gap between analogue and digital

Unfortunately, all the knowledge generated over the centuries in the analogue world is not directly transferable to DLs. Quite often, the direct implementation of features that make sense in the real world can be counterproductive in the digital world. Some issues in the design of DLs are a direct result of the fact that some unquestionable requirements in the 'real' library cannot be applied or simply do not exist in DLs. Here is a short list of issues that need to be taken into account by designers:

- *Sound issues:* The use of sound is very limited in 'real' libraries, due to silence being required by the majority of users. These sound restrictions are not an absolute requirement in the digital context because users do not normally share the same physical space. A choice of background music may improve the speed of reading or data search, and it can also make the whole experience much more pleasant. The use of sound can open the door to a number of possibilities, which were previously beyond reach. Some sound applications can help the visually impaired to access information that was previously unavailable to them, by incorporating speech-to-text programs, audio books, etc. Other sound applications, like audiovisual guides or step-by-step instructions, can help children, young people, beginners and inexperienced (or even experienced) users to speed up their learning process and data search. However, sound should be an optional feature within DLs, as they can be used in a public space and sound might disturb other people.
- *Colour issues:* The restricted use of colour is also in the list of unnecessary limits where the digital copies of a certain document are concerned. In the real world, colour printing is much more expensive than black and white. However, this cost difference does not apply in the digital world.
- *Visual impact issues:* There are major differences between colours on paper and colours on electronic displays, which currently are the devices most used for access to visual digital objects. To see the colour of certain objects in the real world, our eyes process light reflected from an object. The intensity of the reflected light is much lower than the intensity of the source light. This is the reason why we see the colours of an object slightly differently, depending on the light source (sun, candle, luminescent light, neon light, etc.). However, the monitors and TV screens are the sources of the light themselves. The light and the colours are much more intense, and prolonged exposure to digital objects (such as e-books or web pages on the computer screen) is more tiring than similar exposure to the real-world objects (books).
- *Customization issues:* In the past, libraries had very little opportunity to customize their services, appearance and databases to suit the needs of specific end-user groups. The freedom in this respect that is offered by DLs is infinitely greater than that of specialized libraries (or sections). A DL can be adjusted to provide personalized services, or can be styled with the brand of large corporate users.

So far, this comparison of digital and analogue libraries shows that, although both serve the same purpose, there are major differences between them that result in some advantages and disadvantages.

The main disadvantages of DLs are:

- Digital objects put a lot of strain on the eyes because the light is not reflected. Additionally, screens have a refresh rate which, if it is below a certain frequency (around 70 Hz), is visible and causes extra fatigue.
- The end-user needs access to the internet via a computer or mobile device.

The main advantages of DLs, some of which are still not being fully exploited, are:

- Users can have 24/7 access and real-time live support around the world.
- Users can use mobile services (for more information see Chapter 15).
- There is the possibility for various software tools (filters for dyslexic users, text recognition, speech-to-text, translators, etc.) that will improve the access and working experience of a diverse range of users (visually impaired, disabled, etc.).

Some recommendations for visual design

Previous studies have shown that the initial seconds that users spend on a website determine whether they will ever return to the site (Information Behaviour of the Researcher of the Future, 2008). Table 4.1 (below) provides information about what should be used and what should be avoided in the general visual design of any electronic source. It also points to a few very common (and annoying) mistakes. These rules are only a guide: any skilled and confident designer can take a risk and break some of them, in order to produce a desired impact on the user.

Table 4.1 summarizes some basic rules, each of which is explained in more detail.

Conclusions

The human–computer interaction in DLs can be considered to be still in its infancy, since this area of research has not yet developed any specific recommendations on the best ways of communicating with human users. It

Table 4.1 *Dos and don'ts for visual design*

Do	Don't	Explanation
Keep it simple and don't overcrowd	Make it very complicated	Keep it simple is the best line of action that any non-professional designer can take. The use of a minimalistic approach has several advantages: 1. Simplicity makes it easier for the end-user to understand the idea of the designer, hence, it is easier for the designer to guide the user towards his/her goal. 2. Simplicity helps to reduce mistakes. Use a predefined colour scheme or predefine your own (max 5–6 complementary colours).
Use subtle colours	Use very bright colours	This is the best way to reduce eye fatigue, at the same time ensuring the right contrast between background and foreground.
Use one font type with up to five font sizes	Use numerous different fonts and sizes	It is extremely hard to maintain consistency in a text display that has multiple font sizes.
Use simple, easy-to-read fonts that provide a feeling of the desired style, without overstating it	Use multiple or different, very elaborate and diverse fonts	The choice of fonts is a very important issue in digital objects. There are two major types of font: serif and sans-serif. The serif fonts have very fine details at the ends of the strokes and are designed for best legibility on paper. On paper the reader can easily discriminate letters as small as 3–4 points (1 point = 1/72 inch). Most serif fonts are not good for digital display because, on the monitor, the edges are blurred and readability decreases significantly. Sans-serif fonts are designed with straight lines and are more suitable for digital displays.
Use Times New Roman (serif) and Arial (sans-serif)	Use Times New Roman (serif) and Arial (sans-serif)	Both Arial and Times New Roman are certainly very well designed and popular and this makes them a popular choice. Well-designed fonts have many features (kerning, size corrections for each letter, width of horizontal and vertical strokes) that make them look good in text. But there is also a downside: being so popular could make them boring.

(continued on next page)

Table 4.1 *Dos and don'ts for visual design (continued)*

Do	Don't	Explanation
Use Bold and Italic sparingly, only to make intended statements	Use Bold and Italic as much as possible because they look very cool	Bold and italic can be very helpful for certain purposes (citations, extra attention, etc.).
Use a hierarchical structure that can guide the user towards the required topic or item	Put all topics and items on the first page so that the user can find everything he needs without having to search for it	The hierarchical structure helps users to achieve their goals more intuitively and with less confusion. The home page of any digital object should be dedicated to the general appearance of the object itself, with a simple menu.
Be consistent. Use the same identifications (colour, style, size, etc.) for identical objects	Use different ideas on every page so as to provide a variety of choices to suit different users and support a diversity of opinions and desires	Use the same identifications (colour, style, size, etc.) for identical objects: it is hard to overemphasize the importance of consistency in simple text documents. It is enormous. Documents that have consistency look better.

is necessary to integrate the findings from human behaviour research, human–computer interaction and user-centred studies of DLs into coherent design guidelines. At the same time, it is also essential to accommodate the technological advances that make the DL a very different space from traditional memory institutions.

References

Börner, K. and Chen, C. (2002) Visual Interfaces to Digital Libraries: motivation, utilization, and socio-technical challenges. In Börner, K. and Chen, C. (eds), *Visual Interfaces to Digital Libraries*, LNCS, **2539**, 1–9, Berlin/Heidelberg: Springer.

Chowdhury, G. G. (2004) Access and Usability Issues of Scholarly Electronic Publications. In Gorman, G. E. and Rowland, F. (eds), *International Yearbook of Library and Information Management, 2004–2005: scholarly publishing in an electronic era*, Facet Publishing, 77–98.

Connell, I., Green, T. and Blandford, A. (2003) Ontological Sketch Models: highlighting user-system misfits. In O'Neill, E., Palanque, P. and Johnson, P. (eds), *People and Computers XVII, Proceedings of The Human Computer Interaction conference HCI'03*, Springer, 163–78.

Dillon, A. (1999) Evaluating on TIME: a framework for the expert evaluation of digital interface usability, *International Journal on Digital Libraries*, **2** (2/3), 170–77.

Duncker, E., Theng, Y. L. and Mohd-Nasir, N. (2000) Cultural Usability in Digital

Libraries, *Bulletin of the American Society for Information Science*, **26** (4), 21–2, www.asis.org/Bulletin/May-00/duncker__et_al.html.

Information Behaviour of the Researcher of the Future (2008) CIBER, www.jisc.ac.uk/media/documents/programmes/reppres/gg_final_keynote_11012 008.pdf.

Ruecker, S., Radzikowska, M. and Sinclair, S. (2011) *Visual Interface Design for Digital Cultural Heritage: a guide to rich-prospect browsing*, Ashgate.

CHAPTER 5

Users within the evaluation of digital libraries

Giannis Tsakonas

Introduction

Digital libraries (DLs) are complex information systems and, as such, they are operated by or involve humans. They are used by people with real needs, competencies, experiences and expectations and they function within environments that aim either to produce or to transform digital resources. One of the ways to measure production and transformation is user studies, and various chapters in this book underline the multidisciplinary nature of this field. User studies help researchers to explore several facets of the socio-technical nature of DLs. Even in the most systemic views of DL evaluation, the users – regardless of their role – are significant participants and provide meaningful information through their perceptions, opinions and cognitive status. It is true, however, that the boundaries between user studies and evaluation activities are not always clear. The ambiguity is caused by the fact that user studies, user-centred design and DL evaluation are pieces of the same jigsaw that make up well-designed DLs. There are definite commonalities between these three areas, as well as critical differences, and this chapter will tackle this issue, firstly by describing how the concept of user fits into several evaluation models, secondly by providing examples of where user studies and evaluation interweave successfully, and thirdly by making an explicit distinction of their roles and contribution in the evolution of DL systems.

The user in evaluation modelling

During the last 20 years the presence and the role of users in DL evaluation has been growing steadily. Paola Marchionni has presented a number of possible ways of involving users in the development of DLs, including users' feedback, facilitation of users' engagement, determination of the DL service's impact and so on, sharing emphatically their potential benefits through examples from the JISC Digitisation Programme (Marchionni, 2009). At the same time, evaluation models that have emerged in the last decade have placed users at the centre of their study, as a result of the changed view of users, from passive 'actors' who only use interfaces and services, to drivers of DL development. Thus, the users are an integral part in several modelling efforts, either formal or informal. Modelling the evaluation of DLs is a process that reveals their most critical constituents in abstracted ways in order to raise case-specific details and constraints. Through modelling one can macroscopically check what are the building elements of an evaluation and how these integrate together, while through advanced modelling techniques one can reveal the rich relationships between these elements.

We will look at three particular models, the Digital Library Reference Model (DLRM), the 5S (Streams, Structures, Spaces, Scenarios, Societies) and the Interaction Triptych Framework. These three models are based on different philosophical and expressive mechanisms but despite this there is some similarity of overlap, and they constitute essential representations of the DL evaluation field.

Digital Library Reference Model (DLRM)

The DELOS Network of Excellence provided EU financial support from 2003 to 2007 to establish a community of researchers dedicated to the advancement of DL theory and practice. It was succeeded by the DL.org project in 2008–10. One of the outcomes of DELOS refined further the Digital Library Reference Model (DLRM) (Athanasopoulos et al., 2010).

The DLRM is a conceptual model that can help DL developers and researchers to build a shared understanding about the scope of DLs and set the foci of research activity. It outlines six major domains, namely architecture, user, content, functionality, policy and quality, as well as three levels of conceptualizations of the systems and architectures involved: the DL as a front-end assuring user communication, a DL system and a DL management system. According to the DLRM, the user is any actor, human or machine, communicating with the DL for a certain purpose. The user can have many identities, which can communicate with the three different levels in the DL universe. For example an end-user can interact with a functionality of the DL (the final product that provides content and services); a DL designer can configure content details in the DL system (the system that is responsible for the provision of the DL). The DLRM employs concept maps as a graphical way to represent the structure of the DL universe, as well as propositions, statements that connect entities of the universe, which form paths. These paths are essential elements of the conceptualization, as they recreate the context wherein an entity is and the properties that govern the entities.

The DLRM represents the evaluation process as a set of abstracted parameters which are located within the Quality domain. More specifically, the Quality domain examines the User domain under the terms of 'user behaviour' and 'user activeness', forming paths such as:

{User behaviour} – *isA* ->{User Quality Parameter} – *isA* ->{Quality Parameter}
and
{User activeness} – *isA* ->{User Quality Parameter} – *isA* ->{Quality Parameter}.

However, the DLRM argues that the user is not only the focus of attention of research but, as a participant that *acts* in these systems, he/she can also assess the quality of the other domains. For instance, a user can express his/her opinion on the usability of a specific service within the DL, which is formally expressed by the following path:

{Actor} – *expressAssessment* ->{Quality Parameter} <- *isA* – {Functionality Quality Parameter} <- *isA* – {Usability}

The (5S) model: Streams, Structures, Spaces, Scenarios, Societies

The 5S model is one of the cornerstones of DL theory. In the seminal work by Gonçalves et al. (2004) it is argued that a DL has five conceptual building blocks, namely Streams, Spaces, Structures, Scenarios and Societies. Similarly to DLRM, the concept of societies does not adhere strictly to humans. However, it mostly refers to users of DLs while they perform actions that conform to some scenarios of use of data (streams) in a space and through some structures. The 5S model provided the basis for the development of a quality model of DLs in 2007 and a tool assessing it, the 5SQual, in 2008 (Moreira et al., 2009). In the quality model, the users and the societies correspond to several criteria, or quality dimensions, such as accessibility and pertinence of data or the reliability of services.

The Interaction Triptych Framework

The Interaction Triptych Framework (ITF), proposed by Tsakonas and Papatheodorou (2008), focuses on the interaction between the main constituents of the DLs, namely user, content and system. ITF proposed a user-centred evaluation model based on the users' views of the system and the content attributes as they interact with these constituents. According to ITF, three categories of metrics are established upon the axes that are formulated by their in-between relationships (see Figure 7.1). These categories are usefulness, which corresponds to the interaction between user and content; usability, which focuses on the interaction between user and the system; and performance, which corresponds to the interaction between system and content. The usefulness and usability categories are within the focus of current research that represents two large areas in DLs, the one being information behaviour and the other the human–computer interaction.

Findings from an ITF study (Tsakonas and Papatheodorou, 2008) reported that in Open Access environments usefulness can be predicted if the DL supplies 'relevant, levelled and widely covered information', while its usability levels can be predicted if the system satisfies the attributes of ease of use, learnability, aesthetics and terminology.

These are only three of the most popular models that have modelled work on DL evaluation in recent years. They help developers and researchers to comprehend certain facets of content features and users' interactions with the system; however, it is important to remember that any evaluation they acknowledge is dependent on the users' context, and this is an area which most likely will be integrated in user models in the future.

User studies and digital library design and development

In this section we will examine how user studies are situated within evaluation procedures and how user studies, user-centred design and evaluation relate to one another.

As highlighted in Chapter 3, user-centred design is governed by two approaches: user analysis (in the early stages of a project) and, later, usability research (Normore, 2009). While there are other important user-oriented areas, such as usage and usefulness, that one can investigate, these two approaches seem to be the norm in the user-centred design of DLs.

Figure 5.1 presents a typical DL development timeline. Evaluation in DLs can be either formative, which means that it can be conducted while the DL is still under development, or summative, which means that it is conducted once the DL has been delivered and is in use. Usually, the user requirements analysis is done prior to the initiation of the project, most likely seeking information about *what people think or like*, their needs and preferences. A significant part of the data gathered will focus on the content and the functionalities of the DL and how these correspond to the users' needs. Examining previous user studies in similar contexts will be useful in prioritizing design issues. Important tools for the researcher to support development are typical portraits of personas (see Chapter 10) or stereotypical situations (scenarios), which inform the first prototypes (first circle in the figure).

As the development of the DL progresses the inventory of methods increases and the researcher can involve more classes of representative users. It is expected that expert researchers can provide assistance when the DL has been refined, giving their insights on the quality features that the system is acquiring (for more information see Chapter 7), while test users can provide feedback that helps in the recognition of flaws in the interaction design. Dorward, Reinke and Recker (2002) provide an illustrative example, as they followed a mixed methods approach, including needs assessment, prototype testing, expert reviews and so on, to gather data and inform the design of their Instructional Architect system. In their case, expert researchers provided guidance towards augmenting search interfaces and improving navigation through auxiliary screens, while the users suggested enhancements in the system interface and required that content and services should meet 'their immediate needs'. During formative evaluations, the researcher may return to previous stages of development and adapt their findings, thus altering the status of the DL (Figure 5.1, second and third circles denote different development ratios).

After the delivery of the DL the researcher will be most interested in *what people do or have already done and how* and, specifically, in interactions with the system services, interface elements and content choices. The researcher will be seeking actual patterns of use and usage without, however, excluding further gathering of users' perceptions (fourth circle hosting two evaluations). Many evaluation studies explore the ways that users interact with information retrieval services and interface architectural and design issues. In order to gather this data the researcher will focus on the recorded aspects of activity, such as time of task completion, errors and so on, or the observed aspects of user performance, such as selections or patterns of interactions. Summative evaluation can also include outcomes of assessment studies, which concentrate on the long-term effects that the DL has on the users. As DLs correspond to particular societal and cultural settings, an evaluation is extended to measure their impact on a long-term basis.

Finally, in this developmental course, the researcher has to decide on several critical issues. For example, the choice of an approach – qualitative or quantitative – during evaluation is one of these critical issues, and the choice could be different along the various stages. This will depend on the goals and the planning of the evaluation and, most specifically, on whether the study has the scope to extensively explore a certain issue, such as usage, or whether it aims to understand the users' fundamental reasons and motives. There are certain trade-offs that the researcher has to make, as well as certain dependencies, which are reflected both in the methods and the tools one selects and in the analyses and the inferences one can make.

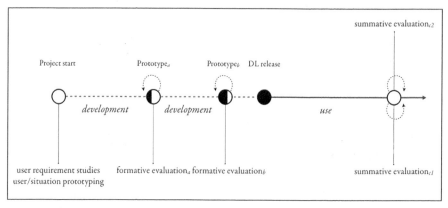

Figure 5.1 *A time-line of design and evaluation of digital libraries*

Case study 5.1: Clarity information retrieval system

One illustrative example for integrating user studies early in the design and using feedback to inform interventions is the study of the Clarity information retrieval system, a project funded by the EU to develop an interactive cross-language information retrieval system for rare languages (Petrelli, 2008). Petrelli reports on the results of a longitudinal user-centred evaluation, following a research plan that included several formative and summative studies. At first, the Clarity researchers worked on user requirements through contextual enquiry and interviews, and on system requirements through paper prototypes. This allowed the researchers to move towards bridging the various conceptual misfits between users and developers. For instance, it was shown that users were interested only in simple search processes that involved query submission and results presentation, while the developers had included advanced functionalities in the prototypes, such as sophisticated controls and visualizations.

The progress of the project included the examination of user performance in laboratory settings, using test collections, pre-set queries, questionnaires, logs and observations. These user-centred tests revealed areas of possible system improvement, which were associated with system performance (speed in response time) and content presentation (lexical/semantic aspects of multilingual results presentation). Subsequent testing allowed the researchers to identify, through comparisons, if the interventions they had made were effective. Finally, a formative evaluation that involved domain experts was conducted to explore again the improvement of the system (through pre-set queries) and the effect that it had on users.

Dealing with misfits

Iterative evaluation guarantees that the overall evaluation results inform the re-design and can be reused in subsequent stages, reflecting thus the benefits of revisiting axes of interaction among users, content, system and evaluation itself. This iterative mode of evaluation, regardless of the time-frame involved, is based on the findings of earlier studies, the changes in technological setting, of the user population and so on. This iteration is necessary in order to lessen the misfits between users' and developers' conceptual models. Saracevic (2004) has outlined the 'user versus the digital library' hypothesis, which is synopsized to the conclusion that 'in use, more often than not, digital library users and digital libraries are in an adversarial position'. Michael Khoo reported on ways in which he qualitatively explored the different 'technological frames', or the different views, of the users and developers of the Digital Water Education Library, a subject DL for water. Through iterative exploration and analysis he confirmed that:

> Users frame their understanding of a new technology in terms of how it fits in with their existing 'traditional' practices, while developers are often more concerned with the possibilities afforded by new systems.
>
> (Khoo, 2005)

Blandford and Attfield (2010, 57–67) have proposed the Conceptual Structures for Information Interaction methodology, where the macroscopic and abstracted view of the main interaction components can aid the identification of the conceptual misfits, and the factors that cause them. The misfits can be classified in three broad categories, namely:

1 user concepts not represented in the system
2 system concepts that the user has to know about
3 user and system concepts that are similar, but non-identical.

Blandford and Attfield (2010) also clarify that, in the case of operating DLs, one needs to also collect system-centred data to support the formation of a panoramic view of the conceptual misfits.

Users inside the digital library evaluation

The previous chapters have laid the basis for a fundamental distinction. While users are important participants in DL evaluation, user studies are not identical to evaluation studies. The purpose of the developers and researchers is not to evaluate the users, but rather to highlight areas of improvement or to inform and document decision making. There are other *user-centred research fields*, such as information behaviour or social informatics, that have an increased interest in assessing and explaining user performance.

On the other hand, DL evaluation employs *user-based* methods to support user-centred design. In user-centred design, evaluation is a phase that could provide useful information to achieve the goal of qualitative use of DLs. Toms (2010), quoting Gould and Lewis, names three basic principles that support user-centred design, namely, focus on the user, assess and evaluate through the design and development phase, and use iterative design to constantly improve the system. User-based evaluation corresponds to the second principle and, when preceded by user studies that help developers to recognize key beliefs, skills and behaviours, it facilitates the design of user-accessible and friendly systems.

However, users are a vital element not only during design, but also within evaluation. Users understand and express each evaluation perspective in various different ways. They have their own experiences, structured diachronically through numerous channels, and thus they respond differently to the criteria that researchers propose. Xie (2006) tested how users generate their own criteria and how these correspond to the criteria from existing models and from experienced researchers. He found that users evaluate DLs purely subjectively (whereas a researcher is acting objectively), based on their own experiences, and that they prioritize criteria associated with the quality of content. More specifically, it was found that users 'placed more emphasis on the ease of use of the interface and high quality of the collection in evaluating digital libraries', where, among the important collection quality features were listed coverage, authority, accuracy and currency. With this specific study it was highlighted that conceptual misfits are diagnosed not only in the relationship between the user and the developer, but also between the user and the researcher.

One of the most important differences between user studies and evaluations is the scope of research. According to Reeves et al. (2003, 3–4) 'evaluation questions are much more closely linked to specific decisions that have a more localized, less "generalizable" scope'. This is an explicit differentiation between evaluation and other forms of research that narrows the results and the effects of the study to an idiosyncratic level. The results are definitely informative for other initiatives, but cannot be considered generic enough to represent categorical properties of DL components or processes.

Conclusions

The DLRM has made it clear that the user is not only an *object* of a study, but also a *subject* in a study. The user in evaluation is an acting entity that uses the actual object of the study, which in turn can be either the content (data, metadata) or the system (features, services, algorithms, design elements). While both fields - evaluation and user studies - involve users, they share common elements of scientific querying, such as user recruitment and instruction, data triangulation and so on (Blandford and Bainbridge, 2009). Conducting user studies often involves carrying out evaluation work. It is important to keep some independent variables stable so as to allow valid comparisons that will lead to conclusions about the changes that the DL has succeeded in implementing. In this chapter it has been shown that studying users is a process distinct from involving them in DL evaluation. However, the connection between DL evaluation and user studies is multi-fold and grounded in the type of research, the methods and the time-frame in which each study is happening and, of course, in the scope of the research. Users are important parts of DL engineering. Acknowledgement of the potential effect of their involvement in design and evaluation phases will enable them to lead development towards higher levels of user friendliness and satisfaction.

References

Athanasopoulos, G. et al. (2010) *The Digital Library Reference Model*, http://bscw.research-infrastructures.eu/pub/bscw.cgi/d167719/D3.2a% 20The%20Digital%20Library%20Reference%20Model.pdf.

Blandford, A. and Attfield, S. (2010) *Interacting with Information*, Morgan & Claypool Publishers.

Blandford, A. and Bainbridge, D. (2009) The Pushmepullyou of Design and Evaluation. In Tsakonas, G. and Papatheodorou, C. (eds), *Evaluation of Digital Libraries: an insight to useful applications and methods*, Chandos Publishing, 149–72.

Dorward, J., Reinke, D. and Recker, M. (2002) An Evaluation Model for a Digital Library Services Tool. In *Proceedings of the 2nd ACM/IEEE-CS Joint Conference on Digital Libraries*, New York: ACM Press, 322–3.

Gonçalves, M. A., Fox, E. A., Watson, L. T. and Kipp, N. A. (2004) Streams, Structures, Spaces, Scenarios, Societies (5S): a formal model for digital libraries, *ACM Transactions on Information Systems*, **22** (2), 270–312.

Khoo, M. (2005) Tacit User and Developer Frames in User-led Collection Development: the case of the digital water education library. In *Proceedings of the 5th ACM/IEEE-CS Joint Conference on Digital Libraries*, New York: ACM Press, 213–22.

Marchionni, P. (2009) Why Are Users so Useful? User engagement and the experience of the JISC Digitisation Programme, *Ariadne*, **61**, www.ariadne.ac.uk/issue61/marchionni/.

Moreira, B. L., Gonçalves, M. A., Laender, A. H. F. and Fox, E. A. (2009) Automatic Evaluation of Digital Libraries with 5SQual, *Journal of Informetrics*, **3** (2), 102–23.

Normore, L. F. (2009) Characterizing a Digital Library's Users: steps towards a nuanced view of the user, *Proceedings of the American Society for Information Science and Technology*, **45** (1), 1–7.

Petrelli, D. (2008) On the Role of User-centred Evaluation in the Advancement of Interactive Information Retrieval, *Information Processing & Management*, **44** (1), 22–38.

Reeves, T. C., Apedoe, X. and Woo, Y. H. (2003) *Evaluating Digital Libraries: a user-friendly guide*, University Corporation for Atmospheric Research.

Saracevic, T. (2004) Evaluation of Digital Libraries: an overview. In Agosti, M. and Führ, N. (eds), *Workshop on Evaluation of Digital Libraries*, Padua: DELOS.

Toms, E. G. (2010) User-centered Design of Information Systems. In Bates, M. J. and Maack, M. N. (eds), *Encyclopedia of Library and Information Sciences*, 3rd edn, CRC Press, 5452–60.

Tsakonas, G. and Papatheodorou, C. (2008) Exploring Usefulness and Usability in the Evaluation of Open Access Digital Libraries, *Information Processing &*

Management, **44** (3), 1234–50.

Xie, H. I. (2006) Evaluation of Digital Libraries: criteria and problems from users' perspectives, *Library & Information Science Research*, **28** (3), 433–52.

PART 2

Methods explained and illustrated

CHAPTER 6

Questionnaires, interviews and focus groups as means for user engagement with evaluation of digital libraries

Jillian R. Griffiths

Introduction

Evaluation of online systems, services and resources, and latterly digital libraries (DLs), has a long tradition of improving the state of the art in information retrieval (IR) technology. The traditional system-oriented experiments for IR system evaluation provide a measure of system performance in terms of items retrieved and relevant to a given query. Yet today's end-user interactive DL environments demand user-oriented measures of usability and user behaviour, perceptions and preferences (Harter and Hert, 1997; Su, 2003). User satisfaction is often used to evaluate a system from the users' perspective and, as Gluck (1996) notes, 'in spite of the definitional and operational inadequacies these two traditional measures [user satisfaction and system performance] have led to considerable research and notable improvements' (p. 92). Controversy surrounding the user satisfaction approach arises mostly from the very nature of 'satisfaction', a user state determined by the influences of many factors – be they elements or characteristics of the system, the users or the task situation (Griffiths et al., 2007; Al-Maskari and Sanderson, 2010). Melone (1990) argued that it is this lack of attention to the theoretical underpinnings of the user satisfaction construct that has led to disagreements amongst researchers regarding its definition, method of measurement and research findings. In spite of the debate, user satisfaction holds considerable value and appeal as a construct for user-centred system evaluation within both the IR and the information systems literature.

This chapter identifies practical applications of methods that elicit user engagement with the process of evaluation, using experience with the DiSCmap project for illustration.

The DiSCmap project

The 'Digitisation in Special Collections: mapping, assessment and prioritisation' (DiSCmap) project, funded by the Joint Information Systems Committee (JISC) and the Research Information Network (RIN) and run jointly by the Centre for Digital Library Research (CDLR) and the Centre for Research in Libraries, Information and Media (CeRLIM), took a collaborative approach to the creation of a user-driven digitization prioritization framework, encouraging participation and collective engagement between LIS professionals and patrons (Birrell et al., 2011). Between September 2008 and March 2009 the DiSCmap project team asked over 1200 intermediaries and end-users a variety of questions about which physical and digital special collections they made use of and what criteria they felt must be considered when selecting materials for digitization. This was achieved through focus groups, interviews and two online questionnaires.[1, 2]

Aims and objectives

The overarching aim of the DiSCmap project was to provide recommendations for a strategic approach to digitization within the wider context and activity of leading players in both the public and commercial sectors. In doing so, DiSCmap also sought to identify priority collections for potential digitization housed within UK Higher Education Institutions (HEIs) (within libraries, archives and museums, as well as faculties and departments); to assess users' needs and demands for special collections to be digitized across all disciplines; to produce a synthesis of available knowledge about users' needs with regard to usability and format of digitized resources.

Specific objectives were:

- to survey and consult with both direct end-users (researchers, teachers, subject-specific societies) and intermediaries (librarians, curators and collection managers) to gauge their views on the collections to prioritize for digitization
- to devise a list of priority special collections as candidates for potential future digitization, based on users' needs and demands
- to produce a synthesis of previous and current studies that have focused on identifying researchers' needs with regard to issues of the usability and consumption of digital resources.

Methods and implementation

In order to achieve the aims and objectives, DiSCmap used a combination of several methods for user studies:

- web-based questionnaire applied to gather responses from intermediaries
- end-user survey (achieved through a combination of web-based questionnaires, focus groups and telephone interviews)
- analysis of the findings from the intermediary questionnaire and the end-user survey, involving quantitative methods and qualitative analysis
- synthesis of a framework of criteria for the assessment of the 'prioritization status' of a potential collection.

Sampling and surveying users of digital libraries

Engaging with users of DLs is often challenging, due, in part, to the constraints on data collection imposed by the fact that the library has a population that may be distributed worldwide. Participation rates are thus often lower than researchers would like. Adopting a flexible approach to the elicitation of data from users is critical to the success of user evaluation, so, if a questionnaire approach has failed to yield sufficient responses, then follow-up interviews and/or focus groups may be employed to enrich the data collected.

Initial questions must also be addressed when considering user engagement (and again, this is difficult when potential users are distributed internationally), such as: 1) What do you need to know to achieve the purpose(s) of the study? 2) What is feasible to ask, given the time and resources that you have available? 3) What is the purpose of your work – what are you trying to achieve and why is it being done? 4) Whom is the library principally targeted at and how can the data be collected? Consideration of data analysis is critical at the design stage of an evaluation in order to 1) identify the most appropriate data collection approach to adopt; 2) design the data collection instruments in accordance with the approach adopted; and 3) avoid wasting time, due to collecting more data than can be analysed.

Development and deployment of questionnaires

Questionnaires provide a method of gathering large quantities of data, both quantitative and qualitative, in a relatively simple, structured and resource-efficient way. Although the questionnaire itself can be deceptively difficult to design well, it is easy to distribute, does not require too much time or effort to complete, and can be analysed fairly quickly to provide a useful snapshot (or a baseline for longitudinal work) or, if administered repeatedly, comparative data about services over a longer time span. For longitudinal studies, questionnaires can be very useful because they help to maintain a common structure between different data collection exercises, as well as having the obvious benefit, for impact studies, of addressing individuals' experiences. The disadvantages of a questionnaire approach include low response rates, with people often suffering from 'questionnaire fatigue', and that there is no chance to ask a follow-up question if the initial answer is not sufficiently revealing.

In order to gain a comprehensive picture of current digitization priorities for special collections within UK HEIs, DiSCmap adopted a two-fold strategy centred on the deployment of two discrete but complementary questionnaires, thus:

- one questionnaire was sent to intermediaries – i.e. librarians, archivists and curators (Appendix I)[2]
- another was sent to the scholarly community of direct end-users (Appendix II).[2]

The respondents' knowledge necessarily influenced the level of detail provided; this highlighted differences between the ways in which intermediaries and end-users understand the notion of a special collection, which the project was able to incorporate into its analyses. Each questionnaire was designed in recognition of the differences between the groups; for example, intermediaries – but not end-users – were asked about the extent and age of nominated collections, while end-users – but not intermediaries – were asked about their use of special collections for research and teaching and their views on the provision and accessibility of such collections.

After the questionnaire had been piloted with a purposive sample of intermediaries, content analysis was used to ascertain the emerging digitization criteria most popular within that group. Based on this, subsequently canvassed intermediaries were asked not only to provide reasons for digitization but to select from a 'top five' list of criteria for digitization those which they found most relevant to their particular nominations.

The user questionnaire adopted a different approach, suggesting a wide range of possible reasons for digitization, derived from a combination of the findings resulting from analysis of the intermediaries' pilot questionnaire and of the analysis of six existing frameworks: The National Library of Australia's *Collection digitisation policy* (National Library of Australia, 2008); Cornell University Library's *Selection Criteria for Project Digitization* (Cornell University Library, 2005); the DIGIT-STAG Digitalization report (DIGIT-STAG, 2002); the MINERVA initiative's *Good practices handbook* (MINERVA Working Group 6, 2004); JISC's *Digitisation Strategy* (JISC, 2008); the New Zealand National Digital Forum's Digitisation position paper (New Zealand National Digital Forum, 2007). It should also be noted that, whilst this questionnaire was primarily aimed at end-users, some intermediaries did wish to engage with this survey – thus their responses were also included.

The user survey was informed by: 1) the results of the intermediary survey (described in Section 4.2.1 of the DiSCmap project report), 2) the findings of the interviews with intermediaries and 3) critical evaluation of related studies. This enabled the development of a list of criteria for digitization of special collections. Additionally, advice was taken from the members of the Advisory Board on further areas of investigation to include. A pilot questionnaire was tested with colleagues in CeRLIM and CDLR and, following final adjustments, the survey was released for one month (Appendix IIa).[2]

Distribution to UK universities was achieved utilizing a database of contacts – compiled for the intermediaries' survey – which contained an identified intermediary from each higher education library, to whom was e-mailed a request to distribute an invitation to staff and students of their institution to participate in the online survey. In total 196 universities were contacted. In addition, related professional bodies were also invited to participate and postings were made on the DiSCmap Facebook group, other related groups on Facebook (12 in total) and on the project website and discussion forum. As a result of this distribution 179 responses were received. Results of this online survey are presented in the Final Report[1], with additional detailed analysis being provided in Appendix VI.[2]

Interviewing and focus groups

Interviews can gather quantitative and qualitative data. However, as interviews are generally conducted in person by the researcher, it is possible to gather richer qualitative data than can be achieved using the questionnaire method, and they allow the interviewer to ask follow-up questions. Conducting interviews allows for much greater focus on specific issues and greater flexibility, and this method is often used in conjunction with questionnaires to provide an overall picture and detailed consideration of certain areas of interest. Interviews may also be structured to ensure that like is compared with like.

In the DiSCmap project, five intermediary participants were interviewed from a range of institutions across the UK HE community. It was initially hoped that engagement with intermediaries would occur through a variety of methods, but it was found that the most successful was via interview. Social networking was explored, but at the time of the interviews social media was not used with sufficient consistency to form the main data collection approach. A Facebook group was set up with links to the discussion forum at Strathclyde.

The results of these interviews identified: 1) digitization criteria important to intermediaries, 2) criteria thought to be important to end-users and 3) views on the impact on teaching and research of the digitization of special collections. The interview schedule used can be seen in Appendix IIb of the Final Report.[2]

It was agreed with the project advisory board that the subjects to be included for the focus groups would be the biological life sciences, history and sociology. Two focus groups were to be held in Manchester (history and sociology) and one in Glasgow (biological life sciences). To this end, participants from universities located within a reasonable travelling distance were invited to attend and in total 221 historians, 159 sociologists and 214 biological life scientists were invited to participate. However, efforts to recruit participants to these focus groups were largely unsuccessful, with only one focus group taking place for historians (plus one interview for a participant who was unable to attend the focus group but wished to participate). One participant accepted the invitation for biological life sciences and was subsequently interviewed. No academics accepted the invitation for sociology. The focus group/interview schedule used can be seen in Appendices IIb and IIc of the Final Report.[2] The History focus group was extremely useful and gathered very rich data which contributed significantly to the project. But low response from the biological life scientists was disappointing. Arranging focus groups to take place at a subject-related conference or workshop might alleviate difficulties in recruitment, that is, rather than expect participants to come to the researcher, the researcher should go to the community with which they wish to engage.

Greater success with focus groups, and an example of the richness of the data that can be obtained, may be seen in the RIN-funded study *Communicating knowledge: How and why researchers publish and disseminate their findings. Supporting paper 2: Report of focus groups findings* (Fry et al., 2009), where 10 focus groups were undertaken, plus interviews, which covered 6 broad disciplines, 11 subject disciplines with 87 participants.

Conclusions

Evaluations of services that do not, at some point, include their users are setting themselves up to fail. Engagement with users is challenging but needs to be embedded within the development of DLs throughout their lifecycle and may be supported by use of other approaches to evaluation, such as expert evaluation methods, usability testing and wider understanding of user behaviours and the different approaches to research that this entails. As Marchionni (2009) observed, 'Recognising that users are co-producers of a resource's value, to the extent that its value is determined by how much a resource is used, the best projects have approached user engagement as a lifecycle process taking place before, during and after the creation of a digital resource and informed by a strategic approach including a range of activities aimed at soliciting users' input in a two-way exchange, where users shape, at various points and in various degrees, the development and creation of a digital resource.'

For the DiSCmap project engagement with users resulted in new insights in understanding the differing ways in which direct end-users and inter-mediaries viewed special collections, in that the project uncovered a key area where a difference in perspective exists in the understanding of special collections between the two groups consulted. Intermediaries (with due professional care) were, for the most part, highly specific in their provision of descriptive detail about the collections that they nominated as priority cases for digitization. End-users (understandably) had a tendency to be vague, often nominating discrete 'sub-' or 'super-collections' for digitization. This revealed that the granularity of collections is understood in different ways by intermediaries and by end-users. One significant conclusion to be drawn from this finding is that, when providing a digital resource to end-users, intermed-iaries should seek to accommodate both these understandings of its relevant context; the digitized resource should not only enable end-users to identify the context of a given object in the sense of the collection to which it physically belongs, but it should also allow them to view its relationship to relevant 'sub-collections' or 'super-collections', with the capacity to view related items or groupings – for example, '19th century newspapers' or 'incunables'.

DiSCmap also demonstrated that the needs across domains are different, and that the distribution of subjects across the nominated collections revealed, unsurprisingly, a higher level of interest in the digitization of arts and humanities material. This echoed the findings of the Loughborough study (JISC, 2008). One possible approach here would be to undertake further subject-specific studies on user needs.

The assessment of service and resource quality has developed significantly in recent years. We have robust sets of performance indicators that provide the basic 'picture' of library performance and, beyond that, we have ways to explore the customer experience, to find out how users feel about the services and resources they use and to use these insights to provide better-managed services. Brophy (2004) has suggested that, as a profession, we may be moving beyond individual techniques in an attempt to synthesize the different approaches towards measurements of impact, to get back to the essential question of 'do libraries and their services do any good?'. The challenge is to continually strive to seek, and understand, the evidence that they do.

Notes

1   Full details of the DiSCmap project can be found at
    www.jisc.ac.uk/media/documents/programmes/digitisation/discmap_final_
    report_211009_final.pdf
2   A full list of appendices can be found at
    www.jisc.ac.uk/media/documents/programmes/digitisation/discmap_final_
    report_appendices.

References

Al-Maskari, A. and Sanderson, M. (2010) A Review of Factors Influencing User Satisfaction in Information Retrieval, *Journal of the American Society for Information Science and Technology*, **61** (5), 859–68.

Birrell, D., Dobreva, M., Dunsire, G., Griffiths, J. R., Hartley, J. R. and Menzies, K. (2011) The DiSCmap Project: digitisation of special collections: mapping, assessment, prioritisation, *New Library World*, **112** (1/2), 19–44.

Brophy, P. (2004) The Quality of Libraries. In *Die effective Bibliothek*, K. G. Saur, 30–46.

Cornell University Library (2005) *Selecting Traditional Library Materials for Digitization*, Report of the CUL Task Force on Digitization, www.library.cornell.edu/colldev/digitalselection.html.

DIGIT-STAG (2002) *Report of the Meeting of the Digitalization of Natural History Collections STAG of GBIF*, www.gbif.es/ficheros/Digit%20final%20report%20.pdf.

Fry, J., Oppenheim, C., Creaser, C., Johnson, W., Summers, M., White, S., Butters, G., Craven, J., Griffiths, J. and Hartley, D. (2009) *Communicating Knowledge: how and why researchers publish and disseminate their findings. Supporting paper 2: Report of focus groups findings*, RIN.

Gluck, M. (1996) Exploring the Relationship between User Satisfaction and Relevance in Information Systems, *Information Processing and Management*, **32** (1), 89–104.

Griffiths, J. R., Johnson, F. and Hartley, R. J. (2007) User Satisfaction as a Measure of System Performance, *Journal of Librarianship and Information Science*, **39**, 142–52.

Harter, S. and Hert, C. (1997) Evaluation of Information Retrieval Systems: approaches, issues, and methods. In Williams, M. E. (ed.), *Annual Review of Information Science and Technology*, **32**, 3–94.

JISC (2008) *JISC Digitisation Strategy*, www.jisc.ac.uk/media/documents/programmes/digitisation/jisc_digitisation_strategy_2008.doc.

Marchionni, P. (2009) Why Are Users so Useful? User engagement and the experience of the JISC Digitisation Programme, *Ariadne*, **61**, www.ariadne.ac.uk/issue61/marchionni/.

Melone, N. P. (1990) A Theoretical Assessment of the User-satisfaction Construction in Information Systems Research, *Management Science*, **36** (1), 7–91.

MINERVA Working Group 6 (2004) *Good Practices Handbook*, www.minervaeurope.org/structure/workinggroups/goodpract/document/goodpractices1_3.pdf.

National Library of Australia (2008) *National Library of Australia Collection Digitisation Policy*, 4th edn, www.nla.gov.au/policy/digitisation.html.

New Zealand National Digital Forum (2007) *Digitisation Selection Work: Position Paper*, http://ndf.natlib.govt.nz/downloads/NDF%20Digitisation%20Selection%20Work%20edited.pdf.

Su, L. T. (2003) A Comprehensive and Systematic Model of User Evaluation of Web Search Engines: I. Theory and background, and: II. An evaluation by undergraduates, *Journal of the American Society for Information Science and Technology*, **54** (14), 1175–223.

CHAPTER 7

Expert evaluation methods

Claus-Peter Klas

An expert is a person who has made all the mistakes that can be made in a very narrow field.   (Niels Bohr)

Introduction

Comprehensive, generalizable evaluations of digital libraries (DLs) are rare. Where evaluation does occur, it is generally minimal. Saracevic (2004) analysed around 80 evaluations to conclude that, both in scientific research and in practice, thorough evaluations of DLs are rather the exception than the rule. The complexity of DL systems can be identified as one reason for this. Examining them in their entirety is not straightforward. Even when attempting to do so, we lack scientifically accepted concepts, approaches and models. Another reason is the allocated funding in DL projects. Evaluation is always a 'must have' stated by the funder, but is rarely supported by adequate resources. These reasons are, unfortunately, still valid at the time of writing.

In this chapter the method of expert evaluation is presented and shown to be one possible way of addressing such problems. Expert evaluations are heuristic or qualitative in nature, as opposed to quantitative evaluations, which aim to provide statistically significant results. Heuristic evaluations (Nielsen, 1994) are common in usability engineering, where user interfaces are evaluated by a small group of experts on the basis of their conformity to certain usability principles (heuristics). Expert evaluations differ from other types of heuristic evaluation in that they lack *pre-defined* heuristics. The experts are free to provide any comment, on the assumption that their views will be informed ones. Some examples of the 10 general heuristics defined by Nielsen are visibility of the system status, error recognition, error prevention, user control (support undo and redo), aesthetics and minimalistic design.

The advantages of such an expert evaluation are fast and cost-effective results, in contrast to the more expensive types of qualitative user study, which require a larger number of evaluators in order to reflect a representative result. We can distinguish further between two types of expert evaluation: in the first case, the experts themselves are the evaluators, conducting the evaluation and providing the results. In the second, the experts are monitored by evaluators, who lead the evaluation and assess the results.

Even without pre-determined heuristics, a framework is needed to structure the knowledge gained, to define appropriate goals and to allow comparability of results. Such a framework consists of various factors. The first factor is the actual task, which is based on an information need. Tasks can vary in complexity and are determined by the pre-existing foreknowledge and prior experience of the searcher with respect to the information need and the type and number of objects to be found in the DL which relate to that need. More foreknowledge makes an information need easier to resolve. In other words: to what extent is a searcher able to express the unknown?

The same applies to the number and type of the 'to be found' objects. If an information need can be answered with exactly one object (a 'known-item search'), this is clearly easier than to find many objects, or unknown ones. Depending on the type of evaluation, the experts should either undertake tasks of similar complexity, or the opposite - tasks of great difference, covering a wide spectrum of search usage.

The next factor is the actual target group of the DL. A DL, if not actually designed for a specific target group, should support different groups such as pupils, students, researchers, leisure searchers or others. Of course, task and target group should reflect each other – evaluators should be experts from the same community as the intended audience.

The third factor is to ensure that the results are structured and comparable along a given schema or framework. Several frameworks exist – some for practical, some for theoretical purposes. In the following section two of these will be described.

Finally, the period in the development of the DL must be considered. Expert evaluations can be performed at almost any stage of development; however, a *formative* evaluation will be carried out during each stage, sequentially, while a *summative* evaluation is done at the very end.

Two expert evaluations are presented below: that of The European Library portal, undertaken as part of the EU DELOS Network of Excellence projects, and, as part of a German national project, the assessment of the DAFFODIL virtual DL.

Case study 7.1: The European Library

The European Library (TEL) (www.theeuropeanlibrary.eu) offers free access to the resources of the 47 European national libraries. TEL provides a common access point to over 150 million catalogue entries. It not only provides core DL services, like search and browse, but supports user interaction with enhanced functionalities, such as making connections between and across information systems. Within the DELOS Network of Excellence (www.delos.info), experts were tasked with helping to improve TEL services and, within the improvement of the user interface, to undertake an evaluation exercise to provide feedback on the areas of design, navigation, functionality and visualization (Klas et al., 2007).

Grouped according to the four factors listed above, a summary and lessons learnt are described below.

Tasks

In order to perform an evaluation as reflective as possible of real-life situations, when assessing functionalities within TEL a specific framework was used describing work-task situations (Hansen and Karlgren, 2005). It was enhanced into a contextual framework description called SDWS (Simulated Domain and Work-Task Scenario).

For each scenario, a two-level description framework was created. The scenarios were derived and designed from real-life work-tasks similar to the simulated work-tasks described by Brajnik, Mizzaro and Tasso (1996) and Borlund (2000). However, the TEL tasks tried to incorporate slightly more natural search-task situations.

The two-level scenario and description were designed as follows: the first level contains a short description of the domain and of general work-tasks or routines usually performed within this domain. The second level contains a *situational description* including the topic of the query and a search-task description. In this way, by following the structure of the scenarios, participants gain a broader understanding of the actual information-seeking situation they are evaluating, as well as of how they relate it to the system and its functionalities. The three task topics shown in Table 7.1 on the next page were designed and every expert chose one to be applied.

Framework

In order to structure the findings of the expert evaluation of the TEL website we

Table 7.1 *Summary of tasks used within the TEL evaluation*

Task	A	B	C
General description			
User group	Researcher	Leisure searcher	Leisure searcher
Domain	Historical research	Historical research	Prehistoric religions in Europe
Work task	Research on historical events such as the Crusades in Europe	Finding information about pilgrim paths in Europe, maybe also forgotten paths, in order to explore their paths and sites	Exploration of prehistoric matristic religious symbols and artefacts that have been 'integrated' into Christian symbolism and artefacts in European countries
Situational description			
Topic	Historical Crusades (first to fourth)	Pilgrim paths	Black Madonnas in Europe
Search task	Textual and visual information on the historical Crusades (first to fourth), including contemporary reports, but not novels or fiction	Search for textual and visual information about pilgrim paths in Europe, especially the Jacobus path, but beginning from Northern Europe. Find interesting paths and cities along the ways.	I am going to travel through mid-Europe next summer and would like to read some books and see other material about Black Madonnas.

applied the criteria of the Interaction Triptych Framework (ITF) (Tsakonas and Papatheodorou, 2006) (see also Chapter 5). Although the ITF is not intended for evaluation work, its simple yet comprehensive approach allowed a useful summarization of the findings. ITF assumes that the main DL constructs (namely users, system and content) develop a dialectical relationship. Three evaluation categories are defined on the axes that are created while the constructs interact, which are usefulness, usability and performance. Each category of ITF aggregates a set of attributes (see Figure 7.1). While this is a top-down approach, we also used a bottom-up approach to investigate the technical abilities of TEL. The functionalities that TEL provides, such as linking with other services or sharing results, are essential for the enhancement of the information life-cycle.

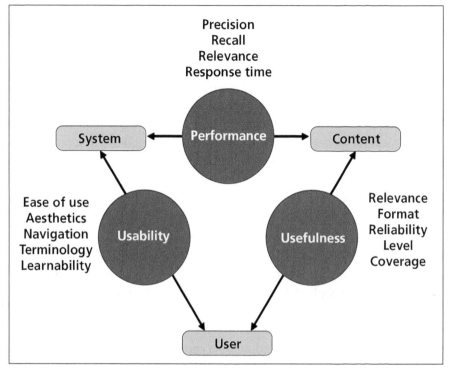

Figure 7.1 *Interaction Triptych Framework*

Findings

During the study, each section of the TEL website was analysed using all listed evaluation categories. A selection of typical examples from the study is presented here, with respect to *usefulness, usability* and *performance*. These apply not only to the TEL interface, but also to any DL.

Usefulness

The usefulness of a DL is dependent on main attributes like coverage of a specific domain, reliability of services (e.g. being accessible online 24/7) and the relevance of the objects within it. Since the providers of TEL are the national libraries, the reliability and coverage of content can already be considered satisfactory. The main items stored are bibliographic references, but complete digital items, including maps, paintings, old books and manuscripts, are also included. These are specially placed under the category 'Treasures'. In some cases thumbnails attached to bibliographic records permit users to see the items, although not in a full multimedia format. TEL can be used to search for references with specific topics or tasks, but it seems best suited for known-item searches, based on title and/or author search.

Usability issues

- *Terminology:* The meaning of a term and relationships between terms are usually biased and clear to developers of the portal, rather than to the user. In TEL, several such terminology problems were identified, e.g. it could not be determined what 'default list of collections' meant, as no description was given. Another example was the link called 'see online'.
- *Navigation:* Links on web pages should be clearly labelled and have functionality. Examples like the 'see online' button did not provide the obvious function. Another point with browser applications is the intuitive usage of the 'back button' inside the web browser. When looking at a detailed window, the back button should stay in an appropriate context; it needs to remain application aware and jump to the previous page, not the previous website.
- *Ease of use:* Here the evaluators should look at inconsistencies, hyperlinks or sequences of working steps, e.g. to fulfil completeness in a result set, to have hyperlinks to details or not – consistency in the interface is essential and applying inconsistent approaches might confuse the user. The classic working steps would be, to search, find items and follow them to a detail view. This process should be clear and easy to use.

Performance

The performance category focuses on the relationship between content and system. It describes, for example, access and search timing as well as the quality of the results returned. Here, Google search is, of course, the state of the art with respect to search time – usually milliseconds – yet other parameters also drive performance. For example:

- Precision and recall values indicate the quantity of relevant documents returned with respect to a given query. A system should present the most relevant items at the top of a results list.
- Response time. Here the expert evaluators found that TEL was taking more time to search the complete catalogue (22.06 sec) than the respective national library's catalogue (4.06 sec). Questions of usefulness and purpose then arise.

The TEL evaluation aimed to expand the knowledge of the TEL team about design deficiencies. Expert evaluations, especially in terms of human–computer interaction (HCI), are usually classified under what is termed predictive evaluations (Hilbert and Redmiles, 2000), applied mainly during the initial phases of the design. Here, a reverse route was followed in order to extend the set of methods employed and to give the TEL team more findings and data on which to ground their design interventions. Expert reviews are able to provide data from the DL and the graphical user interface experts' perspective, as well as to propose specific improvements and to predict their costs (Reeves, Apedoe and Woo, 2003). The findings of this evaluation are enlightening and may bring to light potential problems, rather than those which actually exist, especially in terms of user interaction. The TEL evaluations described above gathered results suggestive of a greater number of issues than did previous exercises. This clearly shows the depth that can be achieved when expert evaluation methods are used. ▪

Case study 7.2: DAFFODIL evaluation

DAFFODIL is a virtual DL system targeted at giving strategic support to users during the information-seeking and retrieval process (Fuhr et al., 2002; Kriewel et al., 2004). It provides basic and high-level search functions for exploring and managing DL objects, including metadata annotations over a federation of heterogeneous DLs. For structuring its functionality, the concept of high-level search activities for strategic support as proposed by Bates (Bates, 1979, 1990) is employed.

Based on empirical studies of the information-seeking behaviour of experienced library users, DAFFODIL integrates many functions to raise information competence and sustainable information seeking and searching and places the user at the centre of this process. A comprehensive user evaluation showed that the system supported most of the information-seeking and retrieval aspects needed for a computer scientist's daily work (Klas, Fuhr and Schaefer, 2004). It was shown that, if the user's task becomes more complex, the user is more efficient and effective with such a sustainable system.

Within this evaluation, one of three evaluation phases was conducted with search experts. Three computer science professors and three librarians served as expert test persons in the domain of computer science. It was assumed that these experts would know and use a variety of search tactics in their daily work and that they would be familiar with several other DL systems to which they could compare DAFFODIL. We therefore expected that the experts would be able to make profound comments. In the experts' evaluation version of DAFFODIL all of DAFFODIL's tools (such as the meta-search tool, the detail viewer, the personal library and the extraction tools) were enabled and the experts received an introduction to these tools.

Tasks

The topics of the task were chosen individually by the test subjects to reflect a current professional interest, so as to ensure familiarity. The librarians chose tasks (e.g. identifying relevant papers) and compared DAFFODIL intuitively with their own library system, whereas the professors focused more on their research domains, identifying relevant authors or searching for their own publications (e.g. with respect to comprehensiveness of results returned).

Framework

The overall framework for handling the complex DAFFODIL evaluation as a whole was that proposed by Saracevic and Covi (2000). They define five dimensions in order to describe and classify an evaluation:

- Construct: describes the element that can be evaluated, like user, system and data collection. It corresponds with the ITF (see Figure 7.1).
- Context: considers social, institutional and technical factors.
- Criteria: these are the criteria to measure – for example time (in minutes), using a clock. Also relevance and precision can be used here to measure performance.
- Methodology: this dimension describes the evaluation methodology, like structured interviews, analysing log data, experiments or video monitoring.
- Measures: to calculate the evaluation values of certain criteria we need evaluation metrics. A typical value to calculate effectiveness is time. User satisfaction is also an important measure.

From this model we can derive guidelines for preparing and implementing a practical evaluation, so as to reduce complexity. Also, the repetition and the comparability of results are facilitated. The proposed dimensions answer the key questions that arise in an evaluation:

- Why evaluate?
- What is to be evaluated?
- How should it be evaluated?

Findings

During the summative evaluation (ranging from 30 minutes to two hours) all experts concentrated on the task and intuitively used the provided tools. The librarians were positively surprised by the rich functionality and that most of the information-seeking and task-solving tactics they usually used were available within DAFFODIL. Asked about missing services, two named merging of results lists, and one missed categorization by general keywords associated with documents. Some of the positive comments made were: 'Daffodil is an expert-system, since it not only retrieves information, but also mediates the knowledge on the tactics to the user', or 'Daffodil's functionality goes beyond today's systems'. The academics searched for a current personal work task and tested the tools according to their background, starting from known items. Finding what they expected, they started to trust the system.

Overall, the experience of the evaluation of DAFFODIL showed, first, that even complex evaluations are feasible and, second, that the feedback is really valuable for refining the system. This again shows the depth that can be achieved when expert evaluation methods are used.

Conclusions

Expert evaluation is a feasible method for cost-effective and valuable DL evaluations. On the one hand, developers, decision makers and project funders receive a sophisticated rating essential for further development of their systems. On the other hand, the users receive an effective and efficient service to drive their information needs. Both expert evaluations described in this chapter brought with them their own complexities, requiring detailed consideration of the appropriate methods and models to deploy. DL evaluation is still rather undefined, and often neglected as a result – hence expert evaluations take a significant amount of time for preparation, implementation and post processing. However, the outcomes (for example, comparing the previous and current versions of the TEL search capabilities) show the positive results that such work can generate when the findings are applied. As methods and modes of DL evaluation continue to be refined, with best practice identified and acted upon, so too will be the benefits, functionalities and task-solving capabilities of DLs.

References

Bates M. J. (1979) Idea Tactics, *Journal of the American Society for Information Science,*

30 (5), 205-14.

Bates M. J. (1990) Where Should the Person Stop and the Information Search Interface Start?, *Information Processing and Management,* **26** (5), 575-91.

Borlund, P. (2000) Evaluation of Interactive Information Retrieval Systems. Doctoral dissertation, Åbo, Finland: Åbo Academi.

Brajnik, G., Mizzaro, S. and Tasso, C. (1996) Evaluating User Interfaces to Information Retrieval Systems: a case study on user support. In Frei, H.-P., Harman, D., Schäuble, P. and Wilkinson, R. (eds), *Proceedings of the 19th Annual International ACM SIGIR Conference on Research and Development in Information Retrieval* (SIGIR '96), Zurich, Switzerland, 18–22 August, 128–36.

Fuhr, N., Klas, C.-P., Schaefer, A. and Mutschke, P. (2002) Daffodil: an Integrated Desktop for Supporting High-Level Search Activities in Federated Digital Libraries. In Agosti, M. and Thanos, C., *Research and Advanced Technology for Digital Libraries,* LNCS **2458**, Springer, 157–66.

Hansen, P. and Karlgren, J. (2005) Effects of Foreign Language and Task Scenario on Relevance Assessment, *Journal of Documentation,* **61** (5), 623–38.

Hilbert, D.M. and Redmiles, D.F. (2000) Extracting Usability Information from User Interface Events. In *ACM Computing Surveys,* **32** (4), 384–421.

Klas, C.-P., Fuhr, N. and Schaefer, A. (2004) Evaluating Strategic Support for Information Access in the DAFFODIL System, *ECDL* **2004**: Springer, 476–87.

Klas, C.-P., Kriewel, S. and Fuhr, N. (2007) An Experimental Framework for Interactive Information Retrieval and Digital Libraries Evaluation, *LNCS* **4877**, Springer, 147–56.

Kriewel, S., Klas, C.-P., Schaefer, A. and Fuhr, N. (2004) Daffodil - Strategic Support for User-Oriented Access to Heterogeneous Digital Libraries, *D-Lib Magazine,* **10** (6), www.dlib.org/dlib/june04/kriewel/06kriewel.html.

Nielsen, J. (1994) Heuristic Evaluation. In Nielsen, J. and Mack, R. L. (eds), *Usability Inspection Methods,* John Wiley & Sons.

Reeves, T. C., Apedoe, X. and Woo, Y. H. (2003) *Evaluating Digital Libraries: a user-friendly guide,* University Corporation for Atmospheric Research, www.dpc.ucar.edu/projects/evalbook/index.html.

Saracevic, T. (2004) *Evaluation of Digital Libraries: an overview,* http://comminfo.rut-gers.edu/~tefko/DL_evaluation_Delos.pdf.

Saracevic, T. and Covi, L. (2000) Challenges for Digital Library Evaluation. In *Proceedings of the American Society for Information Science,* Band 37, S. 341–50.

Tsakonas, G. and Papatheodorou, C. (2006) Analyzing and Evaluating Usefulness and Usability in Electronic Information Services, *Journal of Information Science,* **32** (5), 400–19.

CHAPTER 8

Evidence of user behaviour: deep log analysis

David Nicholas and David Clark

The methodology

What is deep log analysis?

Everyone who uses a digital service leaves a record of their activities on the particular platform they used, be that a mobile phone, laptop or iPad. This record, which is best thought of as a digital footprint, is automatically stored on the computer server as a log. The log provides a huge treasure trove for researchers and practitioners who are interested in how people seek, search, navigate, use and act upon information. Deep log analysis then involves processing, relating, evaluating and making sense of this data on behalf of businesses, libraries, policy makers and senior managers. It is called 'deep' to distinguish it from transactional log analysis, which is essentially an activity (hit or download) counter.

Deep log provides very detailed and bespoke usage analyses of digital information services of all kinds. Deep log transforms the *activity* data found in the logs into information-seeking and usage behaviour; then, with the aid of other information held in the logs, online questionnaires and third-party data sets, like Scopus, information-seeking and use data are transformed into *user* behaviour by relating it to demographic, attitudinal and then *outcome* data, enabling satisfaction and success to be established – a real breakthrough. As we shall see, deep log analysis goes well beyond Google Analytics, the closest most people get to deep log analysis.

Why the need for deep log analysis?

Because of the massive scale and rapid speed of the digital transition, which is now impacting on all aspects of our lives (work and social), we badly and urgently need to know what is going on in the virtual information space because that is where most of the action is, and the challenge (and need for deep log analysis) is occurring remotely, anonymously and dynamically. Interviews, observation and questionnaires – the traditional library and information science (LIS) research methodologies – on their own do not work well in the digital environment because people have problems remembering when and what they did in the virtual space, which, of course, covers a myriad of platforms, including mobile and smartphones, digital interactive television, touchscreen information kiosks, and desktop and laptop computers. There is a pressing need for a new methodology for the new information environment we find ourselves in, and this method needs to be evidenced based. To this end, CIBER (Centre for Information Behaviour and the Evaluation of Research) developed deep log analysis as a powerful methodology over the last decade. Deep log analysis, as previously mentioned, is a form of transactional log analysis, and was originally developed for studying the performance of online library catalogues (OPACs). Remarkably, despite the undoubted success of the methodology – employed in user evaluations of Europeana, ScienceDirect, OhioDirect, Oxford Journals Online, The Times Online, Emerald, and MyiLibrary among others – very few researchers have adopted it.

Attractions and problems associated with deep log analysis

The prime attractions of deep log data are that they:

1 constitute what people actually did online; not what they said they did, thought they did (people tend to leave their memories behind on the web) or hoped they would do
2 offer a record that comes free of worries about sampling biases and errors; virtually everyone and everything is recorded (that is, everyone who goes online)
3 provide user/use data routinely and automatically (24/7) without bothering the user one bit (an increasing problem for over-exposed and intrusive methodologies like questionnaires) and are independent of where people are using the service – it could be from home, office, airport or on the move
4 furnish evidence-based datasets of a breathtaking size, a size that the LIS field could hardly have imagined 10 years ago; with deep log analysis you are covering tens of thousands or millions of people, not tens or hundreds.

As with all methodologies, there are downsides to using deep logs:

1 Their great attraction – they produce vast amounts of data – also means that truly vast files of data have to be transferred, managed, stored, manipulated and sifted. And this is by no means a quick or easy task; a lot of computer power and time is necessary; however, fortunately, this is often available on today's laptops and servers.

2 Server logs were never intended to be a record of use, being designed more for monitoring system performance. So to get anything out of them requires quite a bit of effort (parsing) and thought – hence the attraction of Google Analytics for many. This aspect is covered more in the following section.

3 Data is not easily transformed into users and usage. Thus, user identification, usually through IP addresses, is problematic because of multi-user machines, dynamic numbering and robots. Use – typically page views, the main usage currency – is somewhat less problematic, although you have to do a lot of sifting to come up with actual user content page views. This aspect is covered more in the following section.

Technical explanation (the nitty-gritty of log analysis)

As mentioned earlier, log-files were designed not for information research but for system administration: that is both a limitation and an advantage. Log-files monitor the performance of the machine, they tell us how well it is working; they document the origins of break-downs and break-ins. They are also an accounting record: how many users, where from, where to, what do they do, at what cost? This accounting function can be built into the mechanism: for example, it would be a poor order-processing system that did not feed data to stock control and invoicing. But there is also a requirement for what may be called soft accounting: marketing forecasts and monitoring after-sales. We have a need to know, but are less certain of what and when. So we record data speculatively, in the expectation that it may be useful later. Sometimes that post factum analysis may be forensic: identifying a single significant event and thence tracing backward and forward, from point of entry to impact. Or the analysis may be synoptic: mapping influences and predicting trends in a mass of anonymous detail.

In either of these approaches the logging is performed on the server and the records created are of incoming requests to a single website (or possibly a number of websites with a common data controller). An alternative is that employed by Google Analytics, Sitestats and many other similar packages. The logging is originated at the client end, relying on mechanisms incorporated in the web page to forward log data to a central repository. Such methods may enable tracking of users before and after their visit to a specific website, and a pre-packaged range of analysis tools offers the promise of easy creation of reports. But the ability to track users across domains is limited; the valuable information accrues to Google, who holds all the data, not the individual website operator, who does not see the full picture. The essential data is usually stored as 'cookies' and these can, with simple modification to the server log, be included in the log and analysed – but only for that one site. And pre-packaged generic report formats are inflexible. This is particularly important with web pages generated on the fly from database queries, where the website has very few 'pages', each generated as a special and possibly unique edition. The 'deep log' approach is tailored to the specifics of the application: we look at all the data, including the 'cookies' provided by generic log-analysis tools if available, but our analysis of the log-file is not limited to statistical aggregation. Knowing how the application works and who the users are informs our search for unique and site-specific patterns in the data.

A fundamental logging choice, then, is between using an existing facility and designing a specific logging capability into the application. There are considerable advantages to making best use of existing mechanisms such as web-server log-files. They are readily available, the format is well understood; they can be created and processed without incurring significant development work. The disadvantage is that such log-files have their origin as a tool of system administration; a format designed to monitor server performance and security may not be ideal as the basis for market research and user testing. On the other hand, not being designed for the purpose can be an advantage: such data may be considered neutral, it is not proleptic, it may record what we have never thought to ask.

However they are originated, in analysing log-files there are three basic approaches used. The first is user-centric: observe how the website functions interactively and correlate user actions to log records. The second is based on understanding software: what actions within the program mechanism generate a logged event. The third is to start with the logs themselves: data-mining the logs to discover association rules and hence predict patterns of behaviour. Deep log analysis employs all three, but data mining is central to our approach. Not least because it is best suited to the analysis of existing standard log-files.

More information on deep log analysis can be found in Nicholas and Rowlands (2008).

Anatomy of a log-file

A typical log-file will consist of many millions of lines, as shown in Figure 8.1, part a. (Apache common log format).

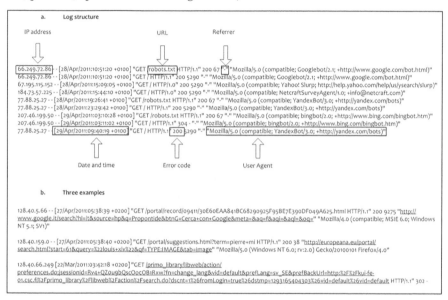

Figure 8.1 *Log structure*

Some of this information is both useful and standard (Date and time, IP address, error code), some may require interpretation (User Agent, URL, Referrer), and some can be thrown away, but what is crucial often requires interpretation in the context of the application. This is particularly the case where much of the information is buried in the depths of the URL query string, as in the examples in Figure 8.1 part b. (the URL query strings are underlined).

Usually each request for a web page is made up of many component files: images, program scripts, stylesheets, etc. In almost all cases our interest is in the 'page-view': the resulting effect of presenting a new page to the user, regardless of how many log entries this may generate. So, typically, the log entries will be much reduced by consolidating and discarding what are in effect duplicate records. Also, in most cases, being concerned only with what the user 'uses', we will set aside page requests that result in error messages. The result is to reduce the log-file to a record of page-views.

Attribute analysis

Each line in the log-file records a request for an item (html file, image, stylesheet, script) from the server. It identifies the user's IP address, and UserAgent (Browser), the date and time, the URL requested and usually the referrer (i.e. the previous web page visited that contained the requested link). It may be convenient to visualize the daily log-file as a very large table, the rows divided into columns for IP, date, time, etc. As is now usual for a website of any size, the file component of the URL invokes a program: the 'web page' is held not as a single html file but is composited on request by the server. The important consequence of this for log analysis is that analysis by 'page viewed' tells us very little. To understand what is being requested and viewed we need to analyse the query string in the URL. Hence we need to decompose the URL into its various components, including the query string, and the query string in turn is then further divided into its components (field=value pairs). Sometimes the values of the fields may themselves be composite and require further decomposition. The referrer column is also in the format of a URL and is likewise decomposed. A similar process can be applied to the UserAgent string. The result is that, after processing, one day's log-file has become a table of perhaps 1 million rows and as many as 4000 columns. In data mining, the columns are usually known as attributes; the first task is to identify useful attributes.

The utility of an attribute, and the value of the information it may yield, takes into account its reliability, ubiquity, frequency and discrimination, and, more subjectively, relevance to the purpose of the analysis. An attribute present in every row is more useful than one that is present only rarely. An attribute that takes a few well defined values is better than one that is almost, but not quite, unique to each row. Some attributes merely restate what we already know. As a result of this assessment a set of useful attributes can be selected. Typically there may be around a hundred that should be regularly monitored. Changes to the standard log-file format, such as adding fields, will create additional attributes.

Case study 8.1: The Europeana Connect project

Europeana was launched in 2008 as a prototype and has run an operating service since October 2010. It currently provides multilingual access to 15 million European cultural objects in 1500 institutions from 27 countries. Europeana is largely a portal/gateway and search engine but has aspirations beyond that:

developing a digital economy, mounting online exhibitions and crowd sourcing. CIBER was commissioned to monitor usage and to determine impact, whether the website was meeting objectives, delivering target audiences and establishing what works. Only deep log analysis could evaluate something on this scale, so this is a wonderful case study to exhibit the methodology.

Log findings

The comprehensiveness, level of detail and precision that log data provide in respect to Europeana are portrayed in this section but, given the constraints of space, this can only be undertaken in a selective manner – many more analyses are on offer, courtesy of deep log analysis (Nicholas and Rowlands, 2010).

Users

Most use was robotic – in fact over 80%. The most common and the most known of these robots was Googlebot. With a prototype site like Europeana there is also a lot of systems use, and this can distort usage patterns significantly, especially given relatively low levels of end-use. It is never easy identifying end-use, but stripping away robots, systems people and rogue users left us with 1 million users of the site in 12 months.

Levels of use and growth

Human users made around 10 million page-views during 12 months. Use was characteristically volatile, varying considerably from hour to hour, day to day and month to month, and this could be put down to the nature of the service, the users and/or because it was a prototype. Hourly use peaked initially at 11a.m. and then built up during the day, reaching a plateau in the evening, which is an indication of high volumes of home and general public use. There were considerable variations between countries, with, for instance, Finland peaking at 10–11a.m. and Portugal at 6–7p.m. Daily use was highest on Tuesdays, and Sundays proved to be as busy as weekdays, which again points to the consumer/leisure profile of Europeana users. As regards monthly use, surprisingly, perhaps, December and March turned out to be the busiest months and summer generally saw a lull in use – the latter could be because Europeana has a large academic following and summer is when schools and universities are closed.

Growth was modest over the first 12 months, the equivalent of a compound annual growth rate of 0.9%. However, once Google was allowed to deep-index the site in January 2011, use grew massively, by something like 160% in a month, and very high levels of growth have been maintained since.

Nationality of use

The biggest EU users were France and Germany, and together they accounted for 40% of use. However, allowing for population size, France, Poland and Iceland performed the best, and the UK relatively poorly. The main 'engines' of growth were Poland (+1.2% over the year) and France (+1.1%); use was more sluggish in Denmark (0.8%) and Romania (0.8%).

The most obvious question to be asked is: 'Were users attracted primarily to their own national collections, or did they range more widely across Europeana, as system designers hoped?'. France proved to be the most insular: 88% of material used was French, but of course the French had plenty of French content to choose from. Poland was the next most insular (77%); Italians, by comparison, viewed only 23% of their own content, and the UK 33%.

Referrer (navigating to Europeana)

Unsurprisingly, Google was the major driver of traffic to Europeana, reaching half of all referrer traffic by January 2011. Users tend to search for 'Europeana' rather than to bookmark it or remember the URL. Google also corrects spelling and the spelling of Europeana is far from straightforward, and that is another reason for using Google! What, then, of social media sites from where Europeana is hoping to gain traffic/publicity? Blogs proved to be the most important source, generating 52,384 page-views over the first year. Blogs were followed in popularity by: Wikipedia (11,099), Facebook (4771), Twitter (1046), YouTube (65) and Flickr (12).

Searching and browsing

Essentially, Europeana is a finding device, search engine and gateway – not a source of cultural content itself (although this is not obvious to the first-time visitor). The Homepage in fact has a very prominent search box, with obvious echoes of Google. A search in the box or a browse (Browse through time, for instance) results in a display of thumbnail images of content with an invitation to 'Click here to view object in Europeana'. An object in Europeana is a catalogue entry – a description, a small but larger-than-thumbnail image and an invitation to 'View in original context'. Original context means opening a new window on the content provider's site that may present larger images, more detailed description, or more of the same now dressed in the provider's livery. Thus, from catalogue to catalogue the user goes, and deep log can record the process.

The Homepage search box was the finding method of first choice with 338,000 searches entered over 12 months. In fact there is much more keyword searching than that, because when people enter their first search on the Homepage they are sent to a second-level page where they can do as many follow-up searches as they like; 2.25 million searches were conducted. That is a lot of searches. As is the case with most scholarly information services, few people utilize the advanced search (3750 page views), even on a portal designed to enhance search.

Of the browsing options 'Browse through time' came in for reasonably good use (243,000 page-views). The 'People are currently thinking about' (wisdom of the crowd) browsing option generated 48,000 query strings. 'New content' obtained few takers. The video clip box (e.g. Art Nouveau) provides a visual approach to search/browse; this is new and we are yet to report on it.

Form of content viewed

Europeana is a multimedia resource, so what do users plump for when searching the gateway? In fact, for video and sound, of which, ironically, there is relatively little (sound and video represent less than 2% of the digital objects). Allowing for relative representation on Europeana, users were 10 times more likely to want sound and video.

Type of platform

There has been an explosion of interest in mobile access to the internet with the introduction of smart devices and, in particular, the iPad. The latter seems to be a natural for looking at multimedia content as presented by Europeana and is a possible winner with cultural tourists. By the end of September 2010, mobile agents accounted for just under 1% of *Europeana* page-views – more than three times the level at the beginning of the period. More recent analysis shows strong future growth. ▨

Conclusions

We have demonstrated the utility of a user methodology for monitoring and evaluating the use of a digital service created by 27 countries in nearly as many languages and used by the whole world. The fact that we can do this precisely, in real time and remotely, in London, with three people (working on it part time) and never have to worry about response rate or co-operation demonstrates the huge attraction of the method.

References

Nicholas, D. and Rowlands, I. (eds) (2008) *Digital Consumers*, Facet.

Nicholas, D. and Rowlands, I. (2010) Unique Perspectives on User Behaviour for Multi-media Content: case study Europeana, *Online Information Conference Proceedings*, London, December 2010, 127–35.

Scopus, Abstract and Citation Database of Research Literature, www.scopus.com.

CHAPTER 9

An eye-tracking approach to the evaluation of digital libraries

Panos Balatsoukas

Introduction

Eye tracking is the process of recording and analysing human eye-movement behaviour in order to investigate the mechanisms that underpin the operation of the human mind when a decision is made to look at any point. The study of eye movements has been used for a long time in psychology and cognitive science research as a means of understanding the cognitive process of reasoning and decision making (Rayner, 2009). In market research eye tracking has been employed as a tool helping to analyse how the usability of products, such as mobile technologies and websites, can be improved (Duchowski, 2007). Recently, information retrieval (IR) and digital library (DL) communities have been focused on the use of eye tracking in order to understand users' behaviour when they search and evaluate information on the web (e.g. Loringo et al., 2008). In the latter case, the use of eye tracking has implications for the design and the evaluation of information systems, such as search engines and DLs.

The aim of this chapter is to explain and illustrate the use of eye tracking for the evaluation of DLs, and it uses examples from the evaluation of the Europeana Digital Library as a case study (Dobreva et al., 2010).

Eye tracking as an evaluation tool

Why evaluate using eye tracking?

There are two main reasons why the use of eye tracking is important for the evaluation of DLs. First, eye tracking can provide a richer and more detailed view of users' behaviour than can other quantitative data collection techniques, such as data logs and screen-recording software. While data logs and screen-recording software record all observable user interaction on the screen (e.g. clicks on a specific link or keywords typed in a search box) the recording of eye movements can show much of what is not observable by the researcher, or non-recordable by traditional software. Examples of this are user behaviour, such as all links that were viewed but not clicked, the exact number of times a user viewed specific interface components, the sequence with which these components were viewed, or the time it took the user to read a piece of text or view a particular image on the screen. Therefore, eye tracking can show the whole picture of a user's interaction with the DL interface because it records both active behaviour (interpreted as mouse-clicks or keystrokes) and inactive visual behaviour during the interaction with the system. This type of information is important in order to obtain an in-depth view of users' distribution of cognitive load and the decisions made.

The second reason is that eye tracking can enable the in-depth interpretation and explanation of qualitative data that comes from think-aloud protocols and interviews. Instead of relying only on users' self-reported data, which often can be subject to post hoc rationalization biases, data collected from eye tracking provide a more objective and real-time map of users' behaviour onscreen. Therefore, eye tracking can be used in mixed-method research designs that examine users' cognitive and visual behaviour onscreen.

What to evaluate

The use of eye tracking can support the evaluation of the usability and usefulness of DLs (see Chapters 2 and 5). Usability refers to the ease of use of a DL and focuses on user interaction with a DL's functions or tools. Usefulness examines the utility or relevance of the results retrieved by the system to the user's needs (Tsakonas and Papatheodorou, 2006). There are unique types of data that can be collected using eye tracking in order to evaluate both the usability and the usefulness of DLs.

What to evaluate for usability and usefulness

Table 9.1 *Evaluation questions using eye tracking*	
What to evaluate for usability	
Indicative question	*Indicative answer*
Q1. Which is the first and the last place the user looks on the interface?	E.g. users should be able to recognize immediately the key elements of the interface.

Table 9.1 *Evaluation questions using eye tracking (continued)*

What to evaluate for usability	
Indicative question	*Indicative answer*
Q2. Which elements of the interface do users tend to look at and which are ignored?	E.g. key interface elements should be made visible in order for users to avoid the risk of making wrong selections.
Q3. How long does the visual scan of the interface last in order to complete a specific task?	E.g. shorter visual search times are usually an indicator of a good level of usability.
Q4. How many times and for how long do users look at various interface elements before clicking on a target element?	E.g. a usable website should reduce users' cognitive load by cutting the time spent on distractive information.
What to evaluate for usefulness	
Indicative question	*Indicative answer*
Q1. How many times and for how long do users view the results retrieved?	E.g. the visual time spent on the search results and the number of results viewed can be used as indicators of a system's usefulness.
Q2. What are the visual search strategies employed by users when they evaluate the relevance/usefulness of the information presented in the search-results interface of a DL?	E.g. the identification of these strategies is important in order to identify appropriate ways of displaying the information contained in the results lists.

How to collect data

The recording of eye movements is made possible through the use of specialized devices called eye trackers. Eye trackers are fixed (desktop) or portable devices with embedded cameras that can sense light reflected from the eyes onto the screen (Figure 9.1). Among the different types of eye-movement data that can be collected using eye trackers, users' fixations are the most common and useful data for understanding visual searching behaviour and any behaviour associated with cognitive activity. A fixation is a stable gaze focused on a specific area. The typical length of a fixation can be 150–600 milliseconds

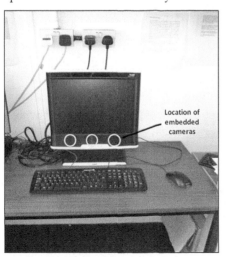

Location of embedded cameras

Figure 9.1 *A desktop eye tracker*

(Rayner, 2009), but longer fixations can occur. Usually, repeated and long fixations on a focus area can be associated with increased cognitive load, due to several factors, such as interest, surprise or difficulty in comprehension (Hughes et al., 2003). In the context of IR research the number and length of fixations has been used to examine the level of users' attention on specific features or areas of search-results lists and web pages (e.g. Loringo et al., 2008).

As well as fixation data, researchers may also collect and analyse data related to users' scan-paths or saccades (Duchowski, 2007). Saccades can be thought of as rapid eye movements that take place between fixations, and last no more than 100 milliseconds (Duchowski, 2007). As opposed to fixations, saccades are usually ignored from the data analysis in IR studies because they can capture little or no information about a user's behaviour. However, when analysed in relation to fixation data (for example, the sequence of fixations and saccades), saccades can produce scan-paths. Scan-paths can show eye movement patterns, such as navigation patterns during the interaction with the search and search-results interfaces of DLs.

How to analyse

Data analysis of eye movements can be conducted both statistically and visually. Statistical analysis involves calculations on ratio types of data, such as the number and length (in milliseconds) of fixations. For example, it is possible to calculate the total or the mean number of times a user fixated on a specific area of the interface. In order to identify the length and frequency of fixations on a specific area of the interface, eye trackers provide the opportunity for researchers to define Areas of Interest (AoI). These are similar to boxes of content and are particularly useful when the evaluation is focused on specific components of a DL (e.g. the search box, or the logo).

Visual analysis of the data is possible through heat-maps and gaze-plots. Heat-maps are graphical representations of users' visual behaviour in which the frequency and length of fixations are represented by the use of colours. For example, a typical heat-map may use red to present an area of high visual activity (i.e. repeated and long fixations), yellow in areas of moderate visual activity and green for areas where only a few and short fixations occurred. Figure 9.2a is a grey-scaled version of a typical heat-map. In the grey-scaled figure, the brighter areas represent increased visual activity, while the darker areas denote areas of low visual activity. Finally, a gaze-plot shows a graphical representation of a scan-path (Figure 9.2b).

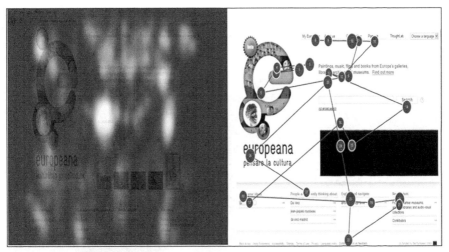

Figure 9.2 *(a) Heat-map (left) and (b) gaze-plot (right)*

Case study 9.1: The Europeana study

The evaluation of the Europeana prototype was identified as a priority within the Europeana v.1.0 project (see Europeana v.1.0). An international user and functional testing study was conducted between October 2009 and January 2010, co-ordinated by the University of Strathclyde, Glasgow. The study aimed to gather feedback from potential users of Europeana (members of the general public and younger users) and make some recommendations for the improvement of the usability of this service.

The use of eye tracking was part of a mixed-method research design that also involved qualitative data collection from focus groups. Data was obtained from a total of 12 participants who used Europeana in order to complete a set of informational tasks (e.g. to find information about their local city). The results presented in this case study came from the analysis of user interaction with the Home screen and the Search results interface of Europeana. Data analysed included the number of fixations made on specific AoI, and calculation of the sequence with which various AoI were fixated by participants during initial exposure.

Home screen analysis

The various interface elements of the Home screen interface were divided into seven AoI (Figure 9.3a). These were: 1. Search box, 2. Images, 3. Welcome text, 4. Navigation bar, 5. Logo, 6. Logo text, and 7. Menu. Figure 9.3b shows that the highest percentage of fixations occurred in the Search box area. This was followed by the Welcome text (which contains a short text about Europeana) and the Navigation bar. The lowest percentage of fixations occurred in the Logo text area (1%).

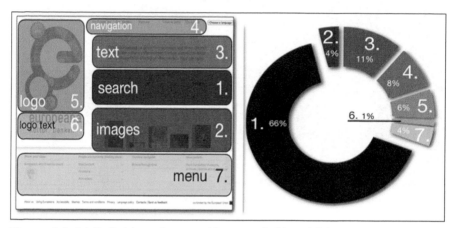

Figure 9.3 *(a) Definition of areas of interest (left) and (b) percentage of fixations per area (right)*

The calculation of the sequence in which various AoI were fixated by participants was based on the use of gaze-plots. Gaze-plots show the order of fixations on the screen (see Figure 9.2). A decision was made to focus on initial exposure in order to find out which AoI were immediately noticed by participants. It was anticipated that the important AoI of the Home screen, such as the Search box, would be made visible by participants immediately after initial exposure. On the Home screen, participants tended to fixate first on the Search box, followed by the Welcome text and the Logo areas. Usually, the areas fixated last were the Logo text, the Images and the Navigation bar.

Search results screen analysis

The analysis of the number of fixations that occurred on this screen showed that the Search box accounted for the majority of fixations. The Search box was followed by the Images area, which received 23% of fixations. The Refined search area and the Result navigation accounted for 15% of fixations each, while the Europeana Logo received only 3%.

Although the area of Images was the second most-fixated AoI, with 23% of the fixations, it was the first AoI that participants in the study fixated during initial exposure. Then, participants attended to the Result navigation area before directing their attention to the Refined search box. The Search box, which accounted for 36% of fixations, was rarely fixated first during initial exposure. This was also the case with the Logo and Navigation bar areas of the Search results screen. Usually, these were fixated last during initial exposure.

Interpreting data for design

The data collected from the eye tracker gave some useful insights into the attention that the various interface elements of Europeana's Home and Search result screens received from participants in the study. The interpretation of this data into practical recommendations for redesign can highlight the importance of using eye-tracking technology in the evaluation of DLs.

Firstly, the findings showed that the Search box, which is the principal tool for using Europeana, received a good level of attention in the cases of both the Home screen (66% of fixations) and the Search results screen (36% of fixations). Although the Search box did not draw participants' immediate attention, in the case of the Search results screen this was normal, because the main purpose of this screen was for users to evaluate the results before deciding to reformulate their queries. Therefore, the data collected suggested that participants' visual search behaviour for keyword searching was served well by the specific area of the interface.

The Image area of the Home screen received a poor level of fixation (4% of fixations) and it was not made immediately visible to participants. However, this was not the case for the Search results interface. The images displayed in the Search results screen occupied most of the space of the interface, received the second-highest percentage of fixations from participants and became immediately visible during initial exposure. The difference between the Home and the Search results screen can be justified by the role that the images played for both interfaces. In the case of the Search results screen, images were the result of participants' search for relevant information. However, in the case of the Home interface, images played a different role, which was merely informational (e.g. to show featured images in the collection or newly digitized material). Although a decision could be made to eliminate images from the Home screen, the fact that these images received a low level of attention from participants and did not distract them from completing the main task of searching for information renders such a decision optional.

The Navigation bar was among the least-fixated areas in the cases of both the Home screen and the Search results interface (accounting only for 8% of fixations). This may be due to its lack of prominence, or because the user does not understand the importance of the Navigation bar. When observing gaze replay it was noted that navigation terms received extended fixation – suggesting that the user might be having difficulty understanding the terms and/or where they would be likely to navigate to.

The Europeana Logo and the supporting text accounts for nearly 25% of the fixations made on the Home screen. As such, it might be expected that the Logo would draw users' attention from competing AoI, like the Navigation bar. Feedback from participants' focus groups confirmed that the Logo was felt initially to be 'too big in the browser' and 'occasionally distracting'. However, a follow-up analysis of the length of the fixations showed that the Logo did not receive much attention. In particular, the total time spent fixating on the Logo and the accompanying text (Logo text) accounted for only 7% of user attention. This suggests that the Logo initially grabs the user's attention, but interest wanes as the user attempts to accomplish a task.

Finally, the Menu area of the Home screen did not receive much attention (only 4% of total fixations, while in the case of immediate exposure it was fixated after the Logo and the Welcome text). Given the importance of the information contained in the Menu (it contains links to featured searches, news and time-line browsing of the collection), further actions should be taken in order to increase its visibility. ▓

Conclusions

The aim of this chapter has been to introduce a new approach to the evaluation of DLs, based on the recording of eye movements. The case study of Europeana shows that eye tracking can be a useful tool in the evaluation of DLs, especially because it records behavioural data that cannot be captured by other traditional techniques (such as data logs and screen-recording software). For example, in the case of Europeana, the number of fixations gave some indication of the level of importance of different AoI during task completion. Similarly, the order in which AoI were fixated during initial exposure disclosed information about their salience or visibility. Based on the interpretation of this type of data, some recommendations were made for improving the visibility of the Menu in the Home screen and of the Navigation bar, and informed the design of next versions of the Europeana interface. Also, as well as design recommendations, the collection of eye movement data helped in the interpretation of the data collected from the focus groups, especially in relation to the use of the Europeana logo.

Besides the benefits that eye tracking can offer in the evaluation of DLs, there are several limitations and considerations that should be taken into account before a decision is made to use this type of technology. First, eye-tracking technology is still expensive and a decision to purchase should follow long-term commitment to and investment in this solution. Also, although data collection using eye tracking is simple, the process of data analysis still remains cumbersome and difficult. For example, many eye-tracking software packages do not support complex statistical analysis of scan-paths. Furthermore, there are still problems in recording the eye movements from certain categories of people, such as those with visual impairments. Moreover, some eye-tracking products do not work with all types of stimuli on the web, such as Flash content. However, aside from these difficulties, eye tracking can provide evaluators with rich data about human onscreen behaviour that could inform the design and development of DLs.

References

Dobreva, M. et al. (2010) *User and Functional Testing: final report*, Europeana, http://bit.ly/JSxUQd.

Duchowski, A. T. (2007) *Eye Tracking Methodology: theory and practice*, Springer-Verlag.

Europeana v.1.0, www.version1.europeana.eu/web/europeana-project/about-us.

Hughes, A., Wilkens, T., Wildemuth, B. and Marchionini, G. (2003) Text or Pictures? An eyetracking study of how people view digital video surrogates. In Bakker, E. M. et al. (eds), *Proceedings of the Second International Conference, CIVR 2003 Urbana-Champaign, IL, USA, July 24–25, 2003* Springer-Verlag, 271–80.

Loringo, L. et al. (2008) Eye Tracking and Online Search: lessons learned and challenges ahead, *Journal of the American Society for Information Science and Technology*, **59** (7), 1041–52.

Rayner, K. (2009) Eye Movements and Attention in Reading, Scene Perception and Visual Search, *The Quarterly Journal of Experimental Psychology*, **62**, 1457–506.

Tsakonas, G. and Papatheodorou, C. (2006) Analyzing and Evaluating Usefulness and Usability in Electronic Information Services, *Journal of Information Science*, **32** (5), 400–19.

CHAPTER 10

Personas

Katja Guldbæk Rasmussen and Gitte Petersen

Figure 10.1 *Maria*

Maria is a school teacher, comfortable with computers and the internet. Happily Googles but also frequently having a specific target for her searches as she prepares for work. She uses her mobile to update her Facebook status, but mostly for calling and texting. Her aim is often to prepare for classes, but also to find new ways of motivating her pupils.
(Personas (short version) from EuropeanaConnect)

The description of 'Maria' (Figure 10.1) is an example of a so-called 'persona'. A persona is a fictional person (Nielsen, 2004, 3), an archetypal user, who represents a major user group for a specific website in terms of needs, goals and personal characteristics. The purpose of personas is to act as 'stand-ins' for real users. Made available in the early stages of the development process, they can guide the development team's decisions about functionality and design throughout most of the development process, without the involvement of actual users. However, it is important to recognize that personas are not used instead of but as a *supplement to* other user testing techniques (Grudin, 2005, 8).

The use of personas gives the development team numerous advantages:

- It helps developers to constantly remember for whom they are creating the product. By asking 'Would Maria use this?' they can filter out personal quirks, 'stand in the users' shoes' and focus on motivations and behaviours typical of a broad range of users, while still relating to users as individuals and evaluating ideas from a user's point of view (Pruitt and Grudin, 2003, 2).

- It helps developers by bringing users to life by putting a 'real' face to rather dry results from user tests and statistics and avoids the trap of designing for an 'average' non-existent user.
- It helps to shorten the design process because designs can be constantly evaluated against the personas, reducing the frequency of large and expensive usability tests.
- It supports communication between members of the development team because design suggestions and decisions can be referred to the personas.

The level of detail in a persona description depends on the context in which the persona is to be used. Typically a persona includes a name and picture as well as demographic details such as age, gender, personality, socio-economic background, education, work, home environment, expectations, interests, etc. It is particularly important to include the persona's goals, tasks and motivation in relation to the site or service that is being evaluated. Although fictitious, personas need to be based on 'real' data about target groups. Data may come from different sources, such as previously conducted user research, web statistics, demographic information in general, knowledge about users' search behaviour, general use patterns on the internet, habits and trends in skill levels and tasks performed, etc. The creation, evaluation and recreation of personas based on quantitative as well as qualitative data about 'real users' is important for avoiding the trap of prejudices (Grudin and Pruitt, 2002, 4).

As such, each persona represents many users and a 'set' of personas represents the spectrum of the target user groups. There is no magic number for how many personas a set should contain, but ideally only the minimum number of personas required to illustrate key goals and behaviour patterns should be used (Pruitt and Grudin, 2003, 2). Though most sites have many different user groups these typically need to be condensed into 3–5 personas – having more will make it difficult for the development team to remember the different personalities of the personas and they will start to blur into one.

Complementing scenarios

According to Nielsen (2009), there are two approaches to using personas. The first integrates scenarios and personas. The second describes personas and scenarios as two separate elements of system design. In the Europeana project the latter approach has been used because it makes it possible to adjust and work with personas and scenarios independently and to combine them in numerous ways.

A scenario is a short story with a setting, a plot or a sequence of actions and events – a 'vision of the future' (Pruitt and Adlin, 2006, 13) – describing a possible use situation where a fictional user (a persona) interacts with the web page. Scenarios can be 'problem scenarios', 'idea generating scenarios' or 'idea testing scenarios' (Nielsen, 2009).

When personas are being developed it is necessary to consider what their needs are for using the website and in what kinds of situation each persona will use the site. All characteristic tasks must be listed, as these are the starting-points for the scenarios. The tasks selected need to be a representative collection of benchmark tasks based on the results of marketing research, needs analysis, concept testing and requirements analyses.

The next step is to tell the story of what will happen when a persona tries to perform a task. What will the persona do, not do or wish to do? All personas should 'go through' all relevant tasks, and every little story represents a scenario. On the way through each scenario it is important to take note of possible needs and potential obstacles, possibilities for improvement (functionally and design related), potential problems with incoherent workflows, need for guidance, filters, lists, etc. These will vary according to their importance for users' experience of the website, and they should be prioritized and integrated in the ensuing development iteration of the website.

Integrated into the developers' daily work, personas represent an important tool for identifying some of the most obvious 'developer mistakes' before testing the website on real users. 'Ask' the personas for advice; let them influence decisions and clarify discussions by asking the question 'How can we develop/improve the feature/site to the advantage of this persona – this kind of user?'.

Personas in the Europeana Connect project
An introduction to Europeana Connect

In 2005 Europeana, a cross-European project, was initiated by the European Commission, with the goal of making Europe's cultural and scientific heritage accessible to the public through the web portal www.europeana.eu. In 2008 the first portal prototype was launched, offering a search platform for exploring the digital resources of Europe's museums, libraries and archives. To secure the usability of web services developed within this framework, it was part of the official project plans that a set of Europeana personas should be prepared as a common work tool for all partners in the project. The work was initiated by a usability team at The Royal Library in Copenhagen and it resulted in the seven personas now accepted and used by the project partners. The steps described in this case study were applied, mostly inspired by Nielsen (2007).

Collecting fundamental data

The first step was to collect as much already available knowledge as possible about users in libraries, archives and museums – on a national as well as European basis. Data originated from multiple empirical sources, such as previous usability tests, observations, interviews, marketing research and national or European reports. This was supplemented with a broad range of statistical information relevant to the creation of personas (for instance demographics, such as population age and education, language and IT skills, media and mobile use). To this were added general theories on psychological attitudes and search strategies (e.g. Kuhlthau, 2004 and White and Roth, 2009). According to the project requirements, the process had to start from already existing personas within the domain. Thus, we also collected a large number of existing personas (76) created and used in different contexts, mainly from Central and Northern Europe.

Contextual and non-contextual details

In the second step all personas were systematized and we started building hypotheses about details that were crucial for the users' experiences with Europeana. It was our assumption that, if we wanted to develop a set of personas that could be agreed upon by all project partners, we would have to start from the basic profiles and subsequently jointly 'dress up' the personas with contextual details that might vary according to national and regional differences.

Therefore, all contextual details were removed from the personas and they were 'condensed' into eight basic profiles based on non-contextual differences in search behaviour (from 'strongly explorative' to 'strongly navigational'; the idea of characterizing search behaviour as 'explorative' or 'navigational' is described, for instance, in White and Drucker, 2007, 21–30) and search literacy (from 'effortless' to 'difficult').

'Dressing up' the personas

In the third step the eight basic profiles were presented to a group of Europeana partners at a workshop facilitated by persona expert Dr Lene Nielsen. Participants discussed the distribution of profiles within a matrix having search behaviour on one axis and search literacy on the other. The matrix aimed at two purposes: first, it helped with the mutual distribution of the profiles, and, second, it focused discussions about which profiles were relevant to Europeana. When the group was satisfied with the profiles' placement in the matrix (see Figure 10.2), details about the areas that need to be presented in the descriptions (Nielsen, 2007), namely *body, psyche, background, emotions* and *attitudes towards technology* were added to the profiles during several iterations. It was important for all of the personas' details to be agreed upon by the whole group and supported by relevant statistics and reports. The group also made lists of possible use situations for each of the personas: in which situations would they use the website and which needs of each persona would lead to a use situation? Each need or situation is the beginning of a scenario, and from these starting-points the group created trustworthy stories about each persona's interaction with the website for the achievement of a realistic goal. Obstacles that might block the way to these goals were identified during the 'playing' of these scenarios. After the workshop all the personas were reviewed by international persona experts.

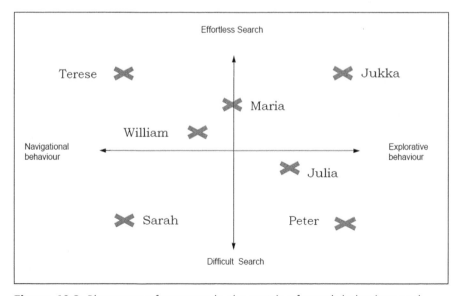

Figure 10.2 *Placement of personas in the matrix of search behaviour and literacy*

Dissemination of knowledge

At the end of the workshop a major concern of the participants was how these personas could be integrated into the Europeana project at all levels. The group who had developed these tools felt very related to the personas – almost talking about them as friends – but knew that they would be different for those who had not participated in the creation process. And if personas are not disseminated to other project participants, 'they are not worth anything' (Nielsen, 2007, 2). The dissemination of the personas combined 'bottom-up' and 'top-down' approaches. The first approach implied that all workshop participants should make an effort to educate developers and designers back home, teaching them how to use personas, how to think in scenarios and use them in use cases. Also, the usability team at The Royal Library committed itself to continuously supporting and guiding project partners in using the personas.

The 'top-down' approach implied the involvement of the main Europeana office. For the purpose of focusing efforts across the whole Europeana project, the office chose four of the eight personas as primary personas (William, Maria, Peter, Jukka). All major decisions in the project are taken by the Europeana office and, as it uses the personas to focus and unify development and services, the work of all project partners will be evaluated in relation to these four personas.

The challenges

One of the biggest challenges in this case was to create a set of personas that, in spite of all national and regional differences, was usable across the European countries participating in the project.

As described in the first part of this chapter, it is fundamental to the persona method that the personas are developed for a specific context, a specific purpose and with regional characteristics. This all influences the choice of attributes attached to the personas. In this case we were faced with a very interesting challenge: would it be at all possible? How should this challenge be approached?

First, it turned out to be difficult to get personas, as well as any information at all, from Southern and Eastern Europe, and this probably had to do with the limitations of language. An even bigger problem was that no partners from Southern and Eastern Europe were able to participate in the workshop where the basic profiles were 'dressed', which otherwise would have strengthened the credibility of the descriptions.

Second, it was difficult to overview the overwhelming amount of data collected. Faced with so much information, it takes many discussions to arrive at the very core of what actually characterizes the different segments of each user group. What are basic characteristics and what is part of the 'decoration'. This was especially difficult when the work had to be based on pre-existing personas. As we did not claim that the personas were representative in the usual quantitative sense, there were no strict rules for what and how much (for instance) statistical information needed to be included in their creation.

In this case, this was determined by the project partners in the workshop held to 'dress up' the personas. It was a condition that all should agree on the details – from name to number of children – attached to the personas, and this dialogue was crucial to avoid the 'stereotype threat'. Stereotypes are embedded in most (if not all) cultures (Burgess, 2003) and often incorporate oversimplified conceptions, or prejudices, and can prevent us from understanding who our users really are and what they really want. By keeping an open dialogue cross-nationally in the process of creating the personas, the project partners helped each other to maintain a critical approach and stay clear of obvious stereotypes. Whenever disagreements or questions occurred, fact was consulted. This resulted in a set of 'pragmatic' personas built on recognizability more than on representativeness.

More quantitative data could be incorporated into the persona-creating process, but at a very basic level. It is the 'softer skills that are most important, such as listening to people and thinking outside existing assumptions' (Spool, 2007). One of the most important purposes of using personas is that they help designers to keep in mind that they are not designing for themselves (Spool, 2007): they are designing for the needs of the people who will actually use the product. Now, four of the personas are being used in Europeana Connect to plan new services; and in the selection, development and evaluation of services, as well as to plan marketing efforts. The personas are 'at work', but this is just the first step in our efforts to spread the method further among designers and developers throughout the Europeana project. ▨

Conclusions: the validity of the persona method

The persona method has gained increasing attention and popularity among software designers and usability practitioners since the method was proposed by Cooper (1999). Today it is considered as more or less a standard component of usability work, used by professional software companies like Microsoft (Pruitt and Grudin, 2003) as well as government agencies such as the Danish 'borger.dk'. Some researchers, for instance Chapman and

Milham (2006), have argued that the persona method lacks validity because of the impossibility of verifying the accuracy of personas and assessing whether a group of personas appropriately represents the population of interests: 'one cannot know whether a persona represents a million people or zero' (Chapman and Milham, 2006, 2).

Even though there may be a certain degree of truth in this argument, it does not change the fact that we, as humans, naturally engage in, care about and remember much more easily when we deal with 'persons' and live stories – be they real or fictional – than when we deal with statistical data or rather 'dry' population segments (Pruitt and Adlin, 2006, 16). Personas invoke this powerful human capability and bring it into the design process – just as on an everyday basis we engage with fictional characters in movies, books and television programmes. Well-crafted personas are generative and, once we engage with them, we can almost effortlessly project them into new situations.

So, even though personas may not be a magic wand, they are certainly a powerful tool for development teams. They are effective in helping the team to gain a common perception of users, rather than to have individual pictures, and help to keep the team continuously focused on and 'addicted' to the users' needs. They do not replace other usability methods and testing with real users, but are a complement to them. Add to this the fact that personas – as opposed to real users – can be available at any time in the development process, whenever there might be a need, ready and willing to help us enhance the quality of the products that we present to real users – whether for testing or for use.

References

Burgess, H. (2003) Stereotype/Characterization Frames. In Burgess, G. and Burgess, H. (eds), *Beyond Intractability*, Conflict Research Consortium, University of Colorado, Boulder, www.beyondintractability.org/essay/stereotypes/.

Chapman, C. N. and Milham, R. P. (2006) The Persona's New Clothes: methodological and practical arguments against a popular method. In *Proceedings of the Human Factors and Ergonomics Society 50th Annual Meeting*, 634–6, http://cnchapman.files.wordpress.com/2007/03/chapman-milham-personas-hfes2006–0139–0330.pdf.

Cooper, A. (1999) *The Inmates Are Running the Asylum*, Indianapolis: SAMS.

EuropeanaConnect (2009) 'Annex 1 – Description of Work (Best Practice Networks). ECP 528001. EuropeanaConnect', Amendment 1.0 of 19/08/2009. European Commission.

Grudin, J. (2005) *Communication and Collaboration Support in an Age of Information Scarcity*, Redmond, WA: Microsoft Research.

Grudin, J. and Pruitt, J. (2002) *Personas, Participatory Design and Product Development: An Infrastructure for Engagement*, Redmond, WA: Microsoft Research.

Kuhlthau, C. C. (2004) *Seeking Meaning: a process approach to library and information services*, 2nd edn, Westport, CT: Libraries Unlimited.

Nielsen, L. (2004) *Engaging Personas and Narrative Scenarios*, no. 16, Department of Informatics, Copenhagen Business School, Copenhagen.

Nielsen, L. (2007) Ten Steps to Personas, *HCI VISTAS*, VOLUME-III, Article INS-24./July 2007, www.hceye.org/HCInsight-Nielsen.htm.

Nielsen, L. (2009) Building Personas for the European Europeana project. A workshop held 12–13.10.2009 at the Royal Library, Copenhagen, DK.

Pruitt, J. and Adlin, T. (2006) Why Personas Work: the psychological evidence. In *The Persona Lifecycle: keeping people in mind throughout product design*, San Francisco: Elsevier Inc., http://research.microsoft.com/en-us/um/people/jgrudin/publications/personas/PersonasTheory.doc.

Pruitt, J. and Grudin, J. (2003) Personas: practice and theory. In *Proceedings of the Conference on Designing for user experiences, New York.*

Spool, J. M. (2007) Making Personas Work for Your Web Site: an interview with Steve Mulder, www.uie.com/articles/mulder_interview/.

White, R. and Drucker, S. M. (2007) Investigating Behavioral Variability in Web Search. In *Proceedings of the 16th International Conference on WWW*, www2007.org/papers/paper535.pdf.

White, R. W. and Roth, R. A. (2009) *Exploratory Search: beyond the query–response paradigm*. Synthesis lectures on information concepts, retrieval, and services, no.3, Morgan & Claypool Publishers.

PART 3

**User studies in the digital library universe:
what else needs to be considered?**

CHAPTER 11

User-related issues in multilingual access to multimedia collections

Paul Clough

Multilingual information access

Increasingly, modern digital libraries (DLs) have to deal with an array of different media types, such as photos, paintings, sounds, maps, manuscripts, books, newspapers and archival papers, and often in large volumes. For example, in mid-2011, Europeana, a portal that provides online access to much of Europe's cultural heritage, contained well over 19 million digitized cultural objects, of which over 60% were images. Of course the challenges faced do not stop at just handling different media types; DLs must also support digital materials that are multi-cultural and multi-language (Borgman, 1997; Oard, 1997). In June 2010 it was estimated that, of the 1.9 billion internet users, 27% used English, 23% Chinese and 8% Spanish (with Arabic ranked 7th) (Internet World Stats). According to Online Computer Library Centre (OCLC), in 2010 its global online library catalogue accessible to users, WorldCat, contained nearly 197 million records for library items in 479 languages from more than 17,000 libraries in 52 countries (OCLC, 2010). More than 57% of records in WorldCat are written in languages other than English. DL infrastructures must therefore be able to handle increasing volumes of multimedia content, and to store and present documents written in multiple language scripts and localized to specific user groups.

Multilingual Information Access (MLIA) addresses the problem of accessing and retrieving information from collections in any language. This covers both technical aspects, such as language identification and character encoding, and the overall access and retrieval of multilingual information. Systems that process information in multiple languages (either queries, documents or both) are called Multilingual Information Retrieval (MLIR) systems (Peters et al., 2012). In such systems documents in the collection exist in different languages and search requests can be made in any language (e.g. as occurring on the web). More specifically, systems that help users to cross the language boundary – querying a multilingual collection in one language in order to retrieve relevant documents written in other languages – are referred to as Cross-Language Information Retrieval or CLIR (Gey et al., 2005; Nie, 2010). An obvious question for MLIR/CLIR is 'Why do users want to retrieve documents they presumably can't read?'. In some cases users are multilingual (or polyglots): they can formulate searches and judge relevance in many languages but want the convenience of a single query; in other cases users are monolingual (monoglots), so want to query in their native language. However, users may be able to judge the relevance of results even if not translated: they may have access to document translation, or the objects retrieved may be 'language independent' (e.g. images).

Apart from being able to index multiple languages, providing cross-lingual access specifically involves translation between the source language (i.e. the language of the user's query) and the target language (i.e. the language of the documents being searched). This can be achieved by:

1 translating the documents into the source language
2 translating the query into the target language(s)
3 translating the queries and documents into a common language (or interlingua).

Approaches based on translating the document collection usually involve translating the documents offline into a number of specific languages in which one assumes that users may want to search. The advantage is that translated documents can be quickly presented to the user for examination; disadvantages include having to store multiple versions of the same document and that accommodating new languages requires translating all documents in the collection, which is time-consuming. Query translation solves some of these problems. However, translation must occur 'on the fly', which can slow the system. In addition, queries are often short, with little context, thereby making automated translation difficult (e.g. due to ambiguity). The translation of queries and/or documents is usually achieved using approaches based on machine-readable dictionaries or using Machine Translation. In addition to supporting the search for specific items, DLs may also want to support more exploratory forms of information-seeking behaviours that involve browsing and exploration. This can be facilitated by translating resources used to organize and manage the content, such as controlled vocabularies and thesauri.

From the users' perspective there are several areas of the search process where they may require support: during query formulation; when exploring the search results and examining individual documents; and during query reformulation and refinement. During query formulation one of the predominant forms of search assistance is query translation: mapping the query from one language into a different language(s). Previous research has shown that allowing the user to monitor and interact with query translation increases the performance of CLIR systems (Oard et al., 2008). Assistance may include helping users to select the correct meaning for an ambiguous word or phrase, allowing users to demarcate phrases and proper names and allowing users to add their own preferred translations to the dictionary for future use (i.e. a translation memory). Once results have been returned users may need help to decide whether or not the results contain any relevant documents. This can be eased by translating document 'surrogates' (e.g. summaries, document titles or key information extracted from the results) into users' source languages. Users may also require help with examining a specific returned result, e.g. by showing a previously translated version or translating the selected document 'on the fly'. Functionality to support query refinement may also be offered, such as automated term suggestion or a 'find me more like this' feature. As one might expect, the degree of users' involvement will depend on their language skills/abilities, the translation resources available for query translation and the design of the user interface and interaction model.

Supporting MLIR and CLIR in DLs has long been recognized as important in providing universal access to digital content. This has been confirmed by many different types of user study. For example, Marlow et al. (2007) investigated the potential need for multilingual access to Tate Online, one of the UK's largest cultural heritage sites, and found that 31% of visitors came from outside the UK and their preferred language for searching and navigating the site was not English. Results from an online survey indicated that the provision of multilingual access would be welcomed by visitors who preferred to interact with content from Tate Online in their native (non-English) languages. Wu, Luo and He (2010) studied the use of multilingual information access by students of Chinese academic libraries. Their findings highlighted the wide use of multilingual resources (most of which were in English and difficult to use) by Chinese students and the need for specialist technologies and translation resources in this domain.

....

Case study 10.1: MultiMatch
....

The following study aims to illustrate a user-centred approach to the design of multilingual access to multimedia document collections. The European MultiMatch project developed a specialized search engine enabling users to explore and interact with online-accessible cultural heritage material across media types and language boundaries (see MultiMatch). The rationale behind the project was to assist users with discovering, interpreting and aggregating content that had previously existed in a dispersed and fragmented nature on the web and in multiple formats and languages.

Cultural heritage content, including images, videos, audio files, RSS feeds and web pages, was automatically gathered from online sources (e.g. cultural heritage sites, educational sites related to cultural heritage, encyclopedic sources and OAI-compliant sources) or provided by participating cultural institutions. This offered a representative cross-section of cultural heritage information: multilingual, dynamic and static and from multiple sources. The content was represented using a conceptual framework (metadata schema and data model, thesauri and rules for mapping between different sources), and a multimedia content management system (see MILOS) was used to store different formats and associated metadata.

Media types were handled individually. For example, key facts were extracted from texts (e.g. names of people and places, dates and times) and used to provide functionality to browse the content (e.g. using timelines and maps). Automatic speech recognition was used to generate text transcripts from audio streams (e.g. podcasts, videos) and to enable standard keyword searching. Videos were automatically segmented into smaller coherent units (shots) consisting of frames, and exemplar frames were selected from each shot and used to visualize retrieved videos. Low-level visual features (e.g. shapes and colours) were extracted from images and combined with accompanying text, if present, for multimodal retrieval. This processing enabled sophisticated forms of searching and navigating, such as using text to search video content and audio files (rather than simply using metadata) and using example images to find similar images in a 'more like this' function.

The design of the MultiMatch system adopted a user-centred approach to incorporate the feedback and views of users (both professionals and more general users) at various stages within the design lifecycle. The first stage, requirements gathering, identified users' information needs and search tasks, resulting in scenarios and use cases. This was followed by the creation of low-fidelity (e.g. paper and HTML-based) prototypes. The final stage developed a fully functional system (shown in Figure 11.1). The resulting system enabled users to search across languages (via query translation); search for web pages, audio files, videos and images simultaneously; and explore connections and relationships between items, places and times. With regard to MLIR support, the MultiMatch system allowed users to:

1 set the locale of the interface (Dutch, Spanish, German and English)
2 search all target languages using English as an interlingua language
3 filter the language of results returned
4 perform interactive query translation (e.g. select/deselect alternative translations for a given word/phrase or add translations to a user-defined dictionary) from a manually specified source language.

The requirements-gathering stage used several sources of input to help understand the nature of searching for cultural heritage material and inform the design of the system (Minelli et al., 2007). This included literature and past research, competitor analyses to identify common features offered by similar sites and services, examining query log files of cultural heritage websites to

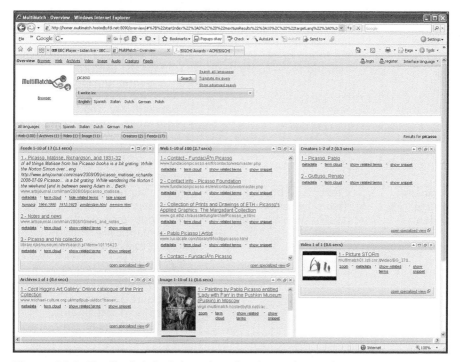

Figure 11.1 *The final default interface for the MultiMatch system*

establish common patterns of search behaviour, and conducting user studies and interviews with cultural heritage experts/professionals and more general users (e.g. tourists) to establish current information-seeking behaviours and the potential need for functionality proposed to be offered by the MultiMatch system. Field studies were also conducted with professionals (academics and image/video professionals) using contextual inquiry: talking to and observing users at work in their own environments. Triangulation of the results of various data collection activities was performed to produce a richer and more complete picture of the nature of search in cultural heritage and the needs of various user groups.

The identification of the information needs of professionals resulted in Table 11.1. Despite the differences in job roles and areas of expertise, many common patterns emerged across all groups of interviewees. The users' needs formed the basis for identifying the system functionalities/requirements for working prototypes. In addition, personas and use case scenarios were developed to illustrate specific users and their use of the proposed system.

Table 11.1 *Summary of user needs and the associated system and interface requirements*

Relevant groups	User need	System requirement
Academic Image Video	Looking for the same material on different sites (either because it couldn't be found or because it needed to be confirmed)	Aggregate multimedia material dispersed across the web and fuse results in a single place. Employ a common ontology to facilitate the exploration of content coming from diverse origins in a unified and organized way. The system will create a new, unique metadata scheme to create common links among the content whilst respecting the original native metadata formats.
Academic Image Video	Search and browse (typically search for a topic and browse through results)	Provide support for both types of behaviour. Organize and sub-divide large results sets into semantically related clusters to avoid duplication of results and to facilitate ease of finding the desired information when the query is ambiguous. To support background research and fact finding, automatically generate summarized descriptions of people and their creations, including names and dates.

Table 11.1 *Summary of user needs and the associated system and interface requirements (continued)*

Relevant groups	User need	System requirement
Academic Image Video	Have support for a variety of searches relating to people, subjects, time and places (who, what, when, where), particularly queries involving two or more of these aspects	Let users navigate semantic relationships between multiple categories (via faceted browsing or some other method). Categories/facets should be logical, intuitive and correspond to the main classes of searches. Utilize specialized thesauri relating to names of people and places to support linguistic variations in these areas.
Academic Image Video	Search for items conveying a feeling, mood, style or other aspect that cannot be easily conveyed verbally	Facilitate content-based retrieval, query by example and multimodal querying.
Academic Image Video	Consult authoritative, quality information sources	Provide information about provenance and facilitate the filtering of results by domain (e.g. exclude Wikipedia results).
Academic Image Video	Be aware of copyright issues	Provide information about copyright; institute a log-in system so that users must register and accept a copyright policy in order to access non-public domain material.
Academic Image Video	Conduct searches in unknown languages	Provide the option of performing and inspecting automatic query translation, thus broadening the coverage of a search and eliminating the need to rely on dictionaries to manually translate terms. Use various thesauri relating to areas in which multiple variations of words exist across languages (e.g. the Getty ULAN for artists' names and TGN for place names). Useful for queries whose spelling varies from language to language (e.g. Raphael in English, Raffaello in Italian).
Academic Image Video	Have assistance to browse documents or results written in foreign languages	Offer the option of automatically translating foreign-language summaries or documents (although the degree and nature of support needed might depend on the media type being searched for).

Table 11.1 *Summary of user needs and the associated system and interface requirements (continued)*

Relevant groups	User need	System requirement
Video	Get a quick overview of a video's content	Provide both textual descriptions and keyframe storyboards to use as summaries. Allow users to retrieve relevant portions of a video clip based on automatic speech recognition transcripts and visual metaphor tools.
Video	Find places in a video where certain words are spoken (e.g. a famous quotation)	Enable keyword searching of video transcripts and the ability to jump into relevant parts of the video.

Conclusions

Multimedia content is one issue that many DLs must address; another challenge is dealing with written content that is expressed in multiple languages and written from the perspective of different cultures. Advancements in multimedia and multilingual information processing will undoubtedly have an important role to play in providing enhanced future information access to digital content. However, despite the obvious benefits of cross-language searching, an analysis of around 150 US DLs in 2007 (Chen and Bao, 2009) revealed that only five (3%) could be accessed using more than one language and no site employed cross-language information retrieval or utilized machine translation. There may be many reasons for this, including lack of demand; the complexities involved in translating natural language, leading to low-quality performance; the lack of translation resources for specific language pairs or domains; the financial costs involved; and the lack of specialist knowledge to implement such functionality.

Multimedia and multilingual content presents the designers of information access systems with many technical challenges, such as processing large quantities of digital material efficiently and effectively, representing various media types in manners that enable a wide range of interaction styles, and supporting the storage and presentation of multiple character encodings and scripts. With the availability of publicly accessible translation resources, such as Google Translate, it may in future become more common to find cross-lingual search in DLs.

However, the problems are not just technical and attention must be paid to the users, especially their tasks and the contexts in which systems are to be deployed, if information access is to be successful. Supporting the individual differences of users, such as language and cultural differences, is becoming increasingly important, especially if the goal is to develop personalized products and services. As Robins states, 'most IR systems are used by people and we cannot design effective IR systems without some knowledge of how users interact with them' (Robins, 2000, 57). User studies are therefore vital for understanding the current behaviours and needs of various user groups and identifying areas where users require assistance (e.g. during query formulation/translation or results presentation and document examination).

References

Borgman, C. L. (1997) Multi-media, Multi-cultural and Multi-lingual Digital Libraries: or how do we exchange data in 400 languages? *D-Lib Magazine*, dlib.ukoln.ac.uk/dlib/june97/06borgman.html.

Chen, J. and Bao, Y. (2009) Information Access Across Languages on the Web: from search engines to digital libraries. In *Proceedings of the American Society for Information Science and Technology*, **46**, 1–14.

Europeana, www.europeana.eu.

Gey, F. C., Kando, N. and Peters, C. (2005) Cross-language Information Retrieval: the way ahead, *Information Processing and Management*, **41** (3), 415–31.

Internet World Stats, www.internetworldstats.com/stats.htm.

Marlow, J., Clough, P. and Dance, K. (2007) Multilingual Needs of Cultural Heritage Website Visitors: a case study of Tate Online. In Trant, J. and Bearman, D. (eds), *International Cultural Heritage Informatics Meeting (ICHIM07): Proceedings*, Toronto: Archives & Museum Informatics, www.archimuse.com/ichim07/papers/marlow/marlow.html.

MILOS Multimedia dIgital Library for Online Search, milos.isti.cnr.it.

Minelli, S. H., Marlow, J., Clough, P., Cigarran Recuero, J. M., Gonzalo, J., Oomen, J. and Loschiavo, D. (2007) Gathering Requirements for Multilingual Search of Audiovisual Material in Cultural Heritage. In *Proceedings of Workshop on User Centricity – State of the Art (16th IST Mobile and Wireless Communications Summit)*, Budapest, Hungary, 1–5 July.

MultiMatch, www.multimatch.eu.

Nie, J.-Y. (2010) *Cross-language Information Retrieval*, Morgan & Claypool Publishers.

Oard, D. (1997) Serving Users in Many Languages – Cross-language Information Retrieval for Digital Libraries, *D-Lib Magazine*, December 1997, www.dlib.org/dlib/december97/oard/12oard.html.

Oard, D., He, D. and Wang, J. (2008) User-assisted Query Translation for Interactive Cross-language Information Retrieval, *Information Processing & Management*, **44** (1), 183–211.

OCLC (2010) *OCLC Annual Report 2009/2010*, www.oclc.org/news/publications/annualreports/2010/2010.pdf.

Peters, C., Braschler, M. and Clough, P. (2012) *Multilingual Information Retrieval: from research to practice*, Heidelberg: Springer.

Robins, D. (2000) Interactive Information Retrieval: context and basic notions, *Informing Science*, **3**, 57–62.

Wu, D., Luo, B. and He, D. (2010) How Multilingual Digital Information Is Used: a study in Chinese academic libraries. In *Proceedings of International Conference on Management and Service Science (MASS 2010)*, 1–4.

CHAPTER 12

Children and digital libraries

Ian Ruthven, Monica Landoni and Andreas Lingnau

Introduction

Online information is now a standard component in most children's information worlds. Children are encouraged to use the internet for education, have specialized online resources created for their entertainment and increasingly have digital libraries (DLs) created specifically for their use (Hutchinson, Bederson and Druin, 2006). Most schools, at least in affluent westernized countries, have computers in the classroom and many nurseries have computers for use by pre-school children.

However, the majority of research on DL interface and interaction design has been on software intended for literate, adult users. Whilst this research has led to many successful and popular systems, the increased use of computers by children has focused attention on information access tools for younger computer users (e.g. Bilal, 2001; Hutchinson, Bederson and Druin, 2006; Bilal and Bachir, 2007). Studies of children's searching behaviour and interaction styles, notably those by Bilal (Bilal, 2001; Bilal, 2002; Bilal and Bachir, 2007), Druin et al. (Druin et al., 2007; Hutchinson, Bederson and Druin, 2006) and by Large, Beheshti and Moukad (1999), have shown that there are differences in how children interact with information systems and that these differences can be exploited to provide child-appropriate information systems.

However, what these studies have also shown is that, beyond a few basic design principles, we don't yet know what are appropriate models for creating children's DLs. The response of most system developers to children's design needs is often to simplify content, to add visual content or to simplify the interaction to a few basic interactions. This approach sees children as simple versions of adults, rather than responding to the specific needs of children using DLs (Large, Beheshti and Rahman, 2002; Reuter and Druin, 2004).

In this chapter we consider the special nature of children as DL users, describing some of the challenges of providing information systems for this large group of DL users, how user studies may inform the design and evaluation of DLs designed for child users and what types of study approaches are suitable when working with children.

Children as DL users

Children are a diverse user group. In addition to commonly investigated individual differences, such as computer experience or searching style, which may affect how a user interacts with a DL, when working with children we also face a range of cognitive and emotional differences: children at different ages have different abilities, different models of the world and different tolerances. DLs designed for one age group may be seen as too childlike by older children, but as too difficult or boring by younger children. Most researchers, and other stakeholders in DL design such as parents, teachers, school librarians and publishers, design for general age ranges. Common ranges are 3- to 5-year-olds, who are pre-literate, 5- to 9-year-olds, who are becoming literate and can interact co-operatively, 9- to 12-year-olds and teenagers. The distinctions are often on the grounds of literacy, but also on the grounds of cognitive and social development and the type of information tasks in which these groups might be involved (Demner, 2001).

Differences in children's psychological and emotional development stages give rise to specific interactive behaviours, ones that must be supported by interaction design. In browsing, for example, we know that children often engage in non-linear search behaviour, following interesting information rather than information that is useful for completing a particular task, resulting in the fact that children are more likely to deviate from their information task than are adults (Bilal, 2001). Children often like to issue queries, particularly as many children's information needs are question based, but struggle with querying interfaces (Large, Beheshti and Moukad, 1999). In particular, children have smaller vocabularies than adults and are less able to generate a good query description of the information they require. Children can also struggle with complex information displays and are more susceptible to losing their way in interfaces with too many special features (Jochmann-Mannak and Lentz, 2010). So, although we want features that engage children in their natural interaction we also want the system to help children structure their information search and to provide external motivation for completing a search. Indeed, one of the goals of a good DL for children is that it should increase children's confidence in their ability to use the system successfully (Bilal, 2001).

Furthermore, unlike adults, who can usually generalize from experience of using DLs, it cannot be taken for granted that children who can solve a specific kind of problem in one domain are necessarily able to transfer that skill to a different domain. On the other hand, children have fewer mental models of what DLs should look like, are naturally inquisitive and will, for example, respond positively to different metaphors or novel interfaces such as tangible user interfaces (Revelle et al., 2005). To allow for child-appropriate DLs, it is vital to find intuitive means of interaction and to provide children with easy-to-use interfaces without the need to learn special commands, interactions or gestures. These needs require the involvement of children as design partners and user evaluators. However, some of the challenges of providing new systems for children also affect how we work with children in these roles.

The role of children in DL design and evaluation

In most research, children have taken on two main roles: as design partners and as evaluators. The former role means involving children in the formative stages of DL design and in contributing to the design of the DL interface, content and interaction. The latter role means involving children as typical end-users of a DL. Neither role should be seen as automatically pertaining to a child: many DLs for children are constructed with no input from children until the final evaluation stage, and many evaluations are conducted as 'expert evaluations' with parents, teachers and other adults speaking on behalf of children.

Within these two roles there are many approaches that can be taken (Druin, 1998), including:

1 *Participatory design*, in which children who are a sample of the intended end-user group contribute to the design of an information system. This form of design helps in prototyping new systems, contributing ideas from a child's perspective, and works best when new prototypes (either system based or paper based) can be developed quickly. This form of design can be useful for quickly eliminating design flaws and unattractive system features but care has to be taken to ensure that the children's opinions inform the design rather than create the design.

2 *Ethnographic approaches*, which cover a range of techniques examining

how children interact with DLs in real situations. Such approaches can be very powerful in eliciting information on how children interact with a DL, how often it is used compared to other sources of information, how children collaborate to find solutions, etc. A particular form of ethnographic work related to design is technology immersion (Druin, 1998), in which a novel product, such as a DL, is introduced into a child's environment to observe how it is taken up and used by a child. Ethnographic approaches have the strong advantage of realism in terms of the data collected; however, it is more difficult to find answers to specific questions – children may never interact in the way necessary to answer a particular design or evaluation question.

3 *Controlled experiment*, which is the classic approach to many DL evaluations. This is mainly appropriate for older children, as will be explained below, but is still a powerful approach for evaluating novel DLs.

User evaluation methodologies and metrics

Working with children as design partners or evaluators raises many challenges and these challenges translate into the style of user studies normally conducted with children. The challenges arise, in part, from:

1 *Children's understanding of evaluation.* Evaluation, and the evaluation component of design activities, requires reflection, reasoning and interpretation. These are activities that older children can engage in because they have the intellectual capability to reason about and interpret their activities; younger children often lack this ability and have difficulty separating an activity, such as interacting with a DL, from the activity of evaluating the interactive episode (Yusoff, Landoni and Ruthven, 2010). Younger children also have far more limited attention spans. Consequently, we need different types of study design for different age levels.

2 *The stronger role of emotion in children's decision making.* For most children, particularly very young children, an activity has to be enjoyable for them to engage in it. If an activity, such as a design activity, is not enjoyable, then the children will not participate. Emotion also impacts on the results of an activity: children are often extreme in their opinions and are often keen to please the adults involved, resulting in overly positive evaluation scores.

3 *The tasks that children naturally perform.* Adults can be asked to perform tasks specifically designed for the design or evaluation activity and many adult evaluations consist of artificial tasks conducted within experimental settings. Children, although they have strong imaginations, can have difficulty imagining tasks that they have not experienced. This means that tasks given to children must be created with care.

4 *The environments in which children naturally interact with DLs.* Children's use of DLs is primarily for education and entertainment. However, within these broad categories there are many situations in which children use DLs. In school, children are often encouraged to work in groups; for entertainment children may use a DL alone or with an adult intermediary. Traditional laboratory studies in which participants are asked to perform tasks in an unnatural environment are unsuitable for children – the unnatural environment alone can interfere with the results of any study – and, consequently, most researchers have chosen to conduct studies within natural environments such as schools, nurseries and children's homes. Many studies involve collaboration as a natural activity for children, and collaboration becomes increasingly more successful as children become less ego-centric, from 5–8 years.

5 *The level of abstraction possible.* Age can affect a child's ability to deal with abstract concepts. Novel approaches to evaluation such as the Sensual Evaluation Instrument objects – a set of eight hand-sized objects designed to stimulate reflection and elicit non-verbal feedback from users (Höök et al., 2006) – can be used successfully by adults and older children (Pasch, 2010) but younger children see the objects as toys, limiting their use as evaluation objects. Similarly, younger children can struggle to understand abstract labels such as 'satisfaction', so we need to use simpler vocabularies in design and evaluation.

User study methodologies and metrics

The research literature describing children's involvement with user studies (e.g. Druin et al., 1999) points to the difficulty of gathering valid data, since verbal communication, both in understanding and in formulating sentences, is not as effective as with adults. This is particularly true for children in the 3–5 and 5–9 age ranges. Consequently, those conducting user studies have been forced to seek methods ranging from interpreting free drawings (Druin et al., 2007) to using visual metaphors (Read, MacFarlane and Casey, 2001).

Children also have problems expressing their feelings in terms of satisfaction (Druin et al., 1999). A third element emerging from previous studies (Sim, MacFarlane and Horton, 2005) is the discrepancy between reported and observed usability when these younger children are asked to provide subjective feedback versus direct observation.

Thus, it is clear that standard tools designed for adult user evaluations and design activities may be appropriate for older children but are not directly applicable for younger children; questionnaires require higher degrees of literacy than is common in young children, interviews require high degrees of reflection and techniques such as think-aloud require high degrees of cognitive dexterity. Nor can we expect younger children to engage in standard experimental procedures such as searching on artificial search tasks, searching for controlled amounts of time, or engaging in procedures such as training or debriefing.

Rather, for conducting user studies with children we need to (a) develop methodologies that allow children to interact naturally with the system being evaluated whilst retaining some experimental control, (b) understand how children express notions of satisfaction with a system and (c) understand what metrics are appropriate for children's DLs. There are still no real standards for children's user studies; however, there are some growing trends. We discuss some of these in this section, referring to 'evaluation' for convenience, although the discussion encapsulates many design activities as well.

Current non-intrusive evaluation methods, such as query log analysis, are commonly used by commercial providers, such as web search engines, to evaluate new algorithms and interface designs. They offer the advantage of allowing a way of longitudinally evaluating a system and providing useful data in the formative stages of design. Interpretations of the logs, however, are usually based on understanding of adults' search behaviour, not children's. As we know that children have different styles of interaction and information seeking, this may mean that we need to interpret interaction logs differently when the system is being used by a child rather than an adult, otherwise our understanding of the success of the system may be flawed.

More commonly, for younger children around the ages of 3–8, studies have focused on emotional measurement tools. Agarwal and Meyer (2009) reviewed two types of emotional measurement tools – verbal and non-verbal emotion instruments – and also discussed the combination of verbal and non-verbal instrument to measure emotion. Examples of verbal instruments include Likert scales, Semantic Differential scales and Pleasure, Arousal, and Dominance Semantic Differential scales. Examples of non-verbal instruments are Emocard, Product Emotion Measurement (PrEmo) and Self Assessment Manikin (SAM).

A particularly well-known instrument is the Smileyometer, which was developed to obtain children's opinions on technology. The Smileyometer, based on a traditional Likert scale but using smiley faces instead of numbers, has proved successful but Read and MacFarlane (2006) indicated that the Smileyometer was a more useful tool for older children, as compared to young children, as too many young children tended to choose the high values and so the data had little variability.

New techniques for design and evaluation activities involving children are constantly being suggested and refined. The more we learn about children, the more we can develop appropriate and useful methods to engage them in research.

Conclusions

Children's DLs are an exciting area of research. Increasingly, many people's first experience of DLs will be as children. Consequently it is important that we should be able to design and evaluate child-appropriate DLs as the first stage in their experience of learning the value of DLs and how to get the best out of these useful repositories.

Concentrating on emotion and system logging has given some good insights into children's opinions on new DLs. Use and reuse of DLs over time can also provide useful information on what children actually enjoy using – an important aspect of any child-centred product. However, there is still a way to go in defining reusable, generally accepted approaches to user studies for children.

References

Agarwal, A. and Meyer, A. (2009) Beyond Usability: evaluating emotional response as an integral part of the user experience, *Proceedings of the 27th International Conference on Human Factors in Computing Systems, CHI 2009, Extended Abstracts Volume.*

Bilal, D. (2001) Children's Use of the Yahooligans! Web search engine: II. Cognitive and physical behaviors on research tasks, *Journal of the American Society for Information Science and Technology,* **52** (2), 118–36.

Bilal, D. (2002) Children's Use of the Yahooligans! Web search engine: III. Cognitive and physical behaviors on fully self-generated search tasks, *Journal of the American Society for Information Science and Technology*, **53** (13), 1170–83.

Bilal, D. and Bachir, I. (2007) Children's Interaction with Cross-cultural and Multilingual Digital Libraries: I. Understanding interface design representations, *Information Processing & Management*, **43** (1), 47–64.

Demner, D. (2001) *Children on the Internet*, www.otal.umd.edu/UUPractice/children.

Druin, A. (ed.) (1998) *The Design of Children's Technology*, Morgan Kaufmann.

Druin, A., Bederson, B., Boltman, A., Miurqa, A., Knotts–Callaghan, D. and Platt, M. (1999) Children as Our Technology Design Partners. In Druin, A. (ed.) *The Design of Children's Technology*, Morgan-Kaufmann, 51–72.

Druin, A., Weeks, A., Massey, S. and Bederson, B. B. (2007) Children's Interests and Concerns when Using the International Children's Digital Library: a four country case study. In *Proceedings of Joint Conference on Digital Libraries (JCDL'2007)*.

Höök, K., Sharp, M. and Laaksolahti, J. (2006) The Sensual Evaluation Instrument: developing an affective evaluation tool. In *Proceedings of the SIGCHI conference on Human Factors in computing systems (CHI '06)*.

Hutchinson, H., Bederson, B. B. and Druin, A. (2006) The Evolution of the International Children's Digital Library Searching and Browsing Interface. In *Proceedings of Interaction Design and Children [IDC'2006], Finland*.

Jochmann-Mannak, H. and Lentz, L. (2010) Children Searching Information on the Internet: performance on children's interfaces compared to Google, *ACM Workshop on Accessible Search Systems at ACM Sigir 2010*.

Large, A., Beheshti, J. and Moukad, H. (1999) Information Seeking on the Web: navigational skills of grade-six primary school students, *Proceedings of the 62nd ASIS Annual Meeting*.

Large, A., Beheshti, J. and Rahman, T. (2002) Design Criteria for Children's Web Portals: the users speak out, *Journal of the American Society for Information Science and Technology*, **53** (2), 79–94.

Pasch, M. (2010) Improving Children's Self-report in User-centered Evaluations. In *Proceedings of the 9th International Conference on Interaction Design and Children (IDC '10)*.

Read, J. C. and MacFarlane, S. J. (2006) Using the Fun Toolkit and Other Survey Methods to Gather Opinions in Child Computer Interaction, *Interaction Design and Children, IDC2006*, Tampere, Finland, ACM Press, 81–8.

Read, J. C., MacFarlane, S. J. and Casey, C. (2001) Measuring the Usability of Text Input Methods for Children. In *People and computers XV: Interaction without frontiers. Joint Proceedings of HCI 2001 and IHM 2001*.

Reuter, K. and Druin, A. (2004) Bringing Together Children and Books: an initial descriptive study of children's book searching and selection behavior in a digital library. In *Proceedings of American Society for Information Science and Technology Conference (ASIST)*.

Revelle, G., Zuckerman, O., Druin, A. and Bolas, A. (2005) Tangible User Interfaces for Children. In *CHI '05 Extended Abstracts on Human Factors in Computing Systems*.

Sim, G., MacFarlane, S. and Horton, M. (2005) Evaluating Usability, Fun and Learning in Educational Software for Children, *World Conference on Educational Multimedia, Hypermedia and Telecommunications*.

Yusoff, Y. M., Landoni, M. and Ruthven, I. (2010) Assessing Fun: young children as evaluators of interactive systems. In *ACM Workshop on Accessible Search Systems at ACM SIGIR 2010*.

CHAPTER 13

User engagement and social media

Jeffery K. Guin

Introduction

Digital libraries (DLs) are created to preserve collections while providing users with greater access to their content. The evolution of the world wide web during the 21st century has changed expectations among these users regarding how, and in what ways, they consume this content. Compared to other fields with a cultural heritage focus, DLs are collectively more advanced in their attitudes towards user engagement. Their history of building tools that encourage access to content and, in some cases, facilitate communication with other users, parallels the history of the web itself, resulting in a natural migration to social media as a way to further serve users.

As progressive as DLs have been in social media adoption, an invisible barrier still separates source material and the online users seeking to connect with it. Libraries are beginning to reimagine the traditional gatekeeper role with an eye on social curation: can the historical integrity of content be preserved along with user-contributed information? Is there potential future value in comments that seem superfluous now? How can more valuable expression be encouraged among users?

Social media, or Web 2.0 as it was commonly known during its emergence in the mid-2000s, refers to an evolution and standardization in web-based programming that reduces the technical expertise and expense needed for individuals to create or share online content and collaborate with others to publish or modify text and multimedia objects with enriched web functionality. In these collaborative environments users may add contextual metadata to an item or a collection, modify descriptions, contribute and edit multimedia, embed library media on their own websites or interact conversationally around library content. The products arising from these technologies are organized and ranked by search engines according to their popularity, the effectiveness of their metadata or their relevance to niche or targeted audiences. This is a departure from historically scientific means of tracking physical publications in libraries, or the menu-driven navigation in traditional websites.

Types of social media

Blogs (WordPress, Blogger): Blogs are websites that feature timely entries containing text commentary or multimedia. These platforms are known for their ability to easily incorporate other forms of social media using embedded code. They also allow for data portability between multiple social media platforms. The informal nature of blogs can provide DLs with the opportunity to engage audiences on a personal level. Blogs are also useful for aggregating other social media outputs into one platform – see, for example, the blogs on DL topics by the University of Glasgow and Lorcan Dempsey.[1]

Microblogs (Twitter, Tumblr): A microblog offers a platform for short messages and headlines from news items, usually with a link to a source with further description. Many DLs use Twitter to update their followers about new content and services and to answer questions about collections – see, for example, UNESCO's World Digital Library, the popular New York Public Library and individual digital librarians like Jason Clark.[2]

Social Bookmarking (Delicious, Digg): Social bookmarking is a method for internet users to organize, store, manage and search for records of resources online. Libraries can bookmark links related to a specific subject within their collections and use common tags to aggregate them within, with a persistent link. Themed social bookmarking pages can provide valuable starting places for users and the media to begin research about a particular topic related to library content.

Wikis (Wikipedia, PBWiki): Wikis are platforms that facilitate collaborative encyclopedic documentation. The largest of these platforms, Wikipedia, provides a method for DLs to bring more attention to their collections by adding new entries and contributing to the entries of others. Wikipedia is based on the open source software MediaWiki, which can help DLs to collaborate on bibliographies, policy documents and media-rich contextual experiences around special collections. For an example of a Wikipedia–library collaboration see the Personendata Project between German Wikipedia editors and the German National Library (DNB).[3] The DNB openly publishes its name authority files, and through the use of a unique numeric identifier allows the creation of standardized hyperlinks leading from Wikipedia articles to the corresponding records in its library catalogues. This makes them more readily accessible and visible to users.

Multimedia sharing (Flickr, YouTube and iTunes): Multimedia is the form of DL content most suited to active social media engagement. Many libraries already share their images on the photo-sharing website Flickr. Libraries use YouTube to post historical films or tutorials regarding the use of their online collections. Less frequently, libraries use audio podcasts to connect conversationally with their audiences or to share historic audio recordings.

Social networks (Facebook, Ning, BuddyPress, LinkedIn): Social networks are platforms that integrate elements of many other social media types into a common interface. Members may group socially in a variety of ways according to common interests. A DL may create a Facebook account that allows others to 'friend' it for direct communication, or an organizational page that Facebook users can 'like' in order to interact with its public content. This allows the library to quickly engage an interested audience around relevant content and conversation.

What is 'social' interaction?

While the concept of social media encompasses the brands of YouTube, Twitter, Flickr and Wikipedia (along with agenda-driven offshoots like Wikileaks) in the popular imagination, the potential for its implementation in DLs is less clear. The democratization of information has blurred the concept of what a library is, particularly on the web. The DELOS Digital Library Reference Model (DLRM) defines a DL as 'an organization, which might be virtual, that comprehensively collects, manages and preserves for the long term rich digital content, and offers to its user communities specialized functionality on that content, of measurable quality and according to codified policies'. As the speed of internet connections increases and the cost of producing and digitizing quality media decreases, these qualities are increasingly defining social media services as well, on a much larger scale. Because search becomes the first tendency of people seeking information and social media content is often highly ranked in search, DLs are grappling with the concept of how to remain relevant in the digital landscape without losing their identities. Individuals, non-profit organizations, governmental agencies and even corporations are now establishing their own DLs alongside traditional libraries.

However, DLs and social media platforms have different systematic capabilities and motivations for creating content and interacting with the public online. They also have different levels of social authority (i.e. power and reputation). Traditional libraries retain the advantages of established content and curatorial processes, with a historical position of respect that enables them to preserve primary sources, with the full trust of their users. The approach, cost and purpose behind patron interactivity with digital collections is also quite different. Libraries with an established history of creating digital archives and online communication services are often 'locked in' to using expensive proprietary (or legacy) technologies. Newcomers to the DL space have the advantage of building on open source software and the ease that application programming interfaces (APIs) bring to integrating social media functionality. However, use of popular social media tools does not ensure user engagement, just as the use of proprietary legacy tools does not preclude it. The measure of social media functionality in a DL setting might be ascertained by the quality and quantity of opportunities for users to engage with content.

Case studies

....

Case study 13.1: Library of Congress

....

In 2007, the Library of Congress (LOC) entered a pilot partnership with Yahoo! to bring some of its historic collections to the image-sharing website Flickr. Library personnel initially identified four project features 'that increase awareness of the Library and its collections; spark creative interaction with collections; provide LOC staff with experience with social tagging and Web 2.0 community input; and provide leadership opportunities to cultural heritage and government communities' (LOC, 2007).

During the pilot programme, between January and October 2008, staff uploaded 4615 photos to Flickr. The images garnered more than 7166 user-contributed comments and 67,176 tags. In the programme's five months the library saw a 20% increase in visits to its own Prints and Photographs Online Catalog (PPOC). Existing staff took turns monitoring the Flickr stream, eventually updating more than 500 PPOC records with information provided by users (Springer et al., 2008).

The LOC's large number of photos with no known copyright required a conceptual evolution in the structure of Flickr itself. The company already offered a variety of Creative Commons licences, along with the default All Rights Reserved. It responded by creating The Commons, an area of Flickr where about 50 cultural institutions contribute images for free use. The Commons clarified a philosophical grey area for other libraries, which then began to engage in the social service and innovate on their own. ▒

Case study 13.2: Miami University Library

Among the libraries migrating to Flickr was the Miami University Library in Ohio, which quickly ran into obstacles when trying to port its large number of images to Flickr. Personnel programmed scripts to enable the library's website to interact with Flickr's API and to allow for quick and efficient uploading of images and metadata such as titles, subject headings, tags and hyperlinks back to the library's collections. The scripts have allowed the Miami University Library's Digital Initiatives department to automate the upload of more than 5000 images, resulting in 200,000 views within a year (Michel and Tzoc, 2010). The library has also made these automation scripts available to the larger community so as to help others encountering the same problems of uploading large collections. ▒

Case study 13.3: The Royal Commission on the Ancient and Historical Monuments of Scotland (RCAHMS)

Sharing individual innovation for the greater good is also the concept behind a user-centred photo sharing initiative by the RCAHMS. The organization 'collects, archives, interprets and disseminates information on the architectural, industrial, archaeological and maritime heritage of Scotland'. Its mission necessitates strong partnerships with collections-based institutions primarily focused on technical documents, maps, survey data and images. The advancement of digital technologies and web interactivity led it to adopt an open approach to also accepting user-contributed content. The Commission now allows direct public contributions to its online image collections and through its Flickr presence. In a project funded by the Royal Society of Edinburgh, RCAHMS has partnered with the University of Edinburgh, National Museums Scotland and the National Galleries of Scotland to hold a social media training series for the Scottish cultural heritage sector. The collaborators are establishing a research agenda for museum and gallery education for the digital age, with the further goal of informing policy and practice in the use of social media. RCAHMS is also sponsoring research at the University of Edinburgh to explore the role of users in contributing to the public online presence of cultural institutions, the ways in which users might contribute to the 'making' and 'unmaking' of public archives and the ways in which a global public learns and constructs meaning from institutions' digital collections (Graham, 2011). ▪

Case study 13.4: National Library of Australia's Trove Initiative

The National Library of Australia's Trove Initiative uses social media tools to promote and drive users towards its content, replicating social media functionality throughout its web pages. Trove's Twitter content is presented in an informal style that balances conversation, retweets and has new content announcements that build relationships with users while suggesting opportunities for engagement within its collections. Trove's 'one search' portal retains the simple design of Google's home page, even as it semantically provides access to the holdings of more than 1000 institutions. Featured directly under the search box are links that quantify user engagement and provide immediate opportunity for contributions by visitors. For example, Trove uses crowd sourcing to help transcribe its digital archive of newspapers. Once logged in, a user can select a portion of any newspaper image from the digital collection and transcribe it immediately using his or her web browser. The user can also edit content provided by others (NLA, 2011). This functionality incorporates features common among photo-sharing sites and wikis via a simplified interface that directly informs the library's own metadata. Popular social media tools are used to support deeper engagement with the library's own site, rather than a parallel setting for parts of its content. For example, Trove's YouTube channel features exclusive 2- to 3-minute tutorials that describe simple ways in which users can contribute contextual information. Trove further encourages this concept of content ownership by providing code to allow bloggers and webmasters to embed its search engine on their own sites. The site specifically states this idea in its document 'How to Utilise Trove in Your Organisation':

> The National Library has acknowledged that changes in user expectations, technology and the wider environment mean that some users do not expect to be passive receivers of information, but rather contributors and participants in information services, and thus able to share their ideas and information. Trove enables this by giving users the ability to tag, comment and correct content, and organise their results. People can upload their own

images into the service. Users are encouraged to give feedback and engage with content and this is driving the future development of the service.

(Campbell, 2010)

In at least one case, the National Library of Australia's emphasis on crowd sourcing resulted in a grassroots movement among its users to have a direct influence on its digitization priorities. Trove user Donna Benjamin began the #digitisethedawn movement after realizing that *The Dawn* – an Australian feminist publication from the late nineteenth century – was not online and was not in the NLA queue to be included in its digital archives. She was told that the cost to fast-track such an effort would be about AU$7500 and decided to raise the funds herself, since 'This is a significant publication from a significant Australian, and there is no reason this publication shouldn't be online.'

The story has historical resonance given that *The Dawn*'s publisher, Louisa Lawson, played a role of democratizing information production by and for women through her publication. Benjamin, an open source advocate, created the website www.digitisethedawn.org through her company, Creative Contingencies, to focus her efforts to raise funds and support for the project. She also used Twitter to create greater awareness of Lawson's cultural impact and generate conversation around the fund-raising activity. Support from organizations such as Google Australia/New Zealand helped the group to surpass its goal of raising the necessary funds by International Women's Day, 8 March 2011 (Benjamin, 2011). Members plan to remain active by contributing metadata as *The Dawn* becomes available on Trove.

Case study 13.5: University of Houston Library

In the autumn of 2010, the University of Houston Library in the USA took a more direct approach to engaging its users with more than 15,000 images in its digital collections. Conceptualized as a short-term experiment for an internship, the project took a user-oriented approach to incorporating the collections into social media environments. Michelle Reilly, head of digital services at the University of Houston libraries, said the project was designed on the 'realization that students seem to start their search at Google, and they end up at Wikipedia. We'd like them to finally end up with us' (Kolowich, 2011).

The library identified which of its digital assets had the most potential impact within Wikipedia. These items were placed on Wikimedia Commons, which is similar to Flickr Commons in that it provides a pool of media with no copyright restrictions. These media assets can then be easily incorporated into Wikipedia articles, and receive greater exposure from bloggers and traditional publishers who monitor the site to augment their content outside of Wikipedia. The library took the further step of making its own users aware of its contributions to the Commons and provided simple tutorials for them to begin contributing content to Wikipedia as well.

Additionally, the library looked for images that lent themselves to rich categorizations. Wikimedia Commons requires that all images uploaded have at least one 'category'. Richly categorized items – materials with a large number of specific categories attached – are more discoverable by other Wikipedia editors and are more likely to be used and reused in Wikipedia articles. The library took the rich categorization concept a step further by cropping images to provide impact and context for multiple Wikipedia entries. For example, project intern Danielle Elder found a photo dated to the early twentieth century featuring a well-dressed woman and a baby on a porch. She cropped the photo to emphasize the woman's elaborate cloche hat and added it to a related entry on Wikipedia, which hosts an active group of authors who specialize in period costume. The image was viewed more than 5000 times in a 30-day period (Westbrook, personal communication; see also Elder, Westbrook and Reilly, 2012). This type of multi-purposing of photos functions as a form of metadata comparable to the 'notes' feature of Flickr, yet more suited to the streamlined interface of Wikipedia.

The University of Houston also engaged its existing users in its Wikipedia project, challenging them to discover which images were contributed from the library. The library provided simple tutorials on how to contribute to articles on the site and incorporate Wikimedia Commons content into entries. The Houston Library's prioritized engagement resulted in Wikipedia becoming its third-largest referring site – consistently drawing more users to the collection than the library's own web page, or any of its other social media channels. ▪

Curating a user-integrated identity

In the recent past, a library's identity was formed through the unique content it curated. Users intentionally inhabited a physical space with the collections and interacted with its knowledgeable personnel in order to have access to the content. As users increasingly access digital information through a common online search experience, they may scarcely be aware of a library's role in housing a document, or an individual document's context within a larger collection, depending on where and how they access it and the links that may or may not be instantiated. The web now offers DLs an opportunity to establish an authoritative identity around their content with a social space, rather than a physical one.

The LOC reports that pages for its Flickr images can rank 10 pages higher in a typical Google search than does its own corresponding image page. Much of this is due to the preference that search engines give to frequent commenting and user-contributed tagging. In 2010 the LOC agreed to archive the entire Twitter archive because of its cultural value (Raymond, 2010). Yet few of its own users' Flickr comments find their way back to be preserved in the original LOC image catalogue. Each day, DLs must make value judgements by which one instance of an expression is archived in its entirety while another is only partially retained. Concern for credibility prevents these institutions from fully integrating social media and realizing its unmitigated benefits. This results in a paradox in which the concept of a gatekeeper is dissonant with the interactivity that attracts more visitors when the same image is presented in a social media context: the surety of sharing their authentic voices and knowing that the words are sufficiently valued to be preserved. To overcome this, Zarro and Allen (2010) proposed a classification system 'to manage contributions and mitigate information overload issues' and strengthen the value of metadata contributed to the LOC's images on Flickr.

Conclusions

Constructing experiences for discovery

The technological tools already exist to move DLs further towards a better balance of medium, message and resources. Social web APIs, website plug-ins and freely available open source code provide great opportunities for the embedding of social content within library websites, as well as disseminating conversations across broader networks, which can serve as a driver to original content. For example, most open source content management systems allow users to comment from their Facebook accounts and, optionally, post the comment to their Facebook profiles.

The University of Houston is constructing a similar interface with the Flickr API so as to allow comments on a Flickr image to appear on the corresponding image page within the library's own website. According to R. Niccole Westbrook, digital photographs technician at Houston, the library is also actively developing functionality within its CONTENTdm infrastructure to let users create their own multimedia exhibits from its online content. Users will be able to add their own narrative and then grab and embed code in order to feature their creations on their own websites.

This kind of digital story-telling, as fashioned by a library or its users, is a powerful tool of engagement as stated in the book *Library 2.0 and Beyond*:

> Digital stories can help us expose and tap into the deeper human needs that libraries traditionally have helped society address. Chief among those needs is the need for community ... Learning is social, showing that community is essential to learning. Libraries aren't quiet anymore.
>
> (Diaz and Fields, 2007)

Digital libraries alone have the unique depth of resources to create authoritative, media-rich environments on their own platforms. Even small DLs have the potential to craft the kind of interactive contextual experiences that most prompt sharing among users of social media.

Towards a sustainable future

A strong institutional approach to taxonomy continues to determine the exposure of collections among potential users. Consistent organizational branding within metadata and persistent linking to the original source further establishes a library's authority online. The true test of whether digital collections are truly available is how quickly and efficiently these users are able to find them, as compared to other sources that may be less credible but more accessible through search. The benefits of search engine optimization strategies like these provide one measure of return on investment, as cultural institutions are increasingly being required to prove their relevancy.

As the Digitise the Dawn project demonstrates, the most sustainable implementation of social media in DLs right now may be externally initiated. Some libraries already allow content popularity to drive their digitization efforts, including policies to offer priority digitization for volumes requested through interlibrary loan, as an alternative to exposing them to increased wear.

The next iteration of engagement for libraries throughout the USA, including the LOC, is the Digital Public Library of America. The concept borrows from the Trove project, as well as the Europeana project, which aggregates search from European DLs. The result will be a collaborative approach to digitizing archives so that duplication is minimized and DL content of every kind is available in a consistent, user-friendly interface.

Notes

1   University of Glasgow Library,
    http://universityofglasgowlibrary.wordpress.com/; Lorcan Dempsey's Weblog,
    http://orweblog.oclc.org/about.html.
2   UNESCO's World Digital Library, http://twitter.com/#!/wdlorg; New York Public
    Library, https://twitter.com/#!/nypl; Jason Clark, https://twitter.com/#!/jaclark.
3   http://blog.wikimedia.de/2008/11/26/wikipedianer-in-der-pnd-redaktion-
    der-deutschen-nationalbibliothek.

References

Benjamin, D. (2011) Supporters Page, *Digitise the Dawn* (blog),
    http://digitisethedawn.org/supporters.
Bernales, B. (2011) What Is a Social Authority? *Life and Business Guide 101, Tips,
    How-To's and News*, 3 April, www.bjornbern.com/what-is-social-authority.
Brauer, M. and Bourhis, R. Y. (2006) Social Power, *European Journal of Social
    Psychology*, special issue, **36** (4), 601–16.
Campbell, D. (2010) *How to Utilise Trove in Your Organisation*,
    www.nla.gov.au/openpublish/index.php/nlasp/article/view/1664.
Diaz, K. and Fields, A. M. (2007) Digital Storytelling, Libraries and Community. In
    Courtney, N. (ed.), *Library 2.0 and Beyond: innovative technologies and tomorrow's
    user*, Libraries Unlimited.
Elder, D, Westbrook, R. N. and Reilly, M. (2012) Wikipedia Lover, Not a Hater: har-
    nessing Wikipedia to increase the discoverability of library resources, *Journal of
    Web Librarianship*, **6** (1), 32–44.
Graham, P. (2011) Skype Conversation with Philip Graham, RCAHMS.
Kolowich, S. (2011) Wielding Wikipedia Inside Higher Education, 11 April,
    www.insidehighered.com/news/2011/04/052/college_libraries_use_wikipedia_
    to_increase_exposure_of_their_collections.
Library of Congress (2007) *The Library of Congress Strategic Plan: 2008-2013*,
    www.loc.gov/about/strategicplan/2008–2013/StrategicPlan07-Contents_1.pdf.
Michel, J. P. and Tzoc, E. (2010) Automated Bulk Uploading of Images and
    Metadata to Flickr, *Journal of Web Librarianship*, **4** (4), 435–48.
National Library of Australia (2011) *Participating in Digitised Newspapers and More…*,
    http://trove.nla.gov.au/general/participating-in-digitised-newspapers-faq.
Raymond, M. (2010) The Library and Twitter: an FAQ, *The Library of Congress Blog*,
    28 April, http://blogs.loc.gov/loc/2010/04/the-library-and-twitter-an-faq.
Springer, M. et al. (2008) *For the Common Good: the Library of Congress Flickr pilot proj-
    ect report summary*, www.loc.gov/rr/print/flickr_report_final_summary.pdf.

Zarro, M. and Allen, R. B. (2010) User-contributed Descriptive Metadata for Libraries and Cultural Institutions, *Research and Advanced Technology for Digital Libraries*, **6273**, 46–54.

CHAPTER 14

Significant others:
user studies and digital preservation

Kathleen Menzies and Duncan Birrell

We can't solve problems by using the same kind of thinking we used when we created them.

(Albert Einstein)

Introduction

A temporal paradox lies at the heart of digital preservation: that the only sure criteria for evaluating the success of today's preservation systems depend on assessing the usability of the digital objects they preserve by *future* end-users – those unknown but significant others for whom we preserve data. It is probable that the difficulties inherent to digital preservation techniques and the user-led evaluation work assessing them will persist across time. The digital preservation (DP) community must therefore address questions about who its end-users will be 10, 50 or even 100 years from now. One way to tackle this problem is to answer the deceptively simple question 'Who are our end-users *now* and what are *their* wants and needs?'. Only then can we begin to imagine how these will change.

When being evaluated by users, DP frameworks and systems must be demonstrated to a wider range of user groups than many conventional user studies address, including data creators, curators, consumers and a variety of potential customer organizations, comprising not only *end-users* but *intermediaries* from multiple sectors possessing distinct operational and conceptual requirements. As the creation, provision and complexity of digital objects increases and evolves, so too does the distribution of user types.

Preservation is inevitably intricate. Inbuilt hazards relate to scale (e.g. the quantity and variety of digital objects requiring preservation), speed (preservation research occurs within a rapidly shifting and multi-faceted technological environment) and incoherence (e.g. a lack of consensus on best practices and preferred methods).

To some extent, the significant contextual or symbolic aspects of items and their probable use have always been important to knowledge organizations. Yet in a *digital* library these aspects *themselves* become targets for preservation (Chowdhury, 2010). All of this is to say that evaluating DP work with users is fraught with complication.

While established means of user testing form an important component within the overall armoury of DP evaluation, new methods and models are being developed in order to keep pace with the ever-evolving thinking of users. Some of these new approaches are explored in this chapter.

DP and user studies

Recent user studies in the area of digital preservation (and digital libraries) have increasingly embraced mixed methodologies which deploy not only the qualitative elements of traditional user studies (questionnaires, semi-structured interviews, case studies and focus groups – see Chapter 5 for examples) but also methods borrowed from the social sciences, such as ethnographic analysis, user profiling, capturing of temporal characteristics, and sophisticated assessments of information behaviour (see Chapters 6–10). Together, these might be said to comprise a *multi-dimensional* approach to user evaluation.

Users in DP

Studies looking into the role of DP users tend to be either small scale and sharply focused, investigating some distinct aspect of a preservation system (e.g. metadata application or the ways in which researchers use objects), or large, multi-national efforts addressing a combination of technological and socio-technical factors (see examples below). Typically, work is primarily qualitative, including attitudinal, behavioural or cognitive aspects within case studies or modes of assessment that incorporate *some* quantitative data-gathering activities (see Snow et al., 2008). Although striving for objectivity, the primary approach of DP and user evaluations will always (as with much of information science) be qualitative rather than empirical. The selection of subjects is not randomized and variables cannot be strictly controlled. Numerical data is not always suitable for in-depth statistical analysis. Validity is often therefore inferred through content analysis, cross-comparison, or the matching of community requirements against system functionalities and capabilities. This is an approach that fits well with aspects of software development and design.

Evaluating systems in DP

DP projects aiming to deliver tools or applications can logically combine qualitative and semi-empirical user-centric approaches with software development methods including iterative design, prototyping and the use of established development models that also prioritize or involve the user by requirements analysis, customer or software requirement solicitation and goal modelling. Any decomposition or analysis of system structures and efficiencies can then be done in relation to those identified needs and requirements. From this software-engineering perspective, DP system evaluations can form cost-effective 'pilot studies to scope future work' or validate 'the basic soundness of core parts' (Buchanan, 2009).

The British Library combined user-centric development methods for the design and evaluation of a web interface for its Archival Sounds project. Having already consulted widely on user needs in relation to content selection, it sought input from 'representatives of user communities in the development of the service'. Key decisions pertaining to technical issues such as preservation technologies and the implementation of standards remained in the hands of the project team and its expert technology suppliers (Digital Preservation Coalition, 2010).

However, it is important to distinguish between 'usability' in the context of end-user experience or user-interface design, and the concept of 'meaningful usability' in the context of long-term DP. The former, which focuses on capturing real-time interactions between end-users and systems, can be productively incorporated *within* the developmental stages of a DP system; but the long-term needs of DP design and evaluation are more complex. DP incorporates more facets than simple usability – for example, maintaining the integrity and provenance of digital objects. Most importantly, it operates on larger time-scales (Katre, 2010).

Scale in DP

The CASPAR (Cultural Artistic and Scientific knowledge for Preservation, Access and Retrieval) project created a series of models, tools and techniques based around the OAIS Reference model (CCDS, 2002) to ensure the preservation of digital objects and associated information regardless of technological change. The project team consulted users at the requirement solicitation stage, using a combination of survey methods and a variation of established system-design methodologies (CASPAR, 2006) during and after the commencement of development work. Concurrently, an external review committee assessed the project's outputs, providing comment iteratively. The project also deployed case studies intended 'to validate the CASPAR approach [...] across different user communities' (CASPAR, 2009).

Another example of innovative user engagement comes from the PLANETS (Preservation and Long-term Access through Networked Services) project. The distinctive contribution of PLANETS was to adopt an intricate combination of 1) established system design methodologies; 2) proven methods of user engagement and evaluation; and 3) qualitative and ethnographic social science techniques (cf. Snow et al., 2008). One instrument employed by the project team was a *user diary*. These were issued to selected participants, who were asked to log their research activities at a series of set intervals over an agreed time period, adding a longitudinal element to the assessment. At later stages, structured interviews and discussions allowed for an 'affinity analysis' – within which the priorities and attitudes of researchers working with digital items across three distinct domains were categorized and analysed in comparison with the data from the user diaries. Results were grouped accordingly into various 'themes', becoming the basis of a DP meta-model that informed system design and functionality.

This willingness to innovate and to seek experimental solutions to the inherent problems of DP has resulted in the formulation of exciting and interdisciplinary methodologies for DP user studies.

The EU-funded SHAMAN (Sustaining Heritage Access through Multivalent ArchiviNg) project, which forms this chapter's case study, built on these methodological techniques and concepts to evaluate a set of 'next generation' preservation tools, consulting users in detail throughout.

Case study 14.1: SHAMAN demonstration and evaluation

This case study focuses on three principal user-oriented aspects of SHAMAN's evaluation strategy:

- the function of usage scenarios and use cases in SHAMAN's demonstrator design
- the role of users in the SHAMAN evaluation process
- the results of SHAMAN's user-oriented demonstration and evaluation activities.

The role of users in SHAMAN's demonstrator design

A key aspect of SHAMAN is its recognition that the concept of the community is important for DP. The first major challenge in designing the SHAMAN framework was to understand what different users require from a DP system. Requirements gathering was undertaken at the project's outset via questionnaires and semi-structured interviews conducted with 24 individuals from 11 different organizations. A set of usage scenarios, use cases and, eventually, *functional requirements* were produced from these (SHAMAN, 2008). All were central to and incorporated within the development process of the SHAMAN demonstrators (or prototypes) shown to users for evaluation.

Because SHAMAN addresses the preservation of multiple digital object types and their contexts, three specific scenarios were devised to reflect the unique requirements related to different digital objects, institutional needs and practices within libraries and archives:

1 indexing and archiving digital monograph-style publications
2 indexing and archiving digitizations not structured like monographs
3 scientific publishing and archiving of heterogeneous interlinked material.

The specific use cases derived from these informed the delineation of functions required or expected within a conceptual DP system. Use cases included, for example, the deposit of items into a repository or archive, error checking, system administration tasks, keyword extraction, and the management of archived digital objects, as well as search, access and retrieval by end-users. Test collections were made available by the German National Library and Göttingen State and University Library to assist in the enactment and testing of these functionalities.

User needs and working practices, the components of a holistic approach, were as vital to the development of SHAMAN's technical architecture and information models as were practical design questions. The use cases incorporated into SHAMAN's demonstrators were therefore both *domain driven* and *user oriented* rather than purely *technology driven*.

It must be noted that in any requirements-capturing process not all requirements can realistically be met, given the constraints and practicalities of software and system development. However, with user inputs guiding and informing the core of SHAMAN, the constitutive elements of its user-led evaluation were richer and more realistic than otherwise would have been the case.

The role of users in SHAMAN's evaluation process

The aim of SHAMAN's demonstration and evaluation work was to gather insights from potential end-users and customer organizations – through a series of focus-group consultations – about the applicability of SHAMAN's underlying concepts, tools and techniques, and from these to formulate recommendations to aid future development work. Evaluations were undertaken with 27 individuals drawn from three key user groups:

- archivists and librarians managing digital collections
- digital records managers in the heritage and/or public sectors
- managers and administrators of DLs and institutional repositories.

Each of these groups incorporated and represented SHAMAN 'actors' (user types) identified through earlier requirements capturing.

The results of SHAMAN's evaluation

Focus-group consultations were undertaken in three locations: Frankfurt (Germany), Vilnius (Lithuania) and Glasgow (Scotland). Findings pertaining to the evolution of user expectations of DP systems regarding *functionality*, *usability*, *metadata extraction*, *preservation management* and *interoperability* were identified across all groups, using a combination of content analysis and illustrative statistics. SHAMAN's project team learned much from the users who evaluated its work; while some ideas and techniques were validated and confirmed as useful, others were found to need improvement. Indeed, some of the users' suggestions have already been incorporated into revised versions of SHAMAN's models and prototypes.

In terms of DP system functionality, the most important feature (as stated by 51.9% of focus group participants) was data migration for long-term bit-stream preservation, followed by easy, secure access to the preserved digital documents (40.7%). Concerns over the usability and search/retrieval capacity of preservation systems appeared frequently (44.4%). The automatic generation and extraction of all metadata (including preservation metadata) featured highly among user expectations (25.9%). While potential end-users found SHAMAN's context-capturing mechanisms for bibliographic metadata highly relevant, they were also keen to identify the 16 content and technical standards that they would like to see supported by or integrated with the SHAMAN framework (SHAMAN, 2010).

It was clear from participant responses that most were principally interested in how they might incorporate particular *aspects* of the featured approaches into current records management or repository systems. For the majority of organizations, making the whole-scale migration to an entirely new and independent solution was not felt to be feasible; rather, they seek solutions to support *existing* DP efforts rather than to replace them.

In terms of the methodological synthesis offered by the SHAMAN evaluation, user groups found the combination of approaches – including the reference architecture, meta-model and group discussions – helpful and thought provoking, requesting further information on how they might best apply the framework to meet specific organizational goals and requirements. As noted above, their input was invaluable to the SHAMAN team, as in previous work packages with other users. This underlines why evaluations in specialized areas are best undertaken by those who are fully conversant with the domain for which a system is being designed. ■

Conclusions: DP users and DP systems – bridging the gap

Many organizations do not yet have DP policies or technologies in place; as a result, intermediaries and end-users are not always well versed with DP concepts. This inevitably poses challenges for user-oriented requirements-gathering and evaluation work. However, if DP systems are to be successful, it is essential that their design processes – and the evaluation of the complex models, tool-sets and prototypes that enable and support DP work – continue to involve them.

As discussed above, a number of projects have developed mixed methodologies for doing just this. They incorporate techniques drawn from various disciplines that fit within the field of social informatics as much as within system design. Such flexibility is important when we consider the pragmatic nature of work within organizations preserving digital objects – something that is highlighted time and again by users themselves.

Participants at the SHAMAN project's evaluation indicated that it would not be easy to modify their current resource-intensive efforts so as to maintain existing information systems in line with new DP concepts or frameworks. These comments remind us why infrastructure independence has been recognized as vital to the most innovative DP projects; and why realism is as strong as vision when it comes to conceptualizing a domain. More broadly, the comments demonstrate why engaging users throughout a project's lifetime is essential. Another practical example comes from the PLANETS project, which established the Open Planets Foundation to maintain a dialogue with practitioners and industry beyond the project's lifetime – and which is already making some of its software available as a 'plug-in' for existing institutional repository packages (Tarrant, Hitchcock and Carr, 2010).

A potential solution to the problem of *bridging the gap* between the technical development of DP systems and their evaluation and uptake by users is now beginning to crystallize. In addition to the use of mixed, interdisciplinary methodologies for concept modelling and data gathering, a granular and representative understanding of DP end-users has emerged – one that recognizes that the *context of use* can be as significant to long-term preservation as understanding *the context of the digital object* itself.

Those devising DP evaluation should customize and extend it to a representative range of users and audiences, focusing on different sets of functions, requirements and usage in accordance with user type – not just between but *within* communities. The distinctions and complexities of digital objects, their contexts and their users must be reflected at the evaluation stage as well as the design stage. Otherwise we will be left attempting to solve a whole new generation of preservation problems using the same old kind of thinking.

References

Buchanan, G. (2009) *Towards Lightweight Digital Library User Evaluations*, http://dlib.org/dlib/july09/khoo/Buchanan.pdf.

CASPAR Consortium (2006) *D4101. User Requirements and Scenario Specifications*, www.casparpreserves.eu/Members/metaware/Deliverables/user-requirements-and-scenario-specifications/at_download/file.pdf.

CASPAR Consortium (2009) *Report on Evaluation Criteria*, www.casparpreserves.eu/Members/cclrc/Deliverables/report-on-evaluation-criteria/at_download/file.pdf.

CCSDS (The Consultative Committee for Space Data Systems) (2002) *Reference model for an open archival information system (OAIS)*, http://public.ccsds.org/publications/archive/650x0b1.pdf.

Chowdhury, G. (2010) From Digital Libraries to DP Research: the importance of users and context, *Journal of Documentation*, **66** (2), 207–23.

DP Coalition (British Library) (2010) DP Case Notes: archival sounds, *DP Coalition Case Notes*, July 2010, www.dpconline.org/advice/case-notes.

Katre, D. (2010) Long-term UX Policy, *HCI Vistas*, **6**, www.hceye.org/UsabilityInsights/?p=107.

PLANETS Consortium (2008) *Report on Usage Models for Libraries, Archives and Data*

Centres, Results of the Second Iteration,
www.planets-project.eu/docs/reports/Planets_PP3-D2ReportOnUsageModels.pdf.
SHAMAN (2008) *D1.1 – Survey of Users and Providers in Europe and SHAMAN Usage Scenarios and DP Support.*
SHAMAN (2010) *D14.2 – Report on Demonstration and Evaluation Activity in the Domain of 'Memory Institutions',* http://shaman-ip.eu/shaman/document.
Snow, K. et al. (2008) Considering the User Perspective. Research into usage and communication of digital information, *D-Lib Magazine,* **14** (5/6).
Tarrant, D., Hitchcock, S. and Carr, L. (2010) A Complete Preservation Workflow in EPrints (+ Plato) – 10 Minute Summary, *Preservation and Archiving Special Interest Group (PASIG),* 5 July 2010, Madrid, Spain, http://eprints.ecs.soton.ac.uk/21279/.

CHAPTER 15

The shift to mobile devices

Lina Petrakieva

Introduction

Mobile devices are now ubiquitous. From the humble analogue mobile phone that appeared in the 1980s (for the general public), and which was thought amazing at the time, mobile phones have developed now into handheld, pocket-sized, super-slim, multi-touchscreen computers. Mobile phones are now devices with hundreds of times more computational power than anyone could have imagined in the 1980s, even in a personal computer; and then there is all the other technology available in them – digital camera, GPS, connectivity capabilities (Bluetooth, Wi-Fi).

But the use of these mobile devices raises specific issues when usability comes into consideration. As W3C has argued:

> Web sites can more efficiently meet both goals when developers understand the significant overlap between making a Web site accessible for a mobile device and for people with disabilities. Users of mobile devices and people with disabilities experience similar barriers when interacting with Web content. For example, mobile phone users will have a hard time if a Web site's navigation requires the use of a mouse because they typically only have an alphanumeric keypad. Similarly, desktop computer users with a motor disability will have a hard time using a Web site if they can't use a mouse.
>
> (W3C Web Accessibility Initiative)

What does the mobile environment mean for digital libraries (DLs)? In their chapter on 'Mobile Access to Cultural Information Resources', Ross et al. (2004) outlined innovative uses of mobile devices, particularly in the museum environment. A recent study provided evidence on the growing number of users who are willing to use library services via handheld devices: 'A total of 58.4 percent of respondents who own a web-enabled handheld device indicate that they would use small screen devices, such as PDAs or web-enabled cell phones to search a library OPAC' (Cummings et al., 2010).

But how well is the growing community of DL users addressed when information resources are designed? With every new feature come more ideas about what can be integrated into mobile devices, as well as about how to use them, including in the domain of cultural heritage applications. And with the development of mobile connectivity (which allows much faster data transfer), the production of high-quality screens and access to the internet, there seems to be no limit to what can be done on a mobile device. Or is there? There are major differences between providing, accessing and manipulating data on a computer and doing the same on a mobile device; this chapter provides a glimpse into them.

Data

In order to access large amounts of data (such as information from an encyclopedia or database), difficult choices must be made. Either all the data can be downloaded locally to the device and the user can access it without having to depend on a high-speed internet connection; or minimal information can be held on the device and necessary information can be downloaded on request, which relies heavily on having a high-speed mobile internet connection and either a reasonable or no data traffic limit.

When the information is in the form of video the biggest challenge is the size of the files, followed by the choice between local access and download on demand.

Today, mobile devices have much more memory than they did a few years ago, but the amount of memory needed to store data is also increasing. This is due to such factors as the emergence of high-definition video, the higher resolution of photos and improvements in sound quality. All these developments have come at the cost of bigger files and the need for greater data storage capacity on the mobile. The W3C consortium offers a tool that allows a website's compatibility with mobile devices to be checked (W3C mobileOK Checker).

Screen size

Another essential consideration when designing for mobile devices is the size of the screen. Basic as it sounds, this has major implications for the ways that information can be presented and perceived. The convenience of having all the information literally in your pocket is traded against the mobile device's relatively small screen. If the information that is accessed is mostly text based, then screen size is not so important. However, the advantage of DLs is in having access to multimedia data such as photographs, audio and video. When the information contains multiple images, which is typical for DLs, the problem of screen size becomes very apparent.

The layouts of the data on a computer monitor and on a mobile screen (with about one quarter of the pixels of an average monitor) are very different. On a monitor you see not just the information that you are reading, but also the context. For example, someone is interested in an article published in a 19th-century newspaper and wants to access it on a mobile device. DLs provide images of newspaper pages that you can zoom into so as to read the required article. On a computer monitor you zoom in to read an article, but at the same time you can see context – the other articles around it. Is the article amongst serious news and reviews, surrounded by articles about curiosities or on a page of paid-by-publisher articles? The context helps in understanding attitudes, at that time, to the subject matter of the article – information that the article itself does not reveal. If the same article is accessed from a mobile device, the context will not be visible on the considerably smaller screen. It will not be impossible to see it, but a deliberate effort will be required to scroll around the page and view the other articles. This changes significantly the way that the user works with the resource. For example, consulting content in context may be a basic requirement of a persona used in the design of a DL (see Chapter 10). When the DL is used on a mobile device the same environment will not be created. This may lead to confusion, particularly for users who use a laptop and a mobile device interchangeably for the same task. This is the biggest problem when bite-sized chunks of data are provided, because a mobile is handy to use but we lose the bigger picture and the chances are reduced of stumbling upon something important without specifically looking for it.

Platform

Computers have been around for several decades and we have got used to the compatibility issues surrounding access to external data. This area is more mature and standards are in place that help with finding a resolution to a problem.

Mobiles devices capable of accessing external sources of information are relatively new. The compatibility issues that were resolved some time ago for computer systems now have to be resolved for mobiles. Currently, access to the internet from a mobile device is relatively straightforward (apart from some problems with Flash support on some older versions of the iPhone, for example). However, if access is through an app, then all the different mobile device operating systems (OS) need to be taken into account. Table 15.1 shows the world distribution of some of the mobile OS. The figures vary according to different sources and change, sometimes dramatically, in just a few months. But the diversity of OS is clear, especially when one bears in mind that there are just three main computer OS (Microsoft Windows, Mac OS and Linux) and anything else is hardly worth including in the statistics. For mobile OS, there are multiple options, each with a sizeable share of the market.

Table 15.1 *Mobile OS market share, February 2011 (based on Lyons, 2011)*

Region	Apple	Android	Blackberry	Nokia	Sony Ericsson	Samsung	WAP	All the rest
USA	35	27	28					11
Canada	77	8	8					7
Brazil				47	8	21		24
UK	42	12	36					10
France	64	19		6				11
Germany	59	21		8				12
Spain	56	20		14				9
Russia	12			47	12			30
India				71	5	11		13
China	11	3		59				27
Japan	58	23					12	7
Egypt	5			80		4		11
Tunisia	15			47		17		21
Australia	74	11		9				6

Controls

One of the important issues to be taken into account is the type of screen: capacitive or resistive. This may sound too technical, but actually it comes down to the way in which the user interacts with and controls the information flow.

With a resistive screen, one can use either a finger or a stylus. The tip of the stylus is less than 2mm in diameter, which allows for better use of the screen to display information because the controls (icons) can be very small.

Capacitive screens use a human finger as the control (although specialized styluses are available for them; their size is almost the same as an average finger). This means that the use of buttons or icons is limited because they need to be much bigger and occupy a larger area of the screen. To avoid this limitation, finger swiping is used. This may sound like a great way to implement controls, but there are a limited number of movements that can be used. To avoid this constraint, the use of two fingers is implemented.

Generally, people find finger movement on capacitive screens a very natural means of control. On the other hand, from a designer's perspective it becomes very difficult to design because there are a limited number of controls that can be used per screen. The controls also need to be intuitive, otherwise people would need instruction on how to use them, which would take up valuable screen space and could be off-putting. Sometimes the same finger movements and taps can mean different things in different apps.

All of these constraints are not a problem for a small application. But in the design of more complex interfaces, as is the case with DLs, the problems become very apparent. When the application involves typing, it requires a keyboard. Any keyboard that requires the use of a finger to type has to have buttons that are no less than half the size of a human fingertip. To avoid problems with typos, a number of autocorrect tools have been implemented, as any user of a mobile device with a capacitive screen will confirm. With its 26 letters, a few popular characters and the 10 numbers (even when designers put them on a separate screen), the keyboard takes up most of the screen. Thus, when you are typing you usually see no more than the last couple of lines of text. This may result in disjointed text because you can see only the last few lines, as opposed to a larger area such as a whole paragraph.

On a resistive screen, the control buttons and icons can be much smaller and you can therefore have more control options on the same screen. A full keyboard displayed on a resistive screen, where you are expected to use a stylus, uses about one quarter to one third of the screen. There is thus more free screen space and you can see a lot more of the text when you type and have a better perspective on the context. However, for those readers who would say 'Fine, we will all just use resistive screens', I need to add a word of caution: resistive screens are not the silver bullet. Using a stylus can be very good for short periods of time. If you use it for longer the ligaments in your hand can get very tired, and this can be very painful. The stylus is very thin, in order to fit inside the mobile device – but that makes it tiring to use it for prolonged periods of time.

Apps

App is short for application, and usually means a piece of software for use on a mobile device. When a new feature becomes available on a mobile device many designers and programmers find a use for it. The problem is that there are now multiple features and numerous people creating apps. Most people will say that more apps are good news. They may be good when you consider the choice available, but here is the problem: Apple's App Store has hundreds of thousands of apps (about 500,000 at the moment and growing). The Android market also has a couple of hundred thousand apps. How do you go and choose an app? Let us imagine that you are looking for an app to help you search the files on your mobile device (or to do any other task that you can think of). You go to the apps store or market and start searching, and the chances are that you will find apps that do what you need – hundreds and thousands of them. How do you search within your search? How do you pick the one to download? DLs may help users by providing recommendations. Other users' comments on apps are another criterion that can help you to make up your mind to use or not to use a specific app. But there will be negative comments on even the best apps – because people often say they don't like a specific app simply because they have different expectations and different preferences as to how things should be done, rather than because the app doesn't do what it is supposed to do. This has been recognized as a problem, as there are also apps that help you to look for the best apps on the market – but again, with varying degrees of success.

I am not saying that having a choice is a bad thing, but having too much choice – and not having support in the decision making – can be.

What about the future, then?

As the spread of mobile devices grows, the demand for information access from them grows too. Any institution, service or company that tries to provide access for mobile device users needs to take into account all of the issues raised here: what information they wish to make available, how to get the information across to the user, how to approach the design and controls, etc. Some of the big museums have developed apps that vary greatly in price, design and functionality, but that have been created to give users more ways to engage with the museum and to access information about the exhibits. Adoption of this technology has so far been piecemeal and very patchy.

One way to develop a system that can incorporate a bigger number of organizations and institutions and at the same time avoid the patchy results is to involve a consortium. A big project like Europeana could be such a consortium and could establish some standards – for referencing, for example. It could develop an app for the visitors of cultural heritage institutions using GPS that would tell users if the site (museum, library, etc.) is listed in Europeana and then allow them to access information from that site. Information could be accessed on demand, by streaming the data, or a user could choose to download all the available information in one go. One way to help users access more information would be to offer free Wi-Fi at such sites, which would reduce the problem of cost and speed associated with downloading large volumes of data.

Conclusions

As proof of what can be done on a mobile device, this chapter was written on one. The device was an HTC Diamond, running Windows Mobile 6.1. The text was typed in Word Mobile using a stylus and typing on an onscreen full-size QWERTY keyboard. When RSI (repetitive strain injury) struck, I used an i.Tech Bluetooth virtual laser keyboard. There was probably a quicker way to do it, and probably a better way to do it, but this was what I had in my pocket and I am a good representative of the average mobile device user.

References

Cummings, J., Merrill, A. and Borrelli, S. (2010) The Use of Handheld Mobile Devices: their impact and implications for library services, *Library Hi Tech*, **28** (1), 22–40.

Lyons, G. (2011) *Mobile Market Share*, http://connect.icrossing.co.uk/mobile-market-share_6301.

Ross, S., Donnelly, M. and Dobreva, M. (2004) *Emerging Technologies for the Cultural and Scientific Heritage Sector*. DigiCULT Technology Watch Report 2, February. Chapter: Mobile Access to Cultural Information Resources, 91–118, www.digicult.info/pages/techwatch.php.

W3C Web Accessibility Initiative, www.w3.org/WAI/mobile/.

W3C mobileOK Checker, http://validator.w3.org/mobile/.

CHAPTER 16

Resource discovery for research and course design

Zsuzsanna Varga

Introduction

The international movement to build digital libraries (DLs) using millions of out-of-copyright library titles has gained significant momentum in recent years, and Google's mass digitization of several highly regarded research libraries' collections continues to grab the headlines in commercial newspapers. These commercial projects, which cover the collections of such prestigious libraries as Stanford or Oxford universities, have made available masses of high-quality facsimiles of source documents, making a significant contribution to the technologically driven democratization of knowledge. The cultural heritage libraries have an immense potential also for scholarly users in the humanities: they allow access to rare texts or archival material, and biographers, scholarly editors and scholars of pre-modern texts have been the main beneficiaries of the rapid increase in the volume of digital content.

Whilst scholars in established disciplines have used these sources in research, the question of using the material in course design for new, innovative, interdisciplinary and area studies courses at universities is significantly more complicated. Area studies often involve the study of literary or cultural texts that have not been recently reprinted: the primary and secondary sources are either 'old,' or not 'indigenous' to the country where the university is. The material is often held in special collections, interlibrary loans are often unsuitable and good practical editions for teaching purposes rarely exist. Therefore, mass digitization is a useful tool for bridging the geographical or spatial gap for historical diaspora studies, translation history and comparative literary studies, and studies in travel writing. The practical aspects of DLs – and the 24/7 access to these materials that they offer for an unlimited number of simultaneous users – places teaching in a new environment (see Chapter 17).

What are the specific difficulties when designing a course in area studies, based on the digitized content of mass digitizing projects and of individual national libraries? And does the existence of such mass projects make the existence of smaller, more focused collections redundant? These questions were raised during the research into digital material for a scholarly portal providing access to East European travel writing, East Looks West. It is a major research project concerning East European travel writing and has been conducted in the School of Slavonic and East European Studies at UCL, London, under the directorship of Professor Wendy Bracewell since 2001 (see www.ssees.ucl.ac.uk/eastwest.htm). A previous project supported by the Arts and Humanities Research Council, also conducted at the School of Slavonic and East European Studies, which completed the compilation of the bibliography of East European travel writing had already discovered many travel texts and relevant secondary sources in the electronic domain, but it also identified the problem of the visibility of such texts: they normally reside in other, more general collections or in specified collections with other foci. The current project seeks to investigate the reasons for this invisibility and argues that it arises from a disharmony between academic user information behaviour and the provision by DLs. A second aim of the project is to examine the possibilities offered by smaller-scale projects that create true virtual research environments within East European studies.

But how do we design courses? Browsing and course design

The information behaviour of humanities scholars has attracted scholarly interest since at least 1955, and earlier research naturally focused on the behaviour patterns experienced in the physical library. Sue Stone's study 'Humanities Scholars: information needs and uses' (1982) and Rebecca Watson-Boone's 'The Information Needs and Habits of Humanities Scholars' (1994) provide succinct summaries of traditional information-seeking behaviour. More recent research in library and information studies has paid attention to the ways in which humanities scholars use digital resources in their research (Audenaert and Furuta, 2010).

Comparing earlier and more recent observations is particularly instructive because they show the fundamental shifts enabled by text digitization: digital accessibility and searchability has given a new lease of life to bibliographies, subject indexes and periodical publications that earlier were deemed to be difficult to use and obsolete. However, the core researcher needs have remained the same:

- Scholars need a variety of materials for their projects: primary sources (earlier and newer); secondary sources (earlier and newer); other reference sources.
- They continue to use primary sources and reread material from the previous centuries.
- Browsing continues to be an essential research tool for the humanities scholar, whether of titles or bookshelves, and 'grazing' within text (Stevens, 1956).

Course design in a relatively new discipline is, arguably, the most intellectually rewarding aspect of teaching in tertiary education, and bibliographical design and course content are mutually dependent elements. The compilation of any course bibliography, involving a range of texts from reference sources to primary texts, relies on a combination of known-item searches and informed browsing. The stages are the following:

1 identification of texts (generally by browsing)
2 location of the texts in libraries (generally by known-item search)
3 securing or finding access to those sources (generally by known-item search).

The compilation of the East European travel writing bibliography in a traditional library followed the elements described above. The first step, the identification of primary and secondary texts, would start off by using known-item searches, based on author–title combination, and then, as usual, it would alternate this with browsing (Cunningham, Reeves and Britland, 2003). Browsing would include specialized libraries and library subcollections and specialized bibliographies of East European travel writing and anthologies of authors and of country accounts. The potentially most challenging and productive part would be the browsing in the general book collections of major research libraries, which could be based on:

1 keyword searches in the title: especially useful when searching in one language. If titles are in different languages, multilingual keyword lists can be useful
2 Library of Congress subject-heading-driven searches: a very productive method if the record has been given LOC subject headings. Older books catalogued earlier may lack these.

How easy is it to find them?

The research for the East European digital portal started from the researcher's assumption that the following types of digitization projects are likely to contain relevant texts:

1 Major international mass-digitization projects or aggregators of digital content: they digitize masses of out-of-copyright material of primarily North American university libraries, and the richness of these collections means that several travel texts originating from Eastern Europe are also included.
2 European national libraries digitizing their own content: they are significantly smaller because they reflect their own collections. As national-language works dominate the physical book collections and the libraries also operate as the legal deposit libraries of the individual countries, much of their digitization focuses on the 'national treasures'. Generally, national- and English-language interfaces are available.

The searches identified six particularly interesting collections for comparison that contain digitized East European travel writing from the period 1500–2000 (see Table 16.1).

Interface can be intimidating: comparative examination of general collection interfaces: the navigation

The primary assumption about special libraries is that their holdings are organized according to a recognizable system such as the Dewey Decimal Classification or the Library of Congress Classification, and librarians provide short descriptions of their strengths. Taking the primary interface page of collections with known general travel writing content can be instructive: the Corvey Collection, which has one of the world's best travel writing collections, describes the size, origin and character of the collection from the perspectives of scope, history, provenance and language, and describes the organizational principle of the catalogue. Another collection, the Wellcome Collection in London, provides a similar brief description of its unpublished travel writing.

DLs are also expected to provide thematic introductions to their collections, especially as the size of collections can be overwhelming. The overview of the digital collections examined, however, suggests that such descriptions are not necessarily in place and, if they are, they often follow

Table 16.1 *Collections containing digitized East European travel writing*

Resource	Description	Address
Hathi	Portal to digitized collections of 29 North American research libraries. The East European travel writing collection grows at a rate of 50% in six months.	http://hathitrust.org
Project Gutenberg	The oldest DL in the world. Currently it contains no East European travel writing, but its collection grows by hundreds of volumes per month.	www.gutenberg.org
Gallica	Digitized content from the National Library of France, with a significant collection of East European travel writing translated into French.	http://gallica.bnf.fr/
Zentrales Verzeichnis Digitalisierter Drucke (ZVDD)	The central register of digitized works in Germany. Its relevant subsection is the Göttingen State and University Library's Itineraria project.	www.zvdd.de/
National Library of Serbia	The library has digitized a number of Serbian travel texts.	http://eng.digital.nb.rs/zbrika/knjiga/
National Széchényi Library, Budapest	Part of the general collection, with under 10,000 digitized items in June, 2011.	http://mek.oszk.hu

organizational principles not based on recognizable systems. The following strategies have been identified:

1 The use of Dewey Decimal classes as organizing principles of collection description. This model is followed by Gallica and the Széchényi National Library, although neither of the libraries makes any reference to the otherwise highly recognizable categories. Gallica uses the term 'themes', corresponding to the Dewey classes; the theme 'History and geography' incorporates 'Geography and travel'. Széchényi's interface identifies five different sub-collections, condensing the ten Dewey categories into five. Each of the five categories has several subcategories,

although it is difficult to notice that clicking on the five categories leads to further groups. 'Culture, arts, literature' leads in to 'Travelling, Tourism', which allows us to browse related books, including travel writing. Collection description is not provided in either case.

2 Categorizing for popular appeal. Hathi prefers to use the term 'public collections' for a long list of themed collections, but these have been compiled by users to reflect their thematic research, with no controlled terminology. Currently, no 'public collection' relevant to travel writing exists. Project Gutenberg's basic organizational unit, 'bookshelves', is meant to remind the user of bookshops. Travel writing can be found under 'Travel', 'Women's travel journals' and 'Countries'. Descriptions are also lacking. The National Library of Serbia also offers thematic sub-collections, which are primarily based on genres such as old and rare books, posters, music and similar categories. 'Books', however, is a category based primarily on 'agents' whether these agents are authors, such as Jovanovic, or subjects of representation, such as Napoleon. Travel writing titles are located within 'Books'.

3 Collection groupings based on provenance. ZVDD contains several sub-collections, which are organized according to the provenance of the digitized collection. The relevant collection is Göttingen University Library's Itineraria, which can be identified only on the basis of its title, as no further description is provided.

Based on the above, it is reasonable to conclude that the libraries examined do not provide clear pointers to their relevant collections. They may use well-established headings (Gallica), but they do not make their practice clear, whilst others want to make their DLs more 'user friendly' by using collection headings from everyday language. Although this may sound less 'threatening' to the user, most DL users would probably welcome a clear indication of the nature of the sub-collection in terms recognizable from library use.

The user wants to browse the catalogue of digitized texts

Locating the relevant primary or secondary sources in the catalogue is the next step in the process. The least complicated way of searching for items is based on known-item search on an author–title basis, which presupposes previous familiarity with the field. Known-item searches can be difficult, though, when the text is translated and the record does not contain the original title, or when the author names are used in a variant form.

Browsing, the significance of which for humanities in the information retrieval process has been widely acknowledged in research, can be a faster way of identifying objects if the exact details are not known, or it can generate surprisingly useful results. In order to compare the browsing or search functions offered by DLs, it is convenient to survey the basis of search functions offered by electronic library catalogues.

In electronic library catalogues of academic standard, search functions normally allow for a long list of search categories, including author, title subject, shelfmark, ISBN, etc. Furthermore, the MARC record of the catalogue can be searched as a full-text surface by a combination of searches selected by each individual user. In order to make the hits possible, it is essential for the information to be provided at the cataloguing stage: in addition to the basic information, Anglo-American cataloguing standard records note if the book is a translation, often noting the title of the original text, whether in the form of 'uniform title' or in a content note. They also add subject headings, which in our case normally is 'Description and travel'. The retrievability of East European travel writing by browsing largely depends on the above information being included in the records, and academic research libraries would generally follow these standards.

Again, it is useful to survey the metadata practices followed by our digital collections.

1 Provenance of metadata: The source of metadata varies in a number of ways. Most libraries digitize their own collections; hence they provide their own metadata. This applies to Gallica, the National Széchényi Library and also ZVDD, especially as the travel writing collection originates from one contributing library. The situation is slightly more complicated with Hathi, the aggregated site of different libraries, which uses the metadata of contributing libraries, and Gutenberg, which does not clarify the origin of its data, although it is obvious that librarians were involved. The Serbian library does not provide cataloguing information.

2 The standards of the metadata: Standards of metadata imply whether the metadata used in the process of describing objects followed a certain system. Most libraries followed MARC metadata, although several of them in a very limited form, whilst Gallica follows the standards of the Simple Dublin Core metadata, without any clear application profile – in other words, without reference to the digital objects, institution, application or other user community.

3 Search functions: All the libraries examined allow a range of simple and advanced searches within the DL catalogue – apart from the Serbian library. Simple searches normally allow author, title, imprint and language searches, and advanced searches add ISBN/ISSN searches and other search categories. Full-text searches on the MARC records are normally possible. Subject searches are also possible.

Based on our experiences of searches, it is important to consider the extent to which the data provided can respond to the needs of the researcher. As Ross and Terras (2011) point out, the key query terms for academic users are 'individual names, geographical, chronological terms, and discipline-specific terms'. The latter in our case include the terms 'travel' or 'description', references to the nationality of the author, and, in many cases, references to translation. 'Travel and translation' should also be used in different translations. Based on the needs of the scholar of travel writing, the following features of the catalogue records have hindered the productivity of searches:

1 Lack of information about translation: In the DLs examined, the category 'language' is present in each of the collections, but it is an empirical observation on the language of the digitized text. None of the records examined notes the original title in the form of a uniform title or a content note.
2 Subjects and subject headings: The terminology 'subject' is used in all the DLs, but the use and depth of subject headings varies. Gallica, for instance, produces only 25 hits to the keyword 'Description and travel', although it has 4988 items under the category 'Geography and travel', implying that subject headings are practically unused. ZVDD records do not use subject headings at all, and Hathi and Gutenberg records show subject headings only occasionally. The most challenging case is the Széchényi Library, which provides subject headings on its records according to Library of Congress (LOC) standards, but only in Hungarian, making it practically unusable for speakers of other languages. The unpredictability of the existence of subject headings means it is unreasonable to expect to find a representative number of relevant records on the basis of subject searches.

Travel writing and virtual research/learning environments

From a different perspective, libraries and digital collections rarely acknowledge the fact that digital collections can operate as continuously changing and developing resources. This would require a different kind of digitization, a digitization that allowed you to contextualize the primary sources for their examination. As Audenaert and Furuta put it, researchers 'study source materials as an integral part of a complex ecosystem of inquiry that seeks to understand both the text being studied and the context in which that text was created transmitted and used' (2010, 290). Some examples for those in travel writing studies already exist: they are small, scholarly digital collections and are usually based on projects originating from universities, university libraries and research institutions in North America or Western Europe, focusing on travel or travel writing describing one particular region, or focusing on travel writing emanating from a region or by a group of authors. Our findings have identified an excellent example of such virtual research environments: the site of the 'Interuniversity Centre for International Studies of the Adriatic Tour' (www.viaggioadriatico.it/ViaggiADR) covers travels to the Adriatic region. Here, travel writing in East European languages sits next to travel writing in English, German and French. The collection is a rather small one, but it is exemplary in terms of searchability. In addition, it also provides biographical and other secondary sources on the travellers and, finally, it allows the user to visualize some of the travels.

Conclusions

At the outset, the question was raised whether current, headline-grabbing mass digitization projects can serve as the ultimate solution for the academic need to access rare or hard-to-find texts in tertiary education. Our findings have suggested that, although the major cultural heritage DLs have become essential tools in the teaching of the humanities, they do not use their full potential for the support of teaching and learning. The primary reason for that is that the level, depth and homogeneity of metadata are very uneven, despite the major role of librarianship in their design and production. Also, they provide little information about the nature of the collection, which makes them less inviting and inspiring as a suitable research environment for humanities research. It is this factor that supports the need for targeted, carefully planned and designed web portals for the teaching and research of humanities subjects. Some of the following may serve as useful recommendations to the designers of DLs:

- There is a clear need to use the traditional method of collection or sub-collection description on the home page of library collections. This is necessary even when the collection is partly user generated: the Dewey Decimal Classification and other similar organizing systems are commonly recognizable, and also not too technical.
- Contributing libraries need to co-ordinate their own metadata with those of other libraries.
- Catalogue records should use metadata tags that provide the kind of information that would help users to find material. Many researchers find that metadata normally used for book description is an essential component for describing digital text.
- An easy interface with virtual research and learning environments would boost the use of digitized collections.

These findings provide impressions based on a small sample of research on using DLs in tertiary education. To date, the life of DLs has been short and they are still developing. But our knowledge and experience as librarians of physical collections should not be suppressed or marginalized.

References

Audenaert, N. and Furuta, R. (2010) What Humanists Want: how scholars use source materials, *Proceedings of the 10th annual joint conference on digital libraries*, New York: ACM, 283–92.

Centro interuniversitario internazionale di studi sul viaggio adriatico/Interuniversity Centre for International Studies of the Adriatic Tour, www.viaggioadriatico.it/ViaggiADR.

Corvey Collection, http://extra.shu.ac.uk/corvey/catalog/travel/.

Cunningham, S., Reeves, N. and Britland, M. (2003) An Ethnographic Study of Music Information Seeking: implications for the design of a music digital library, *Proceedings of the 2003 Joint Conference on Digital Libraries*, Los Alamitos: IEEE Computer Society, 5–17.

Digital National Library of Serbia, http://eng.digital.nb.rs/zbrika/knjiga/.

East Looks West Project, www.ssees.ucl.ac.uk/eastwest.htm.

Gallica, http://gallica.bnf.fr/.

Göttinger Digitalisierungszentrum, http://gdz.sub.uni-goettingen.de/.

Hathi, http://hathitrust.org.

Hungarian Electronic Library, http://mek.oszk.hu.

Mass Digitization, http://massdigitization.com/#europe.

Project Gutenberg, www.gutenberg.org.

Ross, C. and Terras, M. (2011) Scholarly Information Seeking Behaviour in the British Museum Online Collection. In Trant, J. and Bearman, D. (eds), *Museum and the WEB 2011: Proceedings*, Toronto: Archives & Museum Informatics, http://conference.archimuse.com/mw2011/papers/scholarly_information_ seeking_behaviour.

Stevens, R. E. (1956) The Study of the Research Use of Libraries, *Library Quarterly*, **26** (1), 45–51.

Stone, S. (1982) Humanities Scholars: information needs and uses, *Journal of Documentation*, **38** (4), 679–91.

Watson-Boone, R. (1994) The Information Needs and Habits of Humanities Scholars, *Reference Quarterly*, **34** (2), 203–16.

Wellcome Library, http://library.wellcome.ac.uk/doc_WTX058930.html.

Zentrales Verzeichnis Digitalisierter Drucke, www.zvdd.de/.

CHAPTER 17

Support for users within an educational or e-learning context

Nicola Osborne

Introduction

Learning has often been associated with particular physical spaces, whether formal classrooms or lecture theatres, or more informal spaces such as a workshop or studio. However, learning spaces have been changing, and moving either partly or fully online (Brown, 2005), leading to new and different learning and teaching experiences.

Emergent technologies – from the earliest electronic resources to virtual learning environments (VLEs), communications tools and social media – have enabled a radical shift in how educational space may be defined (Lave and Wenger, 1991) and an increasing blurring of the relationship between learning spaces and the other online spaces a learner may inhabit. Even the most traditional offline course should expect some or many participants to be engaged in the recreational use of social media. Nearly half of all respondents to the 2009 Oxford Internet Survey reported having created a profile on a social networking site (Dutton, Helsper and Gerber, 2009) and this looks likely to rise: the Pew Internet and American Life Project found that 73% of American teenagers used social networking sites (Lenhart et al., 2010).

> For me, the net is a wonderful learning network and for some it is a lifeline and for others it is a tether to their boss or a source of harmful misinformation, disinformation, and distraction. Since when is the world starkly divided into either-or alternatives?
>
> Howard Rheingold (quoted in Anderson and Rainie, 2010, 13)

The modern learning experience takes place in a hybrid space that merges the physical and the digital, the formal with the informal, and increasingly shares responsibility between the educator and the empowered learner. Digital library (DL) providers can engage in new ways with users, changing the ways in which resources are used and valued. However, the rules and behaviours of e-learning and online social spaces are still (and likely will remain) in flux, with privacy concerns and the potential for bullying both important as social media spaces are brought into the e-learning process (Davis and Lee, 2008; Keashly and Neuman, 2010).

The combination of approach, educational style(s) and technologies employed can shape the needs or expectations of the e-learner. For instance flexible e-learning courses can fit well with learner-centric pedagogical approaches but can present particular challenges for those who thrive in a highly ordered structured space. There is not one single format, structure or type of e-learning experience, instead it is a continuum, and tools, including VLEs and specialist DLs, may be employed in radically different ways.

These changes and technologies offer huge potential for enriched and engaged learning experiences, but each new technology creates new challenges and further diversifies the needs and expectations of both educational professionals and learners (e.g. Dutton, Cheong and Park, 2004; Eynon, 2005).

Popular uses of digital resources in learning

Beyond the library walls

Perhaps the most mainstream digital resources for learning are electronic journals, which have rapidly become ubiquitous, thanks to their searchability, accessibility and connectivity to additional materials such as referenced materials, videos or imagery. Increasingly, articles also connect to original data and are moving away from their print counterparts to become transliterate (Thomas et al., 2007) experiences: objects that weave text, audio, video, interactive models, dynamic visualizations and actively updated discussion and reflection on the central academic object.

As electronic journals and e-books have emerged online, the process of reading and interpreting a journal article need no longer be a solitary experience, with online citation and ratings tools (e.g. Mendeley), social bookmarking (e.g. delicious, Evernote) and annotation tools (e.g. A.nnotate, diigo, Google SideWiki), along with discussion spaces and instant messaging, adopted as tools for collective reading. One can share thoughts in real time or asynchronously with fellow learners, whether they are within institutional walls or outside of them. Indeed the openness of current digital environments for learning can be highly complex: learning may be enriched by serendipitous contact with interested outsiders. However, licensed content is usually tied to institutions and it can be highly challenging for educators to remain active in and aware of the diverse formal and informal learning spaces that their students may use. Indeed the interplay between officially approved or recommended academic tools and commercial web tools (both specialist and non-specialist) reflects the ongoing tension between the forces that push at change in learning more widely: what the educators and/or institutions promote or want learners to use versus what learners want to use or, in some cases, find easier to use.

Finding, tracking and sharing electronic resources

The tools and websites that manage access to electronic resources have also become increasingly sophisticated, moving beyond portals and traditional OPACs and catalogue-like interfaces, to federated searches, iGoogle and Facebook widgets and mobile phone apps and sophisticated discovery tools that connect distributed web services 'mashed up' with local resources. The user experience has moved from traditional search and/or browse interfaces to those which promote serendipitous discovery through faceted search, tag clouds, etc.

Connecting electronic resources to teaching and learning

These sit alongside (and in some cases are embedded into) VLEs such as WebCT/Blackboard, SAKAI, Moodle, or Elgg or Ning, in which course notes and DL tools and resources and active class discussion spaces coexist. These resources support and are supported by in-person teaching, tutorials, guidance, etc.

Whilst the delivery of pure e-learning is still a relatively niche practice, this type of hybrid learning experience is commonplace, with students accessing course materials online and using digital devices as part of the learning process, whether laptops at lectures or checking course materials via mobile phones (for the specifics of mobile devices see Chapter 15). Group work is as likely to involve students or colleagues gathering around a computer or smartboard and taking part in a digital and/or online project as to be about working around a flip chart or whiteboard. With mainstream education embracing the DL and online world, it is hardly surprising that learning activities have merged into informal spaces, including social media and gaming environments (e.g. Prensky, 2001; Whitton, 2010), that learners are already familiar with. However, the move to both formal support for learners and informal peer support in digital spaces can risk alienating learners with little experience or confidence with computers or the internet, or those with weaker social connections to their peers.

Beyond the (virtual) institutional walls

When learning communities expand in irregular patterns into informal, often commercially operated, spaces they transgress the boundaries and control of the academy, opening up potential inequalities for learners and greater potential for the circulation of information (and misinformation). The concept of scaffolding students (supporting, encouraging and occasionally pushing for correction by more experienced peers or teachers) as they reach the bounds of their skill levels (Vygotsky, 1978) is an important part of the learning process in physical learning spaces, but in wilder online spaces there may be an absence or subversion (through poor/ill-informed support) of such scaffolding. However, this blurring provides huge opportunities for cross-organizational, interdisciplinary and serendipitous connection and reflection. In addition, participation in learning practices in informal, playful, social online spaces can feel far more intrinsically motivating than traditional learning experiences.

An excellent example of the intersection of informal learning, social media and traditional entertainment has been the phenomenal success of TED (TED Conferences LLC, 2011) lectures online. These short talks, often presented by academics and expert thinkers, elicit blockbusting viewing levels and viral sharing through social media sites. Although the presentation styles of these videos are informal, catchy and brief there is additional appeal in their being artefacts and experiences discovered and shared/curated by the (informal) learner.

Future challenges

The challenge for traditional educational institutions, DLs and educational resource providers is therefore to move away from being driven by technical solutions and instead to consider how best to create more relevant and engaging user experiences. The recent JISC UX2 project addressed such concerns by looking at the needs of library users and exploring various approaches and technologies to improve the user experience (UX) for academic library catalogues (see Paterson and Low, 2010).

To some extent it can be assumed that commercial websites offer UXs that appeal to self-directed learners, as they often encourage a sense of playfulness and openness. However, many learners and teaching staff are experienced and comfortable with existing academic tools and those with more formal structures and significant help and support information. Many user interfaces currently rely on technologies that are not accessible to learners who require accessibility technologies to interpret websites and resources. Equality of access to resources, particularly as learning and library materials move generally online, presents particular challenges for digital resource providers in the development, design or procurement of tools and interfaces.

The intuitive UX of non-academic websites and tools can also be problematic in establishing good information-seeking behaviours in learners. It is therefore increasingly important to engage with these resources, to train learners to differentiate between resources and to emphasize, as appropriate, the authenticity and authority of data or resources provided by institutional or trusted digital resource providers.

In the following example I will reflect on experiences of combining digital resources with social media in order to foster an engaged community and craft a more appealing and accessible online offering. The example will look at the way in which social media raised awareness of the UK OER[1] (Open Educational Resources) initiative and how this has connected to the social media and community building activities, and reuse of digital materials, for the Jorum Service.

Example: Jorum and OER

Jorum is a free online repository for the Higher Education and Further Education sectors in the UK. Jorum is funded by JISC and operated by Mimas,[2] having been jointly developed with EDINA.[3] The service began as a cutting-edge project to create a repository for teaching and learning materials to preserve the outputs of JISC-funded projects and complementary materials such as those created for the National Learning Network (Halliday, 2008). Most of these contributed materials were licensed by their creators for viewing, use and reuse within the UK or within their own institutions.

Jorum appeared at a time of increased use of digital resources and VLEs to support traditional and e-learning courses, but a culture of sharing and reusing materials was only just emerging. In 2008 work began on JorumOpen, a version of Jorum to allow the upload of materials for broader sharing under Creative Commons licences. In particular, JorumOpen was established as the mandated deposit space for materials created under the Open Educational Resources Programme funding calls from JISC and the Higher Education Academy (JISC, 2010).

The OER concept is a worldwide movement to encourage the culture and practice of sharing learning materials. There are large and well-established communities around OER, particularly in the United States, and these communities often provide support and advice through social media sites: for instance, there is a particularly strong thread of discussion about and support on OER via Twitter. These presences also represent the types of blending and blurring that take place between institutional learning objects in the VLE with openly shared educational resources (from colleagues, other institutions, etc.) and with publicly shared materials perhaps not created with any pedagogical purpose in mind (YouTube videos, for instance). This existing community activity presented a superb opportunity for raising the profile of JorumOpen and engaging with creators and users of OER materials. A Twitter account and Facebook presence enabled larger engagement; sharing functionality within JorumOpen has enabled bookmarking and sharing of content to raise its profile and that of the site; and the long-standing Jorum blog was complemented with videos about OER and JorumOpen and highlighting best practice.

One of the most successful methods for raising the profile of digital learning materials within JorumOpen and for encouraging best practice in the creation, use and/or reuse of these materials has been the Jorum Learning and Teaching Competition,[4] with awards presented at the ALT-C Conference[5] in both 2009 and 2010. Creators of learning materials were asked to submit their work and, as this was already openly shared, the links to entered, shortlisted and winning materials could be shared via blog posts, tweets, etc. This helped to identify the range of materials in JorumOpen and demonstrate the ways in which educators are combining their own learning resources with existing materials (such as images and video) and feeding this into pedagogically driven websites or resources for use in their VLEs. This opportunity to focus on the content rather than on Jorum/JorumOpen as a tool has been a superb approach for engaging teaching staff across the UK (and beyond) in the resources and ideas behind OER and the use of learning-material repositories in general. Activity around the competition starts conversations about OER, about specific learning materials and general issues in this space, and encourages sharing of further materials.

The nature of the OER community is such that individuals and institutions tend to be proactively engaged in the use of technology and, as they have elected to become involved in the programme, with the notion of sharing and discussion that take place in public online spaces. It is important to note that this is perhaps not typical of the broader DL or academic community, though there are active online communities around both interest areas.

Some of the most active discussions around OER are also not those on best practice, but differing standpoints on hot topics for the community, such as which Creative Commons are sufficiently open for an ideal culture of sharing and reuse. This raises a challenge for anyone hoping to engage with and learn from their users: it is far easier to trigger activity, comment, feedback and advocacy and to learn directly about the needs of users when they are excited or exercised about an issue, but far harder to engage individuals around less controversial topics. For instance, whilst the JorumOpen OER experience has provided a wealth of rich conversations on licensing, it has not yielded as much community-generated discussion on the most effective pedagogical approaches for creating or using digital resources. This has been addressed through the collection and publicizing of best practice and case studies; however, the underlying tension between engaging on topics of personal interest versus less fiercely debated topics that could contribute significantly to understanding and serving users will be familiar from many other contexts within and beyond the academic sector.

Conclusions

The increasing use of digital resources in the academic sector brings many opportunities and challenges that are amplified by the ubiquity of engagement in online learning and social media spaces.

Historically, much of the interest in developing digital tools and resources has focused on the technical: what is technically possible and what is desirable for funders or policy makers. It is important, as the technology is maturing, to reflect on the role that user needs have and could play in future developments. Taking this approach in academic settings reflects considerably the similar shifts in the commercial sector, where 'Web 2.0' tools have been about a shift from the more rigid sites and services created by commercial providers over long periods of time and towards rapidly developed user-centred services and sites that retain users more through UX than through data lock-in or subscription terms.

Authenticity, authority and trustworthiness have greater importance for users online where traditional marks of authenticity (inclusion in a physical collection, publisher, even crude tools for judging quality, such as cover design) may not be available and where a wealth of competing resources are present. However, the vast array of materials also increases the potential for flexible and accessible routes to learning. If a recommended resource is difficult for a user to access, perhaps there is another related item – a review of a paper, a video about it, a comment by the author – that will enable a richer understanding.

Individuals (students or teaching staff) need no longer rely on colleagues and peers for support, correction and gentle scaffolding, as the online learning space empowers them to discover and access materials, support and peers working across the globe. Though discourses on the democratizing nature of the internet can be rather hyperbolic it is undeniable that digital resources of all kinds are enabling enhanced access to information and a new appreciation of the ongoing nature of learning, whether highly structured or very informal in form.

Notes

1   More information on the UK OER programme can be found on the JISC website, www.jisc.ac.uk/whatwedo/programmes/elearning/oer.aspx.
2   Mimas is a JISC designated National Data Centre based at the University of Manchester, http://mimas.ac.uk/.
3   EDINA is a JISC designated National Data Centre based at the University of Edinburgh, http://edina.ac.uk/.
4   Information on the 2010 competition can be found on the Jorum website, www.jorum.ac.uk/altccompetition2010.
5   ALT-C, the annual conference for Association for Learning Technology, www.alt.ac.uk/.

References

Anderson, J. and Rainie, L. (2010) *The Future of Social Relations*, Pew Internet and American Life Research Center, http://bit.ly/KjS9Gc.
Brown, J. S. (2005) *New Learning Environments for the 21 Century. Forum for the Future of Higher Education Symposium*, Aspen.
Davis, M. and Lee, B. (2008) The Legal Implications of Student Use of Social Networking Sites in the UK and US: current concerns and lessons for the future, *Education & the Law*, **20** (3), 259–88.

Dutton, W. H., Cheong, P. H. and Park, A. (2004) An Ecology of Constraints on e-Learning in Higher Education: the case of a virtual learning environment, *Prometheus*, **22** (2), 131–49.

Dutton, W. H., Helsper, E. J. and Gerber, M. M. (2009) *The Internet in Britain: 2009*, University of Oxford, www.oii.ox.ac.uk/research/oxis/OxIS2009_Report.pdf.

Eynon, R. (2005) The Use of the Internet in Higher Education: academics' experiences of using ICTs for teaching and learning, *Aslib Proceedings: new information perspectives*, **57** (2), 168–80, http://dx.doi.org/10.1108/00012530510589137/.

Halliday, L. (2008) *A History of Jorum, the Learning Resource Repository for UK Higher and Further Education (2002–2008)*, www.jorum.ac.uk/about-us/history.

JISC (2010) *Open Educational Resources Programme – Phase 1*, www.jisc.ac.uk/whatwedo/programmes/elearning/oer.aspx.

Jorum and Jorum Open, www.jorum.ac.uk/.

Keashly, L. and Neuman, J. (2010) Faculty Experiences with Bullying in Higher Education, *Administrative Theory & Praxis*, **32** (1), 48–70.

Lave, J. and Wenger, E. (1991) *Situated Learning*, Cambridge University Press.

Lenhart, A., Purcell, K., Smith, A. and Zickuhr, K. (2010) *Social Media and Mobile Internet Use amongst Teens and Young Adults*, Pew Internet and American Life Project, http://pewinternet.org/Reports/2010/Social-Media-and-Young-Adults.aspx.

Paterson, L. and Low, B. (2010) Usability Inspection of Digital Libraries, *Ariadne*, **63**, www.ariadne.ac.uk/issue63/paterson-low/.

Prensky, M. (2001) *Digital Game-based Learning*, McGraw-Hill.

TED Conferences LLC (2011) *TED: ideas worth sharing*, www.ted.com/.

Thomas, S. et al. (2007) Transliteracy: crossing divides, *First Monday*, **12** (12).

Vygotsky, L. (1978) *Mind in Society: the development of higher psychological functions*, Harvard University Press.

Whitton, N. (2010) *Learning with Digital Games: a practical guide to engaging students in higher education*, Routledge.

PART 4

User studies across the cultural heritage sector

CHAPTER 18

User studies in libraries

Derek Law

Introduction

As long ago as 1981 the doyen of British information researchers, Tom Wilson, stated:

> Apart from information retrieval there is virtually no other area of information science that has occasioned as much research effort and writing as 'user studies'. Within user studies the investigation of 'information needs' has been the subject of much debate and no little confusion.   (Wilson, 1981)

This remains true when we look at the division between traditional and digital libraries (DLs). In truth there are very few true DLs with digital-only content, hybrid libraries with a mixture of resources in all media being much more the norm. And in both digital and hybrid libraries the majority of content consists of digitized versions of existing content rather than born-digital content. Even born-digital content such as journal articles or theses will tend to exist in printed form as well. The interesting question that then arises is how the use of digital tools will allow 1) much better understanding of the ways in which traditional, paper-based libraries are used and 2) a comparison of how they support users, as compared with hybrid and DLs. Although users still tend to think of libraries as collections of books, research has shown that they also value support from librarians in their information-seeking practice. The biggest and longest-running collection of data about university libraries in the UK is the SCONUL annual statistics, which show how the usage of libraries has changed over almost 20 years. Similar data exists for other countries. This data allows some analysis to be made of how library usage is changing. This chapter gives examples of how user and use studies can add to understanding of the library and its role.

User studies

A major change in how libraries and library services are planned and managed has been a shift to evidence-based practice as a tool to support decision making. This first started in medical libraries over a decade ago, but has become a standard approach that is even taught at library school. Using research to support effective library decision making should become part of daily practice to help library managers learn more about their work, to develop better services and to share ideas about best practice. It helps to build a body of professional knowledge that can benefit the entire profession. The so-called EBLIP-process (Evidence Based Library and Information Practice) aims at helping library professionals by working through the separate stages of formulating the significant research questions, searching for the best available evidence to answer the questions, critically appraising the evidence, establishing the value of the anticipated benefits of the action plan that is developed and reviewing and evaluating the effectiveness of that action plan.

Measuring service quality

Perhaps the most popular tool for measuring library service quality as seen from the customer's point of view is the increasingly used web-based LibQUAL survey, a method used to determine service quality in libraries. In recent years, libraries have become increasingly interested in the concept of measuring service quality, and for a number of reasons. With institutions being subject to fierce cost pressures, and a need to justify every activity, academic libraries are now expected to compete with other commercial service providers, such as Google. This new environment has led to the development of a belief that the library should focus on meeting the expectations of today's customers, where their predecessors might have given greater emphasis to building collections for the future. In addition, there has been a more sophisticated understanding of measuring qualitative impacts. While the rise of technology use in libraries provides an enhanced capacity to measure some activity, ranging from the number of people entering and leaving the library to the number of hits on library web pages, this does nothing to say whether the service was and is both useful and valued. The purpose of the LibQUAL survey is to seek, record, analyse and then take action on users' opinions of service quality. Subsequent surveys should then allow an evaluation of the impact of any changes made. The data collected by LibQUAL is sent to a central database that analyses the data and presents it in reports that describe users' desired, perceived and minimum expectations of service. For each of the survey's 22 questions, the user is asked to indicate their minimum service level, desired service level and perceived service performance. LibQUAL then ranks users' perceptions and expectations on a scale to produce 'gap scores', which reflect the difference between the two. LibQUAL simply defines service quality as the customer's subjective evaluation of customer service.

LibQUAL is hugely popular as a tool, no doubt because in part it allows libraries to demonstrate an attempt to be part of an international and neutral standards-based activity. But it also begs a quite fundamental question. LibQUAL's underlying assumption is that only customers can adequately judge quality; all other judgements are essentially irrelevant. Critics of the approach have questioned whether users' service priorities should be the driving force behind the service priorities of academic libraries. So this approach gives strong data using a tested and widely adopted model, but it does conceal an unmeasurable philosophical question of whether all users are equal and whether libraries are concerned only with optimizing services for today's users or whether they have any responsibility to future generations who will use the collections built by today's librarians. Is immediate effectiveness more or less important than long-term contributions? To take a specific example, should a library sell off its special but currently little-used collections on alchemy in order to install the wireless connectivity desired by current users?

Measuring collections

Recurring lessons learned from user studies can influence decisions about the investment of scarce resources in the description of primary materials. A vast number of historical, special and archival collections have been minimally processed. It has hitherto been assumed that researchers will visit the collections and be assisted by specialists who can help with data mining. Such collections are becoming increasingly invisible as discovery becomes an increasingly exclusively web-based process. Changes need to be made to descriptions because researchers look less and less often in library catalogues or archival portals to discover primary resources. There is a growing gap between the expectations of users and historical descriptive practices in archives and special collections. User studies are then critical. From research evidence, the community can determine the optimal data and elements to unite users and materials successfully. Ensuring that 'hidden collections' can be discovered requires appropriate description, not just expert processing, cataloguing and the ability to cross-search networks. The entire discovery-to-delivery process needs to be supported by information systems, including increased access to resources.

The library needs to optimize access for its current users. Simple comparisons of the usage data of print and electronic formats can, for example, help in deciding whether acquiring a text in electronic format affects the usage of the print version of the text. An example here is a study focusing specifically on medical texts. Studies in the literature dealt specifically with general collections and it was not clear if they were applicable to medical collections. It was also not clear if these studies should play a role in determining whether a medical library should purchase electronic texts or whether reserve collections were still needed for print texts. Usage studies were conducted using data from the circulation system and the electronic vendor systems. These focused on (see Morgan, 2010):

- trends of print usage
- trends of electronic usage
- a comparison of electronic usage with print usage of the same title in the reserve collection
- a comparison of electronic usage with print usage of the same title in the general collection.

A study such as this is based firmly on evidence and allows good management decisions to be made.

Measuring user support and trust metrics

User support ranges from the provision of a reference desk to training in information literacy, to the embedding of subject specialists in departments and faculties. Each of these roles is implicitly based on trust: trust that the library staff share a common purpose with users and trust that the advice and support supplied is disinterested. In traditional library systems there are many things that allow trust to be assumed. Librarians are themselves trusted figures, seen as disinterested neutrals who can offer help and advice. Books selected for the library are seen as having some merit or trust because they have been chosen. Some library names – the Bodleian, the British Library – are bywords for things that can be trusted. This is much less true in a digital world, where the measures of trust either disappear or have not yet gained acceptance. A book published by Oxford University Press is trusted to be of a certain standard and quality, while a book by the Tea Party offers a different set of standards and quality, each of which is understood. But a web address such as ox.ac.uk or, even less helpfully, ox.org, tells us nothing of the trust that may be taken for granted. Some web resources such as Wikipedia are used – but not always seen as perfectly trustworthy – and concepts such as the wisdom of crowds are drawn on to establish trust, but the trust placed in traditional libraries and librarians is worth exploring and building on in a more systematic way than has been done hitherto. The need to establish trust metrics has been best articulated by Geoff Bilder in a whole series of conference papers (Bilder, 2008). He studies digital behaviour and compares it with traditional behaviour to identify roles and responsibilities missing in the digital environment. By the same token, one can establish roles and responsibilities to be cherished and strengthened.

Measuring the impact of the library

Interest in the impact of the library on the institution as a whole is fairly recent. Perhaps surprisingly, it seems that libraries have failed to collect the sort of statistics that allow quantitative judgements to be made, and qualitative judgements have therefore been made. A major study has shown that the impact of the library is important at a corporate as well as an individual user level (RIN, 2011). It is possible to show the extent to which the library is a major factor in helping to recruit and retain top researchers, in helping to win research grants and contracts, and is seen as vital to assisting in the research process. As institutional budgets shrink there is evident value in being able to demonstrate that the library contributes positively to the common weal and is worth supporting. This will rely on the collection of sound evidence and data.

Evaluating buildings and cost-effectiveness

One element unique to traditional libraries is the physical library building and optimizing its use. Here again, new technologies allow a better understanding of how libraries are used. For example, a simple study of how users moved into a public library was managed using GIS software. Patrons were observed from a stationary and unobtrusive location. ArcMap (GIS software) was used to develop an image of the floor so that entry routes could be recorded and then later analysed. The evidence provided by the study helped the library to establish what areas would be ideal locations for the placement of marketing materials and a book display. Knowledge of popular entry routes might also be useful in identifying routes that could be enlarged to movement round the building by users. GIS was therefore shown to be a useful mapping instrument for recording and analysing routes taken (Gore, 2010).

Very little thought has been given to the cost of housing and storing print collections. In most UK organizations everything from local taxes to heating bills is top-sliced from corporate funds. However, the green agenda is pointing to proper management of scarce and increasingly expensive resources. Much more work needs to be done on examining user behaviour and, if necessary, modifying that user behaviour – and, of course, in modifying buildings so that they meet user needs but reduce consumption of heat, water and light.

Conclusions

Almost all impacts of the library on users and of the users on libraries can be studied in an effort to improve services and collections. It is now understood that this has to be based on the formulation of questions and the collection of data to answer that question. New technologies provide new tools that allow sophisticated data collection. It is also valuable to collect data according to patterns adopted elsewhere, as this allows comparative analysis to be undertaken both nationally and internationally. Studies can also collect qualitative data in order to better understand how the library is used. Whether a library is traditional, hybrid or digital is perhaps less important than the fact that we now have a range of tools that allow the study of user behaviour and the impact of libraries. Libraries and librarians still have a key role to play in the selection of content for digitization, content description, trust metrics and the creation of the study environment.

References

Bilder, G. (2008) Sausages, Coffee, Chicken and the Web: establishing new trust metrics for scholarly communication, Eduserv Foundation Symposium 2008, www.slideshare.net/efsym/sausages-coffee-chicken-and-the-web-establishing-new-trust-metrics-for-scholarly-communication.

Gore, G. C. (2010) Identifying the Most Popular Entry Routes into a Public Library Using GIS Can Be a Tool to Increase Ease of Navigation and Identify Placement of Marketing Materials, *Evidence Based Library and Information Practice*, **5** (4), 94–5.

Morgan, P. S. (2010) The Impact of the Acquisition of Electronic Medical Texts on the Usage of Equivalent Print Books in an Academic Medical Library, *Evidence Based Library and Information Practice*, **5** (3), 5–19.

RIN (2011) *The Value of Libraries for Research and Researchers*. A RIN and RLUK Report.

Wilson, T. D. (1981) On User Studies and Information Needs, *Journal of Librarianship*, **37** (1), 3–15.

CHAPTER 19

User studies in archives

Wendy M. Duff

Introduction

Traditionally, archivists gained knowledge of their users' needs while conducting reference sessions or exit interviews. With the advent of digital archives, interest in using formal methods to study the information behaviour of archival users has increased. As Hill points out, remote users are often anonymous. 'Physical users are easy to count, able to make their needs known in fairly straightforward ways ... remote users are harder to find out about' (Hill, 2004, 139). Furthermore, users often have very limited understanding of archival descriptive practices or terminology and therefore they require systems that are user friendly and self-explanatory and support independent searching and retrieval. Designing these systems depends upon gaining in-depth knowledge of the information-seeking behaviour of all types of archival users and studying the usability of archival systems.

Archivists have traditionally dedicated little time and attention to studying their users; archivists focus, first and foremost, on the care and preservation of records, and only secondarily on the records' use. Eastwood (1997) suggests that an archivist's primary role is to protect the integrity of records; therefore, providing access to records must come after they have ensured the preservation of records. Moreover, Cook (1990/91) warns against turning the archives 'into the McDonald's of Information, where everything is carefully measured to meet every customer profile and every market demographic' (p. 127). Cook suggests that archivists should not modify their acquisition policies or descriptive practices to meet what users think they need. He posits that archivists provide better service if they meet users' needs, rather than users' wants:

> Every user from the genealogist looking for a single fact or a copy of a single
> document through the most sophisticated researcher using 'discourse'

methodology would benefit from this materials-centred approach to archives. The genealogist should not just be handed the land patent or the record of entry relating to his or her ancestor, even if such service can be a quick one-minute 'strike'. Rather, the user should also be led to information about the contextual significance of that document. What is a land patent; what was the process by which it was issued . . .   (Cook, 1990/91, 130–1)

Types of users

Many studies on archives have focused on one type of user (Sundqvist, 2007), the most popular user types being historians, genealogists and students. This research has revealed how some user groups search for and use records. Duff and Johnson (2002) concluded that a historian's success in identifying, locating and using sources is linked to his/her background and contextual knowledge. For example, one historian who investigated the role of women in the dairy industry used her knowledge of the dairy industry to identify relevant fonds. The historian explained: 'So if it's a very large organization with large producers, the likelihood of me finding a lot of women in there is less. Whereas if it's a small organization of local producers, I might have a good chance of finding women … So I take my knowledge of the subject matter and then use the description of the organization or individual [found in the finding aid] and then I make an informed guess, or informed decision as to whether I think it's worth spending the time to look at it or not.' This historian used her knowledge of dairy-farming organizations and the contextual information about the records' creators to locate relevant material.

Wineberg (1991) found that historians used three heuristics to judge the trustworthiness of information in documents: corroboration or checking with other documents, checking the source of the document and situating the document in time and space. Yakel and Torres (2003) identified three types of knowledge that users need to access and use documents: archival intelligence, domain knowledge and artefactual literacy to interpret records.

Use of images

Research has also investigated the use of archival images. A study of relevance of digital images discovered that students and faculty of American history at Carnegie Mellon University based retrieval decisions on their perceptions of the topic of an image, as well as assessments of image quality and clarity (Choi and Rasmussen, 2002). Scholars and graduate students interviewed by Burns (2006) indicated that they required extremely high image quality and preferred to use analogue collections. A qualitative study of extensive users of the Library of Congress's image collection concluded that users have different expectations of digital collections. Conway (2010) explained that 'Not every user expects or demands a browsing or navigation system that represents completely the relationship among discrete photographic objects, but those who do will find new meaning in context search and discovery' (p. 459). Therefore, some users will require high-resolution images or contextual metadata, but others will not.

Terminology

Numerous studies have indicated that users experience difficulties when encountering archival terminology. For example, the difference between 'Overview' and 'Administrative history' confused users of the Online Archives of California (2009), and a user of the Northwest Digital Archives remarked, about 'Administrative information', 'when I see that word, it seems like it has to do with something that isn't my business, it's for the people who work there, if you want people to click there it should say something like "use information"' (Northwest Digital Archives, 2008, 7). Chapman's (2009) usability study of the University of California's online archival system, however, found that users experienced the most difficulty with terminology appearing without context: for example, 'in menus such as the Series Quick Links and left hand navigation bar' (p. 35); and three-quarters of participants actively complained about the series titles 'Volumes, 1860–1965' and 'Additions received after 1989'. One novice commented, 'Volumes . . . volumes of WHAT?'. An advanced participant, however, remarked, ' "Series"? I just look at the title after "series", I don't know what you mean by "series" there actually, to be honest'. The title of the series followed the label 'Series': even though this user did not know what the term 'series' meant, it did not stop her from understanding the description (Chapman, 2009, 36)

Searching

Digital finding aid or retrieval studies also reveal that users value descriptive information about dates, the location of the material or the retrieval number, and an overview of the collection, as well as the title, documentary form, extent of the material and subject headings (Northwest Digital Archives, 2008; Online Archives of California, 2009; Duff and Stoyanova, 1998). However, many users of the Northwest Digital Archives system were confused by the search results for the basic and advanced searches; they expressed general confusion about how to interpret the results and actually use/view the materials. 'Participants started off the search, at the search box, with a high level of confidence; unfortunately, many got lost quickly and expressed frustration. Once this frustration set in, they ended up randomly clicking, backtracking to the previous page, and quickly reading only as much text as was displayed on their screen (not scrolling to find more).' Fachry, Kamps and Zhang (2010) found that the title, documentary form, author, date and the existence of a digital copy in a results summary helped users to estimate the relevance of material and to determine whether to consult the finding aid, while an overview of the collection helped them to predict the time and effort needed to consult records. Users of digital images determine the relevance of the images on the basis of the title, date, subject descriptors and notes (Choi and Rasmussen, 2002). Fachry, Kamps and Zhang (2010) posit that contextual information influences a user's decision to retrieve more information about records.

Expertise

Users with various levels of archival and computer expertise search differently; for example, users with archival expertise tended to browse the whole finding aid and indicated that they liked to get an overview of the entire finding aid. One expert explained, 'I was trying to figure out how this was organized and where I would go to look for something because this left-hand side where it has "detailed description"... has some highlighted topics. I tried to figure out if those were the only highlighted topics or whether there was going to be more somewhere else' (Prom, 2004, 260). Users with less archival experience tended to click 'a few links or scrolled a few lines into the finding aid, then used the find-in-page function to identify the box in which relevant materials were located' (p. 259). Zhang and Kamps's (2010) study of archival search logs identified expert and novice searches based on the frequency of visits. They suggest that novices spent less time searching than did experts, had more one-click sessions, revised and repeated queries less often, searched by name and clicked less on the results of a query. By comparing descriptions created by archivists with user-generated descriptions, Romijn-Wixley, de Vries and Kamps (2010) found that archivists created more abstract but more systematic descriptions, while users created descriptions with more detail and provided terms that would help to locate information in the archival documents.

A qualitative study of Welsh citizens who use archives suggested that archives users face three challenges: knowing where to look, knowing how to express a need and contextualizing what they find. The report concludes that the 'problem with digital archives seems to be that users lack the support of archivists in formulating queries, identifying archival sources and interpreting and contextualiz[ing] the search results' (ArchifauCymru-ArchivesWales, 2007, 25). Daniels and Yakel (2010) also found that their research participants had problems in formulating search queries.

Finding aids

Researchers have also investigated the effect of the structure of digital finding aids on access. Yakel (2004) revealed issues with multi-level descriptions; users in Altman and Nemmer's (2001) study often lost their way in finding aids; and Daniels and Yakel (2010) observed navigational problems. Chapman (2010), however, found that novices demonstrated an understanding of the structure of finding aids. A usability study of students in grades 4 and 12 (respectively 9–10 and 17–18 years old) compared the use of online finding aids with a prototype search engine that allowed users to browse or search for images directly (Besser et al., 2005). The researchers concluded that participants had a better experience and got better search results with the prototype, but some students noted that the prototype lacked adequate contextual information. An experiment studied the use of three archival access systems that displayed different levels of descriptive detail: a system that displayed only fonds-level descriptions, a system that displayed only item-level descriptions; and one that displayed item descriptions as well as information about the fonds. It discovered that participants preferred the third system, which gave the best results and supported relevancy judgements, navigation and direct access to items (Fachry, Kamps and Zhang, 2008).

Cross-institutional studies

Academic researchers and students have conducted most of the published research on archival finding aids; however, a few cross-institutional surveys have also taken place. Since 1998 the Public Service Quality Group (PSQG) has administered periodic national surveys to gain a better understanding of users' opinions of the archival services in the UK. These surveys provide information about archival users' demographic characteristics and satisfaction (Public Service Quality Group, 2007). The Archival Metrics project builds on the PSQG survey and developed five toolkits to help North American archivists gather data from their users. An evaluation study of the toolkits revealed that although many archivists have downloaded the toolkits, few have implemented them; respondents suggested that a lack of time and technical expertise creates barriers to conducting archival user studies (Duff et al., 2010).

Conclusions

In recent years research has shed light on the information behaviour of archival users, though some findings are contradictory. Overall, the research suggests that novices and experts use different strategies, but one system can serve both. The hierarchical structure of finding aids creates barriers for some users but specific elements facilitate relevancy judgements and hierarchical descriptions can also help to improve retrieval. Multi-level description can also foreground relationships among records – information that is needed by some users. Archival terminology was highlighted as creating difficulties, especially for novice users. Finally, research demonstrates that context supports access to and interpretation of records, but more research is needed in order to better understand this process.

References

Altman, B. and Nemmers, J. (2001) The Usability of On-line Archival Resources: the Polaris Project finding aid, *American Archivist*, **64**, 121–31.

ArchifauCymru-ArchivesWales (2007) *Ask the People: ArchifauCymru-ArchivesWales consultation*,
www.archiveswales.org.uk/fileadmin/arcw/doc/ATP-Final_Report-v2.pdf.

Besser, H., Afnan-Manns, S., Stieber, D. A., Turnbow, D. and Dorr, A. (2005) Finding Aid as Interface? Enhancing K-I2 access to digitized cultural heritage resources through adaptive systems technology: an exploratory study, *Proceedings of the American Society for Information Science and Technology*, **40** (1), 511–13.

Burns, M. A. (2006) From Horse-drawn to Hot Rod: the University of California's digital image experience, *Journal of Archival Organization*, **4** (1–2), 111–39.

Chapman, J. C. (2009) What Would Users Do? An empirical analysis of user interaction with online finding aids, Master's paper for the MS in Information Science degree, http://ils.unc.edu/MSpapers/3544.pdf.

Chapman, J. C. (2010) Observing Users: an empirical analysis of user interaction with online finding aids, *Journal of Archival Organization*, **8** (1), 4–30.

Choi, Y. and Rasmussen, E. M. (2002) Users' Relevance Criteria in Image Retrieval in American History, *Information Processing and Management*, **38**, 695–726.

Conway, P. (2010) Modes of Seeing: digitized photographic archives and the experienced user, *American Archivist*, **73**, 425–62.

Cook, T. (1990/91) Viewing the World Upside Down: reflections on the theoretical underpinning of archival public programming, *Archivaria*, **31**, 123–34.

Daniels, M. G. and Yakel, E. (2010) Seek and You Shall Find: successful search in online finding aid systems, *American Archivist*, **73**, 535–68.

Duff, W. M. and Johnson, C. A. (2002) Accidentally Found on Purpose: information seeking behavior of historians, *Library Quarterly*, **72**, 472–96.

Duff, W. and Stoyanova, P. (1998) Archival Displays from a User's Point of View, *Archivaria*, **45**, 44–79.

Duff, W. M., Yakel, E., Tibbo, H. E., Cherry, J. M., McKay, A., Krause, M. G. and Sheffield, R. (2010) The Development and Testing of the Archival Metrics Toolkits, *American Archivist*, **73**, 569–99.

Eastwood, T. (1997) Public Services Education for Archivists, *Reference Librarian*, **56**, 27–38.

Fachry, K. N., Kamps, J. and Zhang, J. (2008) Access to Archival Material in Context. In Borland, P., Schneider, J. W., Lalmas, M., Tombros, A., Feather, J., Kelly, D., de Vries, A. and Azzopardi, L. (eds), *Proceedings of the 2nd Symposium on Information Interaction in Context (IIiX 2008)*, ACM Press, 102–9.

Fachry, K. N., Kamps, J. and Zhang, J. (2010) The Impact of Summaries: what makes a user click. In van der Heijden, M., Hinne, M., Wessel Kraaij, W., van Kuppeveld, M., Verberne, S. and van der Weide, T. (eds), *Proceedings of the 10th Dutch-Belgian Information Retrieval Workshop (DIR 2010), Radboud Universiteit Nijmegen*, 47–54.

Hill, A. (2004) Serving the Invisible Researcher: meeting the needs of online users, *Journal of the Society of Archivists*, **25** (2), 139–48.

International Council on Archives (2000) *ISAD(G): General International Standard Archival Description*, 2nd edn, adopted by the Committee on Descriptive Standards, Stockholm, Sweden, 19–22 September 1999, Ottawa.

Northwest Digital Archives (2008) *Executive Summary: Usability Testing Round 4, 2008*, www.orbiscascade.org/index/cms-filesystem-action?file=nwda/reports/nwda_utwg_ut4_report_20080312.pdf

Online Archives of California (2009) *Second Round Usability Test Findings*,
www.cdlib.org/services/dsc/projects/docs/oac_usability_apr2009.pdf.

Prom, C. J. (2004) User Interactions with Electronic Finding Aids in a Controlled
Setting, *American Archivist*, **67**, 234–68.

Public Service Quality Group (2007) Survey of Visitors to UK Archives,
www.nca.org.uk/materials/psqg_national_report_2007.pdf.

Romijn-Wixley, J., de Vries, A. and Kamps, J. (2010) Archival Access from the User's
Perspective (abstract). In *Eighth European Conference on Digital Archiving: ECA
2010*.

Sundqvist, A. (2007) The Use of Records: a literature review, *Archives and Social
Studies: A Journal of Interdisciplinary Research*, **1** (1), 623–53,
http://socialstudies.cartagena.es/images/PDF/no1/sundqvist_use.pdf.

Wineberg, S. (1991) Historical Problem Solving: a study of the cognitive processes
used in the evaluation of documentary and pictorial evidence, *Journal of
Educational Psychology*, **83** (1), 73–87.

Yakel, E. (2004) Encoded Archival Description: are finding aids boundary spanners
or barriers for users?, *Journal of Archival Organization*, **2** (1–2), 63–77.

Yakel, E. and Torres, D. A. (2003) AI: archival intelligence and user expertise,
American Archivist, **66**, 51–78.

Zhang, J. and Kamps, J. (2010) Search Log Analysis of User Stereotypes,
Information Seeking Behavior, and Contextual Evaluation. In Belkin, N. J. and
Kelly, D. (eds), *Proceedings of the 3rd Symposium on Information Interaction in
Context (IIiX 2010)*, ACM Press, 245–54.

CHAPTER 20

User studies in museums: holding the museum in the palm of your hand

Susan Hazan

Introduction: the quintessence of the museum

When we visit a library or archive, we typically expect to find printed material: books, publications and documents. However, when we go to a museum – either in person or online – we expect a very different kind of experience. The physical museum invites us to discover exceptional and often extraordinary kinds of objects, and accordingly, when these very same objects are delivered online, they are managed very differently from the way books are managed by libraries, or the way that archives manage hierarchically arranged documents. As the footprint of the physical museum, an online museum is orchestrated to convey the singular and often spectacular nature of the objects, as well as the essence of the physical museum. This means that, as objects and works of art appear on the screen, the website needs not only to communicate the physicality of the objects but also to signify – in some way – the embodied space of the gallery.

As if we have just passed through the physical front door of the museum, the electronic portal signifies entrance to the online museum, and the collections are set up accordingly. Objects are not simply displayed as clutches of atomized objects, but are arranged in thematic order – as a collection or exhibition – according to a chronological logic, historical narrative or provenance, or according to artists or schools of art, in just the same way that they are presented in the physical museum.

The props and cues of the physical museum – catalogues, labels, wall texts and accompanying pamphlets – are presented online as descriptive labels and texts (metadata), serving both to identify the object and to maintain its place within the thematic series. Without these supporting descriptions an object simply gets lost, becomes an orphan, stripped of its role in the series and its place in the collection. These textual descriptions enable the user to discern what he/she is actually looking at. For example, just as colours in paintings need to be reproduced with fidelity in order to accurately convey the quality of artwork, so an archaeological object needs to be set in its historical and anthropological context so as to provide both intelligibility and meaning. The scale of a tiny object, or that of an art installation, can be misleading when they are viewed online; without a clear indication of dimensions or proportions, the qualities of a collection can actually confound, rather than inspire, the visitor. All of these different kinds of information must be made available, including how and why the object came into the museum in the first place.

There are many ways for a museum to persuade us that its online presence is in fact the footprint of the real museum. Websites are branded like the mother institution and provide practical information about visiting; audio and video guides introduce the online exhibitions and, of course, provide an entrée to the collections themselves.

Even the way that the user is conceptualized in this scenario is different. A museum website typically calls its user a 'visitor', thereby strengthening the idea that we are welcomed into the museum and that, once inside the museum, we have a distinct role to play – other than 'using' the web pages. The critical difference between the terms 'user' and 'visitor' perhaps reflects the difference between the information provided (opening hours, ticketing, etc.) and the knowledge (the curatorial orchestration of the collections) that the museum shares with its visitors online.

This chapter focuses on the user/visitor perspective in an online museum scenario.

We will investigate two museum-driven projects, the Google Art Project and Europeana (Europe's Digital Library), being two very different approaches to delivering cultural content online. Both of these platforms bring museum content into our everyday lives, whether through a website on the computer screen or through mobile technologies whereby collections and exhibitions are transported directly into the palm of our hand. In both cases we will look at how content is conveyed when visitors seek answers to the 'who, what, when, where' questions and, just as important, we will investigate how the 'wonder' of the object is delivered – the very reason why these kinds of object are in a museum in the first place.

Google Art Project and Europeana: background

While both the Google Art Project and Europeana deliver cultural content, the two projects have very distinct and very different visions and, consequently, offer diverse user experiences. Europeana has been developed as the gateway to the European Union's (EU) distributed cultural heritage resources. Content is drawn from the 27 EU member states and includes books, maps, recordings, photographs, archival documents, paintings and films from national libraries, museums and galleries, archives, libraries, audiovisual collections and cultural institutions (Europeana factsheet, 2010).

The European Digital Library currently points to more than 19 million objects from over 15,000 institutions across Europe (Angelaki et al., 2010). None of the collections, however, is actually held by Europeana. Ironically, this prestigious library, with a recognizable brand, does not act as the custodian of these collections, hosting within its portal only a thumbnail preview and the metadata – the textual explanations that describe the objects or works of art. Through browsing and searching on Europeana, and after discovering the collections, the user is taken out of Europeana, to the website of the content provider where the digital object resides.

However, this library is a truly European library. With the aim of providing multilingual access to Europe's diverse cultural heritage, Europeana is currently available in all of the 23 official languages of the EU.

The Google Art Project is an entirely different kind of portal. This ambitious project grew out of Google's 20% policy,[1] which offers its engineers '20-percent time' to work on what they are really passionate about. The Google Art Project invites you to explore museums from around the world and to view a selection of their collections in high resolution. At the time of writing there are more than one thousand artworks online and 17 museums are participating in the project.

The three main features of the Google Art Project[2] include:

- a walk-through of the physical galleries using Google's Street View technology
- the Artwork View, where a single work of art selected by each museum is offered in high resolution. This is called the Gigapixel Artwork (7 billion pixels), where visitors can zoom into the image and view it over a platform that 'tiles' the work behind the scenes, delivering the breathtaking images tile by tile, almost in microscopic detail
- a shopping cart/lightbox feature that allows users to select from across the artworks and bring them together into their own, personalized collection.

Transmitting tangibility: the essence of the embodied gallery and the physical object

In order to clarify the different approaches of these two projects and the impact they have on the user experience, we will look at the way Rembrandt's paintings are staged both on the Google Art Project and on Europeana, so as to see how they are presented and to compare how the essence of the artwork, in each platform, is mediated through the screen to the visitor.

Google Art Project

For the Google Art Project both the Rijksmuseum, Amsterdam, and the State Hermitage Museum, St Petersburg have selected a Rembrandt painting as their chosen work of art, the former choosing the *Night Watch* (1642) and the latter the *Return of the Prodigal Son* (1663–65).

The Hermitage (see Figure 20.1) presents its premier work with the full label of the *Prodigal Son* on the panel to the right of the high-resolution image (1663–65, Rembrandt Harmensz van Rijn, 1606–69, canvas, oil, height 262.00 cm, width 205.00 cm), noting its location in Room 254. In addition there is a brief audio clip and a 25-minute video of the work, both in Russian. We can also read a short/long description of the painting (in English) and can follow the link to view this work on the Hermitage's own website.[3] The Google map accompanying this section takes us to Leiden, in the Netherlands, where both the birthplace and place of death of the artist are indicated. Two more links take us to the other Rembrandts in the Google Art Project (currently 23 other paintings) and to the other Google Art Project objects located in the Hermitage (some 23 paintings, mosaics and sculptures). As an online research tool, this is just about as good as it gets. We can quickly gather the basic information that we need about this artwork, as well as being able to inspect it in very high resolution. The cross-links to other Rembrandts and to other works in the Hermitage encourage intuitive searches and clearly frame the work in its historical context.

Each museum has its own section in the Google Art Project, including a link to its own home page, and a comprehensive floor plan on which the rooms containing the museum's other artworks in the project are highlighted and linked. In the Street View route we move around the galleries as if we are perched on the shoulders of the driver as he winds his way through the rooms at just the right height to view the paintings and sculptures. This is the magic of the Google Art Project, the sense that we are actually wandering around a real museum and viewing the collections from the best perspective.

Figure 20.1 *Screenshot: a 'walk-through' of the State Hermitage Museum in the Google Art Project*

However, all the museums in the Google Art Project look exactly the same because they are built on an identical template, and until we begin to inspect the artworks and read the texts it is not always clear which museum we have just landed in. At the Hermitage, the Google map shows the location of the museum, and additional information sections describe the history of the institution and furnish further facts about the museum.

A final link allows you to view the Hermitage's other works in the Google Art Project. But with 17,000 paintings and 600,000 graphical works in the collections, and over 12,000 sculptures, 300,000 works of craft, 700,000 archaeological and 1,000,000 numismatic findings in the Hermitage (according to the information supplied here), the 23 objects in the Google Art Project represent a minute percentage of the whole collection. One can only hope that this is an excellent start to what could be an incredible resource, but clearly the man-hours required to upload all of the Hermitage's collections into such a rich environment would be truly formidable.

Europeana

A search for Rembrandt on Europeana (see Figure 20.2) produces 5916 results. This includes texts (108), images (5790), videos (15) and sounds (3). Limiting the search to the Netherlands we find 447 images and 2 videos. As you type in the term 'Rembrandt' you are prompted to check similar terms (in this case all in Dutch) – e.g. rembrandtplein, rembrandthuis, rembrandttentoonstelling, which narrows the search term to help you find exactly what you might be looking for amongst the 19 million possibilities. Further searches can be initiated by content provider (for example Culture.fr/collections), by country, by type (audio, video or images), by language, by date or by rights (free access, public domain, paid access or various Creative Commons licences).

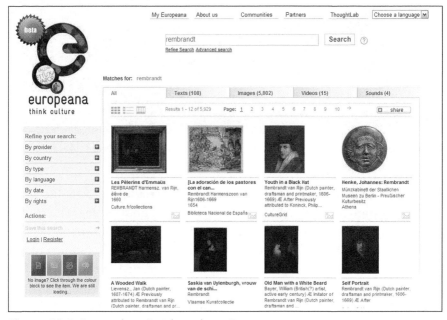

Figure 20.2 *Screenshot: Rembrandt on Europeana*

However, the vast number of results can be misleading. Rather than discovering thousands of paintings by Rembrandt, we find photos of sketches attributed to Rembrandt's students, mere references to the artist in a publication and a host of ephemera that are related in one way or another to the artist. Finding a specific artwork is not quite as simple as one would expect. For example, a search on 'Night Watch' does not bring up the sought-for painting, and unless you have the patience to sift through all the results or know how to spell the title of this famous painting in Dutch, *Nachtwacht*, you won't find it. Once you get to the record page there are links to each line of the description that take you to either Google or Bing for translation. A search for *Nachtwacht*, incidentally, brings up two results, both of which lead to the Rijksmuseum.

Europeana clearly delivers an impressive range of objects. But what about that intangibly vague quality that can best be described as the *wondrous* quality of the object? Can either of these websites deliver anything to convey the auratic quality (Benjamin, 1932) of the art?

Disseminating intangibility: the descriptive qualities of textual metadata

The Google Art Project does offer some measure of the 'wow factor'. The images are gorgeous and it is fun to be able to 'drive' through the galleries and enjoy the art. The 'wow' factor in Europeana lies in the sheer quantity of rich content that lies at our fingertips, and even if you do need to click on the next link to reach the full record and images, searching can be stimulating and rewarding. In both cases, the reward lies also in the textual records and in the descriptions and narratives that are so intuitively accessible.

Conclusions: the loss and the gain

So where has the wonder gone? And how can online environments possibly deliver the aura of the original object and replace the embodied physical experience of the encounter with the real object in the gallery? This is akin, in some ways, to the passionate discussions about the demise of the book. Clearly, an online artwork is not an e-book. There is still a lot of debate about those who treasure the traditional, linear rendering of 'the printed page', even to the point of fetishizing the book. Janet Murray reminds us:

> It is now clear that books will not disappear with the advent of digital genres – they will receive ever wider distribution and broader availability as they are instantiated in networked bits as well as in ink on paper. But bringing traditional books into digital form makes us aware of how much more we want from them than the paper-based versions can offer. We want them to be more portable, annotatable, searchable, and more linked to the world of all the media artifacts they reference: to films, databases, maps, and to the afterthoughts of their authors and the citations of others. (Murray, 2011)

This can only represent a celebration, rather than the demise, of the book, and clearly the 'book', in one form or another, still plays a very central role in our lives. Working in a museum, I am always envious of librarians, who deal with 'symbolic media', as Murray argues, and whose treasures can move almost seamlessly from scroll to codex to movable print to e-page as a simple matter of technology.

Museum curators do battle with symbolic representations of the artwork or archaeological object as they are released into the ether and wish that, like librarians, we could transfer our treasures from the tangible to the intangible in such an effortless way. However, we can't, and we have to make do with symbolic representations of our art on a two-dimensional 'page' that often looks more like a postcard that has been wallpapered onto the screen. Perhaps we should remind ourselves that the alternatives to web pages – the printed book of an exhibition catalogue, a television programme or, even further removed from the wondrous impact of a unique artwork, a radio spot describing an exhibition – are similarly less than inspiring.

I prefer to be able to access my art when and where I want, and I would argue that both of these platforms do an exceptional job in delivering them to me – even into the palm of my hand. With Europeana I can get a dizzying gestalt overview of the richness and breadth of Europe's cultural heritage in one swoop, and with the Google Art Project I am transported, from collection to collection, to some of the world's most fabulous treasures in an instant. There are may be only 17 institutions, and only 19 million objects, out there for me to discover, but right now, when I go searching for art online, I know exactly where I will click to find it.

Notes

1   www.google.com/jobs/lifeatgoogle/englife/index.html.
2   www.googleartproject.com/c/faqs.
3   www.hermitagemuseum.org/html_En/03/hm3_3_1_4d.html.

References

Angelaki, G. et al. (2010) ATHENA: a mechanism for harvesting Europe's museum holdings into Europeana. In Trant, J. and Bearman, D. (eds), *Museums and the Web 2010: Proceedings*, Toronto: Archives & Museum Informatics, www.archimuse.com/mw2010/papers/angelaki/angelaki.html.
Benjamin, W. (1932) *The Work of Art in the Age of Mechanical Reproduction*, www.marxists.org/reference/subject/philosophy/works/ge/benjamin.htm
Europeana fact sheet (2010), http://group.europeana.eu/c/document_library/get_file?uuid=6773c7f5–613c-4d9f-ab6d-95ed10c323bc&groupId=10128.

Murray, J. (2011) *The Book Tomorrow: future of the written word,*
http://focus2011.org/2011/05/the-book-tomorrow-future-of-the-written-word-by-janet-h-murray.

CHAPTER 21

Digital art online: perspectives on user needs, access, documentation and retrieval

Leo Konstantelos

Introduction

Digital art is a manifestation of modern cultural creativity and needs to be represented in the cultural heritage record of our contemporary world. However, current practices within the digital art community reflect a dysfunction between this understanding at a theoretical level and the ad hoc manner in which digital art is collected, described and distributed in online repositories (Konstantelos, 2009). This chapter explores the potential value of digital artwork stored in multiple online sources from a scholarly and educational point of view. In doing so, the chapter presents findings from a three-year research project in the Humanities Advanced Technology and Information Institute (HATII) at the University of Glasgow that investigated the explicit needs of particular communities for digital art discovery, retrieval and documentation from an educational and research perspective. The initial hypothesis postulated that these issues can be addressed by adopting content aggregation, which is manifested in the form of a digital library (DL) collection. A user-oriented approach was employed and data was collected from the target populations of arts and humanities scholars, digital artists and members of the DL community, using a social survey methodology.

Motivation and background

The motivation for this study stemmed from the significance of digital art's inclusion in structured electronic repositories as a creditable asset within the range of informational and cultural material. Waters suggests that

> few institutions have begun to assemble primary source collections of […] digital art and other uniquely digital artefacts that help serve as a record of modern culture for future scholars.   Waters (2006)

Similarly, Hedstrom et al. (2003) discuss the requirement for continuing access to digital content, which will allow future generations to understand the changes in society that have been introduced by the evolution of the internet and the emergence of such manifestations as digital art. This is only possible if such material is collected and maintained in a systematic manner and accessed through effective tools, for the benefit of current and future users.

Why digital art?

'Digital art' is a generic term that is used to describe often dissimilar types of material, and confusion arises with digitized objects. In this chapter, digital art is perceived as born-digital objects, the term referring to a variety of computer-based applications in the field of art and a practice that is not separated from other art forms, but instead associated with other types of artistic presentation and enquiry (Vaughan, 2005). Nonetheless, an array of features constitute digital art as a unique type of material:

1 Digital artworks are an amalgam of traditional and contemporary techniques, with representations ranging from digital images and photographs to multimedia installations. Previous studies to document digital art via extant standards have reported that the unique and particular characteristics of this medium cannot be straightforwardly accommodated (Hanlon and Copeland, 2001; Rinehart, 2004).
2 As Vaughan (2005) explains, digital artworks are infinitely reproducible, since 'every version has equal status by virtue of being absolutely identical; variation does occur [...] only at the point of performance'. Hence, the notion of the 'unique copy' that bestows value to artistic production is obscured.
3 Digital art lacks an identity that has been shaped by a collective memory through the evolution of the field. As Manovich argues, '[digital art] has no memory of its own history, so it can benefit from remembering its past more systematically' (Manovich, 2003). This situation highlights the all-important interpretive role of institutions such as digital museums, galleries and libraries and the imperative nature of their involvement in the information dissemination process.

User-needs assessment methodology

As a front-end evaluation instrument, a user-needs assessment was designed to investigate the documentation and retrieval needs of fine arts and humanities scholars. As little demographic information was available about digital audiences, it was hypothesized that the emergent community of digital art scholars should be evident within the disciplines of fine arts and humanities. Hence, feedback from this community was essential for exploring the research problem. To maximize the potential of the survey, further feedback was sought from digital artists and members of the DL community. The role of each group differed, as it reflected different scopes, research needs and priorities. The identification of informants' roles within the research problem area was pivotal for informing the selection of data-collection instruments, and two types were deemed appropriate: personal interviews and web-based questionnaires. The questionnaire offered distinct advantages when deployed online and proved to be the best method for reaching out to the larger group of fine arts and humanities scholars. Through sampling techniques, the questionnaire allowed for reliable generalizations from the results of a smaller sample to be extrapolated to a greater statistical population. Interviews aimed to extract more focused, nuanced information and were therefore better suited to the qualitative analysis required from digital artists and DL community members.

Selected findings

The web questionnaire collected 466 responses. Interviews were conducted with 40 digital artists and 10 members of the DL community. The results were analysed both independently and in relation to each other. In this manner, comparisons were drawn within the multi-method design and among the feedback from the three study communities, so as to extend the credibility of the findings and deepen the analysis, rather than to provide validation (Turner, 2006). Although variation did exist in the themes identified by each of the three groups, there were more similarities than was originally anticipated. The differences were mainly the result of differing uses of the material, the role of each group in the information dissemination process and the level of maturation of each studied domain, which inevitably influenced the orientation of the responses.

Arts and humanities scholars

The majority of respondents in this group were familiar with digital art and correctly identified the material as 'born digital'. Half the respondents reported acquaintance with digital art and, of these, almost 80% found it necessary to use the material they encountered for the purposes of their academic course. The academic fields most frequently reporting usage were film/theatre/television studies, fine arts, digital media studies, archaeology, architecture and history of art. On the other hand, respondents who had encountered digital art but not found it useful for their studies claimed that this was due to the material's being irrelevant to their field of study. A major part of the analysis involved the investigation of the searching behaviours and related needs that derive from gaps in locating digital art online. Respondents identified a search engine as the preferred method for finding digital art, followed by suggestions of resources from colleagues or lecturers, and use of a digital repository that they trusted. Commonly used digital art-specific resources were ARTstor, deviantArt, Digital Art Museum and digitalart.org. Other items to which participants gave a high score included the need to search multiple repositories before locating the desired digital art material, problems stemming from resources' not being accessible without registration or payment, the lack of a means to eliminate duplicate entries and the existence of links to irrelevant content.

Regarding documentation needs and, in particular, metadata, respondents placed high value on all the metadata elements they were asked to rate. Excluding more generic elements (such as title, creator, date, description and file format, which are common for most digital image materials), the most prominently scored items were: the source where the material can be found, access rights, software and hardware requirements to render the digital artwork and digital art genre.

With respect to the potential of an aggregated collection, the study participants almost catholicly (92%) stated that such a resource would maximize the efficiency of their research on digital art and promote the educational value of the material.

Digital artists

The interviews with digital artists were quintessential to informing this research with the views of the content creators. The studied group included artists active in a variety of digital art genres and therefore the feedback embodied views from equally different practices. Artists predominantly felt the lack of a standardized method for publishing their work. Alternative dissemination channels – which might serve the purpose of publishing one's work – were found to introduce a risk of digital art's being marginalized. The preferred publishing methods included personal portfolios or exhibitions and online repositories. Commonly used repositories were digitalart.org and deviantArt – which coincided to a degree with the resources indicated by the questionnaire group.

Digital artists were asked to comment on the characteristics that distinguish digital art, because these could elucidate features of the DL collection on which emphasis should be placed. The prevalent characteristic was the ease of circulation, as opposed to traditional artistic practices. Other characteristics included the facility to explore artistic styles, due to the capacity of digital media to mimic traditional techniques; the contemporary nature of digital art that attracts the artist's interest; and the capability to create works that integrate technology and art.

Concerning documentation practices, the majority of artists stated that current metadata provisions in online repositories for digital art are inadequate. Artists documented their work in an ad hoc manner, and mainly when submitting material to a repository. This was found to be problematic because the extent of the information that artists provided largely depended on the level of granularity that each repository permitted. Digital artists argued that three fundamental metadata elements should always be present: genre, hosting body and version of artwork. These again coincided with the feedback from the scholars, but in this case revealed the need for digital artists to control who holds their material and how its originality can be safeguarded.

The interviewees were also asked to discuss their preferred methods for preventing unauthorized use of their work and for enforcing intellectual property rights and copyright restrictions. These predominantly included submission in a trusted repository, through public exhibitions (with the expectation that their work will be covered by the intellectual property rights management of the organization owning the exhibition space) or by maintaining a personal database of their artwork. The majority of artists were keen to safeguard their material by using copyright, but at times this was viewed as a hindrance to digital art's reaching its audience. Suggested solutions included allaying copyright restrictions for educational purposes; creating universal access policies; investing in digital cultural institutions as advocates of good practice; and the organization of training events and consultation sessions.

Digital artists commented on the suitability of content aggregation for digital art. Many agreed with the proposed system as a comprehensive solution that promotes dissemination and innovation. Others held that suitability depends on the sources of the material and the extent of representation for artists and genres. A few interviewees raised concerns that an aggregated environment is open to low-quality material. Regarding prerequisites for implementing an aggregated collection for digital art, respondents cautioned that barriers posed by the current state of the digital art market need to be overcome, and support from the community needs to be established.

Members of the DL community

DL representatives agreed with the proposed solution of aggregating content from various repositories so as to make digital art artefacts available and retrievable. However, they cautioned about the trade-off between virtual organizations' need for a distributed IT structure and the corresponding changes necessary for decentralization and incorporation into the organizational strategies. Another recurring theme among the group of interviewees was the perception that digital art can be accommodated as any other information object within a DL. Specific recommendations for metadata standards and DL development platforms were not made, but there was a general understanding that a new standard is not needed: description needs could be accommodated by revising an existing schema.

On the whole, the educational value of digital art was corroborated on multiple occasions in the feedback from scholars and artists alike. Recommendations on required services were suggestive of the suitability of an aggregated collection as a means to strengthen and augment current practices in digital art repositories. The imperative of providing adequate metadata for digital art objects was signalled repeatedly. A common argument referred to the consequences of access permissions and copyright restrictions for information retrieval, and the way in which they can influence the development of a distributed infrastructure. In contrast to the currently employed ad hoc approach, universal policies regulating access rights are pivotal in the definition of quality for DLs.

Conclusions

At the highest level, the aim of this research was to define the prerequisites for the incorporation of digital art material into a structured and formalized management and access system. The lack of understanding as to how such material can be manifested and represented within an organizational environment, and how its incorporation in such an environment can influence the educational outcome, became readily apparent. Systematic, empirical research can provide the digital art community with a roadmap for gathering unique digital artefacts, or can enhance existing collections by defining standardized techniques for collection, documentation and access.

Digital art challenges traditional art description and cataloguing practices. The inclusion of digital artworks in existing DL collections is straightforward as long as they are properly documented. From a user-centric point of view, the problems that need to be tackled relate chiefly to catering for indexing and searching functionality by creating and attaching metadata that explicitly take into account the unique characteristics of the material, such as genres, multiple creators and multiple physical (storage) locations. At the same time, digital artists should understand the benefits of rigorously documenting their products and press online repositories to revise their facilities for the submission of metadata.

Before this study, little was known about the usage of digital art within fine arts and humanities research and teaching. The findings demonstrated that the scholarly potential of the material is far greater than is generally realized. The feedback from postgraduate students elicited high levels of awareness of the nature and meaning of digital art and pinpointed the needs for employing the material in learning and research. Actually doing this is problematic, because potential users have difficulty in locating the material and there is a lack of adequate descriptive information. This chapter has provided an overview of the benefits of a user-oriented methodology for exploratory and descriptive research, emphasizing the strengths of this approach for studying and classifying socio-technical phenomena – especially in under-studied, complex areas where an understanding of users' needs is paramount for the future development of systems.

References

Hanlon, A. and Copeland, A. (2001) Using the Dublin Core to Document Digital Art: a case study, *Journal of Internet Cataloging*, **4** (1/2), 149–62.

Hedstrom, M., Ross, S., Ashley, K., Christensen-Dalsgaard, B. et al. (2003) *Invest to*

Save: report and recommendations of the NSF-Delos Working Group on Digital Archiving and Preservation, http://eprints.erpanet.org/94/.

Konstantelos, L. (2009) *Digital Art in Digital Libraries: a study of user-oriented information retrieval* (doctoral dissertation), University of Glasgow, Glasgow, UK.

Manovich, L. (2003) *Don't Call It Art: Ars Electronica 2003*, www.manovich.com/DOCS/ars_03.doc.

Rinehart, R. (2004) A System of Formal Notation for Scoring Works of Digital and Variable Media Art. Paper presented at the *Electronic Media Group, Annual Meeting of the American Institute for Conservation of Historic and Artistic Works, Portland, Oregon*.

Turner, B. S. (2006) *The Cambridge Dictionary of Sociology*, Cambridge University Press.

Vaughan, W. (2005) Introduction: digital art history? In Bentkowska-Kafel, A., Cashen, T. and Gardiner, H. (eds), *Digital Art History, a Subject in Transition Volume 1: Computers and the History of Art*, Bristol: Intellect, 1–2.

Waters, D. J. (2006) *Middle East Digital Libraries: some principles for development*, www.sis.pitt.edu/~egyptdlw/papers/Donald_Waters.html.

CHAPTER 22

User studies for digital libraries' development: audiovisual collections

Andy O'Dwyer

Introduction

Audiovisual media in the digital domain share many of the basic and fundamental user requirements of other types of collections, centred on a high degree of usability, focused around specific tasks and actions matched to different user groups. However, the delivery of and user interaction with audiovisual collections does have specific considerations that need to be addressed in order to provide and maintain user satisfaction. 'Audiovisual' can be an ambiguous term, as Ray Edmondson observes (Edmondson, 2004); in this chapter we are concerned with collections made up of sound and moving images, such as film and video. User groups for audiovisual collections have many different profiles: the case study in this chapter addresses access to audiovisual content specifically for the personal consumer, the educational sector and media professionals. These are three very distinct groups with separate needs and expectations that need to be catered for in order to ensure a good level of service acceptability. These user groups were the primary targets of a recent project exploring how best to cluster audiovisual material from a number of European archives and provide access over the internet. We illustrate how end-users' needs have been addressed through a task-led approach and by using a requirements-definition process that comprised questionnaires, qualitative interviews and field evaluations.

The cost of providing audiovisual collections in digital form

There is a push to put many audiovisual collections online, and evidence of the great interest of users in this type of material. One of the findings from recent international user testing of Europeana illustrates this:

> Audio-visual content is not as well represented as other material, and users
> wanted more of it.
> (Dobreva et al., 2010, 4)

Various digitization initiatives have come from many quarters. One example is the cultural heritage sector, wishing to share content with the widest possible audience. Another is the commercial sector, where the internet has enabled the full range of providers of audiovisual services, from independent film-makers through to multinational companies selling DVDs and music, to place both new and archive audiovisual material online. They have a common goal in their desire to reach a target audience, and modern search engines really can help to match providers of services with their intended audience – driven in many cases by the commercial ambition of search engine providers to match advertising around search queries directly to targeted audiences. However, many consumers can be left stranded on an apparently relevant site: their search query has landed them on pages that match their search, but the overall experience may fall short of expectations, leading to feelings of frustration and negativity and, ultimately, the departure of the user to other websites.

Many cultural organizations and commercial and national archives with audiovisual media wish to make use of the benefits of digitization, particularly to access a larger online audience for their collections. But entering the online domain can require major changes in internal processes and it can be difficult to get start-up funding. The cost of applying professional digitization techniques to audiovisual material is great, and organizations often need to adopt new workflows as their holdings become more focused on digital storage, display and delivery. These costs, together with the cost of maintaining staff with the necessary IT skills sets, are often a barrier for archives, libraries and museums. A recent study estimates that the costs of digitization, including all the associated and project management costs, are €74 per hour for professional audio and €715 per hour for video. The digitization cost for film, which requires more processes and specialist handling, were estimated to be €2000 per hour (Poole, 2010).

The same report provides an interesting comparison:

> The cost of delivering 100km of main road in Europe is €750m. 100km of main
> road is equivalent to the cost of digitising every piece of audio content in EU
> cultural institutions, or 48% of the total holdings of video (excluding film).
> (Poole, 2010, 1)

There is a concern that much of Europe's audiovisual cultural heritage is in danger of being 'lost' because it resides on redundant formats and the replay devices will become obsolete. Although EC initiatives like PrestoPRIME are actively providing a centralized forum and competence centre to help custodians of audiovisual collections to obtain expert advice, without some grant mechanism being in place it is difficult to see how some of this older material will survive.

Specific requirements for digital audiovisual collections

Online audiovisual collections have specific requirements that need to be addressed if end-users are to experience the full range of possible benefits, whether for work purposes, for enjoyment and entertainment or for artistic reasons. Broadly speaking, these requirements relate to the quality of the viewing and listening experience, and adequate provision of contextual metadata. Essentially, is the consumer receiving the best possible quality of online delivery and end-user interaction? In addition to the type and technical specification of the device used by the consumer, there are many points on the pathway from provider to end-user that can influence the quality of delivery. These issues, which directly shape users' experiences, are explored in the following section.

The technical layer

Typically, the user requirements for online audiovisual content are predicated on the technical and infrastructure layer, rather than informed by a user-centric, task-led approach. There is an obvious reason for this, because without the basic technical and electronic infrastructure that links the consumer with the provider, no service can exist. This technical layer is constantly shifting in terms of what it can offer. Thus the focus from an IT perspective may be on keeping up with the latest speed of delivery and service opportunities. For example, there have been great increases in the size of available bandwidth, which means that audiovisual content can be distributed more efficiently to the end-user. New types of video players and visualization techniques are coming onto the market; the costs of digital storage and servers, on the professional level, and of hardware and software, on the consumer level, have fallen dramatically because of mass production and competition. This affordability means that users are increasingly accessing content from their home, workplace or educational establishment.

They are also viewing or listening to material on a range of portable media devices that are typically 'web enabled' and thus connected to the internet.

This access to content on a multiplicity of devices raises the important issue of the need for contemporary and persistent evaluations of user experiences, because these experiences can change dramatically from device to device. While providers of online digital collections clearly can never cater for every size and shape of screen resolution or every level of audio fidelity, it is incumbent on them to be aware of how these differences shape users' experience. A key reason for this is that a pause in the listening or viewing, or indeed any interruption, may be perceived by the user as a problem caused by the provider (of the digital collection), rather than as something related to the capabilities of the receiving device or to bandwidth considerations. This problem is well understood in the field of online media broadcasting and in the commercial sphere (Amazon, eBay, etc.), where smaller portable devices such as smartphones and tablets access a (mobile) version of the website designed specifically for them (see Chapter 15). This version is usually offered automatically, by detection of the device's operating system. By thus presenting the user with the version of a website that is most appropriate for their viewing device or operating system, usability is maintained. This is particularly important in the commercial sector, which relies, in a competitive market, on presenting users with a slick and efficient process, from navigation and selection through to potential sales.

The factors of bandwidth and the level of technical capability of the intended users are key considerations, as are internet technologies emerging during the design, build and implementation period of any new system. Awareness of these factors will help to avoid introducing services and features that may be imminently superseded. Such a situation can leave the technical administrators of a collection vulnerable to the risks both of growing unreliability as the system becomes outdated and of not matching users' expectations in terms of service delivery quality or the provision of features and functionality. These are just some of the factors that have driven the providers of online digital collections to firefight the immediate technical issues of delivery, rather than to focus on the needs of the user. But I argue that this 'technical linking' and all the necessary steps in the digital chain are now well known. Providers of online audiovisual media need to focus more on the needs and expectations of the user, and to let these point to the most appropriate layers of technical structure, design and features.

Finally, in this consideration of the technical processes in the formative stage of the digital chain that underpin usability, it is worth understanding the basic decisions about the steps needed for the conversion of older analogue material such as film and audio tape. Modern tools and techniques provide far better resolution of picture and sound than did earlier digitization methods, which offered few or no opportunities for enhancement. This is very relevant for older audiovisual collections and the restoration tools that can now turn previously 'unwatchable' content (possibly damaged, scratched or with poor sound) into something of a standard that is acceptable to the consumer. Older archives are likely to hold analogue media such as film and audio reels, plus variants of the wide range of video formats, many of which will have fallen into the obsolescence trap in which no replay device is available to play back the content. Archives may physically hold material but, essentially, it is locked and possibly even 'lost' if there is no means to recover it from a redundant format.

Usability of clustered collections: portals and aggregators

The usability of audiovisual content from DLs and collections delivered through portals (aggregated media) and not specifically targeted at defined and narrow user groups also needs to be considered. This content is made available specifically for a European or 'global audience', where the intended goal is to reach and provide access to the widest possible number of people. The 'donated' content may be the same as that on a provider's own website, but the end-user experience will be different because access is via a portal that is unlikely to be tuned to the same set of users as is the originator's website. Examples of the resulting impact on usability can range from language dependency (see Chapter 11), where the user cannot read the language that the website supports, to the exclusion of the associated metadata and links that different user groups of audiovisual collections would expect to see. For media professionals, for example, copyright information and adequate references on provenance are important. However, when the content is moved from an in-house system to a public-facing portal it is common, either for legal reasons or for space limitations on the receiving portal's site, for only a limited version of the available metadata to be ingested. This and other influences on usability are explored in the following case study on aggregating audiovisual media for online access.

··

Case study 22.1: Video Active

··

The European Commission has fostered collaboration and innovations in the areas of online access to and preservation of cultural heritage. Provision of access is possible through the digitization of collections and their delivery online. With this practice comes the need to ensure that the widest possible set of users is catered for in terms of overall usability. It is likely, with audiovisual materials bundled via a website or portal and displayed to end-users without any evaluation process (see Chapter 5), that it will be difficult for the end-user to navigate through to content, which may be arranged and displayed in an inconsistent manner and with varying amounts of supporting metadata. The user may also be hampered by the fact that content on such sites may be in only the native language of the provider. The EC has made efforts to incorporate multilingual strategies into online collections projects that it has sponsored in the cultural heritage and educational sectors, thereby allowing content to be accessed and understood by a much wider audience. Language support is something that is unlikely to be introduced without some kind of directive at the political level of the EC, backed by sponsorship, because the costs of incorporating multilingual text or subtitling are likely to be beyond the reach of a typical individual collection's service provider. The MultilingualWeb project is a recently funded project that is 'exploring standards and best practices that support the creation, localization and use of multilingual web-based information' (see MultilingualWeb).

Video Active (see www.videoactive.eu) is a good example of a project that is trying to meet the needs of users of audiovisual content and supporting access through tools such as a multilingual thesaurus. In addition to the technical support, videos and photographs are enriched with descriptive cataloguing and specially written articles. A particular difficulty is the clustering of predominantly video material from disparate archives and in a variety of languages from across Europe and placing them online in a usable form. Users can be hampered by the need to search in a particular language or to use a specific video player and software that they do not have permission to use or do not wish to download onto their particular machine at home, in the office or in their educational institution. This is especially relevant in the educational sector, where the software installed on a PC is decided by the administrators and not the individual students or teachers.

Video Active (2006–9) was a three-year project supported by the EU. Its goal was to place online audiovisual content, stored in media archives, that reflected the cultural heritage of Europe.

Comprising 11 content providers and two technical partners, the Video Active project gathered requirements based around the target audiences of the public and cultural heritage sectors, the educational sector and academia, and media professionals. The requirements were collected through online surveys, questionnaires and interviews (see Chapter 6) and sought to understand how the end-users hoped to use Video Active. Partners in the project were interested in discovering the type of content that end-users would like to view, the features and services they would expect to have, and features that would make Video Active relevant and useful. As the project was predicated on the delivery of audiovisual content over the internet, it was also necessary to identify the typical technical framework in which target users operated and the current bandwidth considerations for streaming content.

Legal considerations for some of the content dictated that downloading was not an option. The laws relating to copyright are very uneven across Europe, with differing durations for certain aspects of copyright across music, performance and literary works. This has become a barrier to achieving truly 'open borders' in the online world. The project relied on streaming video to users, and this greatly influenced the user experience because it introduced limitations on how the content could be viewed. It was not possible, for example, to shuttle through the content (fast-forward/rewind) or to home in on a particular sequence, such as an interview. Although the project overcame this to some extent by using clips rather than whole programmes, this became a usability issue for media professionals because streaming content in their workflow could hinder efficiency and was counter-intuitive to their ways of working.

An attractive feature of Video Active is that it provides access to thousands of videos and images based around 34 topics that were chosen subsequently to the requirements stage. Much of the content had hardly been seen since its original broadcast. Material chosen for the project by the various EU archives and placed online needed supporting metadata so as to ensure 1) that it could be searched for and 2) that there was an element of description that both made it meaningful and, where needed, provided additional context. This element of adding context (additional background description) proved to be a valuable experience for the project. For users to appreciate a particular clip, for example, it is important that they understand why it has been chosen by the particular donating archive.

The implementation of a multilingual thesaurus and abstracts in English for all the content helped end-users to interact with the portal more effectively. Terms were translated from English into the different languages of the project partners – French, German, Dutch, Hungarian, Catalan, Danish, Swedish, Italian and Greek. Video Active also demonstrated that content placed online often needs a fresh set of descriptions and cataloguing, focused more on the general end-user rather than for a known (often in-house) set of users who can be familiar with terms and phrases not necessarily known to the public. It also helps if the supporting text is uniform and consistent in character. Considerable effort went into enhancing the overall usability of the materials by updating and standardizing the cataloguing wherever possible, or by adding completely new descriptions where none was present. ▨

Conclusions

The user-related issues addressed by Video Active are not unique, and projects aiming to place content online from disparate archives with a mixed level of cataloguing should consider the use of social tagging (for use of social media see Chapter 13). Work in this area has advanced in a number of projects. The Waisda Game, which was run in 2009 (see Waisda), encouraged the public to tag images, using a competitive approach in which users gained points. Over 2000 people participated and 340,000 tags were applied. The accuracy of the tagging was judged using a statistical approach, and results were first approved by mutual agreement of the gamers and mediated by an information professional. An account of the Waisda Game's success and benefits is provided in Oomen et al. (2010).

Video Active has been succeeded by a follow-on project, EUscreen, which has an enlarged group of content and technical partners. The lessons from Video Active have been carried forward to this project and EUscreen has itself become the audiovisual gateway for the EU portal Europeana.

References

Dobreva, M. et al. (2010) User and Functional Testing: final report, Europeana, http://bit.ly/JSxUQd.

Edmondson, R. (2004) Audio-visual Archiving: philosophy and principles, Paris: UNESCO, http://unesdoc.unesco.org/images/0013/001364/136477e.pdf.

EUscreen, www.euscreen.eu/.

MultilingualWeb, www.multilingualweb.eu/.

Oomen, J., Baltussen, L., Limonard, S., van Ees, A., Brinkerink, M., Aroyo, L., Vervaart, J., Asaf, K. and Gligorov, R. (2010) Emerging Practices in the Cultural Heritage Domain: social tagging of audio-visual heritage. In Proceedings of the

Web Science Conference 2010: Extending the Frontiers of Society On-Line, April 26–27th, 2010, Raleigh, NC, USA,
http://journal.webscience.org/337/2/websci10_submission_23.pdf.

Poole, N. (2010) The Cost of Digitising Europe's Cultural Heritage. A report for the Comité des Sages of the European Commission,
http://ec.europa.eu/information_society/activities/digital_libraries/doc/refgroup/annexes/digiti_report.pdf.

PrestoPRIME, www.prestoprime.org/.

Waisda? *Video Labeling Game: evaluation report,*
http://bvdt.tuxic.nl/index.php/waisda-video-labeling-game-evaluation-report/.

CHAPTER 23

A business-model perspective on end-users and open metadata

Harry Verwayen and Martijn Arnoldus

Introduction

The major European digital library (DL), Europeana, currently holds metadata on 19 million cultural heritage objects that allows for unprecedented resource discovery and links to the actual objects on the sites of 1500 content providers. Metadata in this context refers to the data that describe the key characteristics of the digital content; for instance the name of a work, its creator, date of creation and other background information. Metadata can either be quite simple or extensive and specialized. The cultural institutions that have provided data to Europeana have done so under the conditions specified in the Europeana Data Agreement, first issued in 2009. One of the conditions governing this metadata is that it can be reused for non-commercial purposes only.

Evidence from user research commissioned by Europeana shows that reuse of information consistently comes up as the number one priority for end-users. Work on open metadata is therefore high on the agenda for meeting user expectations and needs, since open metadata is a necessary condition for the reuse of information. To understand better how to combine the wide range of aspirations of Europeana, content providers and end-users, Europeana organized a high-level brainstorming workshop in July 2011; this chapter summarizes its findings.

We will first introduce the concept of a business model that helps to evaluate the potential for value generation in the case of digital cultural heritage. Then we examine in more detail the balance of risks and benefits for cultural heritage institutions. Finally, the chapter provides recommendations on how to overcome the risks.

Business model

In the context of this chapter a business model is understood to be 'the rationale of how an organization creates, delivers and captures value' (Osterwalder and Pigneur, 2010).

The theoretical framework of the business model consists of interrelated building blocks that depict the logic of how the organization intends to deliver value (see Figure 23.1):

1 *Customer segments*: an organization serves one or several customer segments.
2 *Value proposition*: an organization seeks to solve customer problems and satisfy customer needs with value propositions.
3 *Channels*: value propositions are delivered to customers through communication, distribution and sales channels.
4 *Customer relationships*: each value proposition offered to a client group establishes a relationship.
5 *Key activities*: the activities that are required to offer and deliver the value proposition.
6 *Key resources*: the resources that the organization needs to perform the said activities.
7 *Key partnerships*: the partnership network that the organization needs to establish in order to perform certain activities that it cannot efficiently perform by itself.

The building blocks on the Business Model Canvas are organized in a *front end*, the 'what' and the 'who', that defines the revenue-building capacity of the organization, and a *back end*, the 'how', that establishes the cost structure of the organization.

Supply and demand

From a business-model perspective, the aggregation of metadata by Europeana in the period 2008–11 can be seen as an effort driven by the supply side; it has resulted in a repository that currently holds over 19 million metadata records from over 1500 institutions. During this phase, most of the efforts of Europeana were focused on the 'back-end' of the business model: setting up a technical infrastructure for aggregation, standardizing metadata formats and fostering a network of participants. The data were made accessible primarily through the portal Europeana.eu,

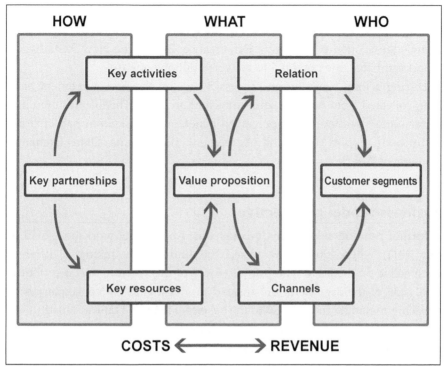

Figure 23.1 *Business Model Canvas (based on Osterwalder and Pigneur, 2010)*

which complies with the legal framework for non-commercial use. With the infrastructure now largely in place, the business-model focus of the organization is shifting to a more user-oriented, demand-driven business model. This requires a very different set of skills, organizational set-up, value propositions and legal framework. During user studies, the ability to reuse information found on Europeana consistently comes up as the number one priority for end-users (the last such report is IRN Research, 2011).

Open licences

This change in focus urges Europeana and participating institutions to review their Data Exchange Agreement (DEA). One of the most important changes in this new agreement is that it calls for a more open licence to govern the metadata held in Europeana's repository. The preferred licensing solution for the new agreement is Creative Commons Zero (CC0), a universal public domain dedication (Creative Commons, 2011). This change of licence is necessary for the development of Europeana's value proposition to users and, additionally, it is deemed critical and urgent for the establishment of a rich, culturally diverse society and a sustainable knowledge economy (The New Renaissance, 2011). The New Renaissance report estimates this potential to be worth billions of euros.

During a long consultation process, views on the new agreement have been collected from libraries, museums and archives. This has resulted in a better understanding of the perceived benefits and risks that participating institutions expect from the Agreement (Europeana Data Exchange Agreement, 2011).

Business-model perspective

A further refining step in this process was a high-level workshop, held in July 2011, where Europeana tested the findings by taking a different perspective on the issue. The primary focus of this consultation was not the legal side of the argument, but instead to investigate the consequences of releasing metadata under CC0 to the *business model* of a cultural institution. While some studies (Deckers et al., 2006; Hargreaves, 2011) and policy documents (EC, 2010; EC, 2011) address the potential macro-economic effects of data, relatively little is known about their effects at the institutional level; hence the main questions that we sought to answer were formulated as follows:

- What is the potential impact on a cultural institution's business model when it starts to release its metadata under CC0?
- What are the main potential benefits and risks of releasing metadata under CC0?
- What can cultural institutions do to overcome the risks and start reaping the benefits?

A typology of the role of metadata in current business models

When discussing the impact on business models of making metadata available openly, the first thing one needs to know is what role metadata plays in current business models. Although the actual (strategic) role of metadata may differ from one provider to another, we suggest that three basic types can be distinguished.

1. Metadata as a key activity – public mission

One of the core activities for museums, libraries and archives is usually to create and maintain descriptive metadata. This can therefore be seen as an integral element of the activities that are needed to operate a heritage institution. As such, it does not need to be related either directly or indirectly to the revenues that the institution generates. It is an integral part of the public mission of the institution.

On the Business Model Canvas this can be depicted as a 'back-end' activity: metadata is created by the organization and made available to the public. The client in this case is the government that funds the organization.

2. Metadata as a key resource – indirect revenue stream

Metadata can also be of *indirect* importance to the income generated by a cultural heritage institution. In this case metadata should be seen as a strategic resource that is important (if not vital) to realizing or maximizing revenues from other value propositions. For instance, metadata can be used as a promotional tool for the actual content (books, magazines). It is thus used for marketing and branding purposes, both of which are important to realizing sales of high-resolution images or to attracting more people to the institution or website. If metadata is used indirectly to generate revenue it is no longer just an activity in business-model terms. Instead it has become a key resource.

In this case metadata is used as a support mechanism for the value proposition, an advertisement for the object, and, if it is made available through the appropriate channels, this will lead to income from users (professionals who need high-resolution images, for example, or individual end-users who are activated to visit the library or museum to view the original object).

3. Metadata as a core value proposition – direct revenue stream

To some cultural heritage institutions (primarily national libraries), metadata is an important commodity that they can use to generate *direct* income. If metadata is sold or licensed to other heritage institutions – or perhaps even to (professional) users – it is part of the core value proposition of the institution. For example, the German National Library sells (tax-exempted) metadata to the library network in Germany. The National Library is aware that this activity will diminish over the years, when descriptive metadata can be found for free elsewhere. It is a matter of time, and requires a new perspective on the value of the services offered. Take as an example the British Library, which recently released 2.6 million records as Linked Open Data under a CC0 licence (see BL, 2011). The British Library also sells metadata directly, which, as it says, is 'worth millions'. It was able to take this step by creating a product/service differentiation that allowed for the open publication of its data in RDF format, while commercially exploiting its full MARC21 records.

Metadata in this model *is* the value proposition to a distinct (professional) user group that is willing to pay for the service. As one of the workshop participants stated, 'Most potential income should be seen as phantom income. But the fear of loss of this potential is very real.'

Risks and benefits of innovating the business model

These three types of metadata value provide different starting-points for metadata providers. It is hard to tell up front how deep the impact will be (either positively or negatively). In the following section we summarize the main potential benefits and risks; we will also provide some thoughts on how they balance out in each of the models outlined above.

Potential benefits and risks of open metadata

Ten major potential benefits emerged during consultation:

1 *Increasing relevance*: open metadata can be used in places where online users congregate (including social networks), helping providers to maintain their relevance in today's digital society.
2 *Increasing channels to end-users*: providers' releasing data as open metadata increases the opportunities that users have to see their data and content.
3 *Data enrichment*: open metadata can be enriched by Europeana and other parties and can then be returned to the data provider. Opening the metadata will increase the possibility of linking that data and the heritage content it represents with other related sources/collections.
4 *Brand value (prestige, authenticity, innovation)*: releasing data openly demonstrates that the provider is working in the innovation vanguard and is actively stimulating digital research.
5 *Specific funding opportunities*: releasing metadata openly will potentially

give providers access to national and/or European funding (Europe and most national governments are actively promoting open metadata).

6 *Discoverability*: the increased use and visibility of data drives traffic to the provider's website.

7 *New customers*: releasing data openly offers new ways to interact with and relate to your customers.

8 *Public mission*: releasing metadata openly aligns the provider with the strategic public mission of allowing the widest possible access to cultural heritage.

9 *Building expertise*: releasing metadata openly will strengthen the institution's expertise in this area, which will become a marketable commodity.

10 *Desired spill-over effects*: institutions and creative industries will be able to create new businesses, which will strengthen the knowledge economy.

The potential risks of open metadata could be summarized as follows:

1 *Loss of quality*: the high-quality metadata provided will be divorced from the original trusted source and corrupted by third parties.

2 *Loss of control*: institutions will no longer be able to control the metadata if anyone can reuse or distribute it.

3 *Loss of unity*: metadata will become scattered across the digital universe when it should be (contextually) kept together.

4 *Loss of brand value*: by releasing data openly the institution risks being associated with reusers with whom it does not want to be associated.

5 *Loss of attribution*: by releasing data under an open licence institutions will not be credited as the sources/owners of the metadata.

6 *Loss of income*: institutions are afraid that they will not be able to replace current revenues from metadata with other sources of income.

7 *Loss of potential income*: in future, institutions may think of a way to make money from the metadata; if they release it openly now, someone else may do this.

8 *Unwanted spill-over effects*: institutions find it unfair that others should be able to make money with the metadata that they provide.

9 *Losing customers*: if data are openly available customers will go elsewhere to get the information they are looking for.

10 *Privacy*: there are privacy restrictions on the use of certain data.

Conclusions

As one of the professionals observed, the single most important risk that cultural heritage institutions run is to miss out on the digital transition that is reshaping our modern Western society.

....

Case study 23.1: Get rid of the yellow Kitchen Maid

....

The Milkmaid, one of Johannes Vermeer's famous genre pieces, depicts an intensely intimate scene of a woman quietly pouring milk into a bowl. During a survey the Rijksmuseum found out that there were over 10,000 variations to be found on the internet, mostly bad, yellowish reproductions (see Milkmaid Vermeer).

> People simply didn't believe the postcards in the museum shop were showing the original painting. This was the trigger for us to put high-resolution images of the original work with open metadata on the web ourselves. Opening up our data is our best defence against the 'yellow Kitchen Maid'.
>
> (Europeana business model workshop participant, July 2011)

We suggest that three specific issues need to be addressed:

1 *Spill-over effects*: opening up data should be seen (again) as an important part of the *raison d'être* of our public cultural sector. Instead of measuring success by the amount of commercial revenue institutions are able to secure from the market, new metrics should be developed that measure the amount of business developed (spill-over) based on data made openly available to the creative industries. This requires a change on a policy level.

2 *Loss of attribution*: heritage institutions are the gatekeepers of the quality of our collective memory, therefore a strong connection between the object and its source is felt to be desirable. There is a fear that opening up metadata will result in a loss of attribution to the memory institution, which in turn will dilute the value of the object for end-users. Investigations need to be made on a technical, legal and user level to safeguard the level of integrity of the data.

3 *Loss of potential income*: it has been established that a very limited number of institutions currently earn a significant income by selling metadata. It has been argued that the loss of this income can be averted by product

differentiation: data can be made available openly in RDF format so that it becomes suitable Linked Open Data, while full MARC21 records can still be marketed under commercial terms. A larger issue is the fear of losing the *opportunity* to sell data in the future, when data is openly available for everyone to use. This requires a change of mindset and the acknowledgement that the reality of the web in the 21st century is that we are all invited to create new, commercial services based on open data.

There is a strong conviction among heritage professionals that the benefits of open sharing and open distribution will outweigh the risks. In most cases the advantages of increased visibility and relevance will be reaped in the short term. In other cases, for example where there is a risk of loss of income, the advantages will come in the longer run and short-term fixes will have to be found. All of this requires a collective change of mindset, courage to take some necessary risks and a resolute willingness to invest in the future of the society we serve and participate in. ■

Acknowledgement

A more detailed publication on the issues addressed in this chapter is H. Verwayen and M. Arnoldus (2011) *Get rid of the yellow Kitchen Maid: A business model perspective on open metadata*, Europeana White Paper 2.

References

BL (2011) Free data services, www.bl.uk/bibliographic/datafree.html.

Creative Commons (2011) *The Power of Open*, http://thepowerofopen.org/.

Deckers, M., Polman, F., te Velde, R. and de Vries, M. (2006) *Measuring European Public Sector Information Resources (MEPSIR report)*, http://bit.ly/qSryyi.

EC (2010) *Unlocking the Potential of Cultural and Creative Industries*, http://bit.ly/bgBcoG.

EC (2011) *Open Data and the Re-use of Public Sector Information*, report from the workshop Digital Agenda Assembly June 2011, http://bit.ly/gLslcA.

Europeana Data Exchange Agreement (2011).
http://version1.europeana.eu/web/europeana%20project/newagreement/.

Hargreaves, I. (2011) *Digital Opportunity: a review of intellectual property and growth*, www.ipo.gov.uk/ipreview-finalreport.pdf.

IRN Research (2011) *Europeana Online Visitor Survey*, http://bit.ly/nTgxf6.

Milkmaid Vermeer, Search results for images on Google, http://bit.ly/mRoOfp.

Osterwalder, A. and Pigneur, Y. (2010) *Business Model Generation,*
www.businessmodelgeneration.com/book.

The New Renaissance (2011) *The New Renaissance: report of the Comité des Sages.*
Reflection group on bringing Europe's cultural heritage online,
http://ec.europa.eu/information_society/activities/digital_libraries/doc/
refgroup/final_report_cds.pdf.

PART 5

Putting it all together

CHAPTER 24

And now ... to the brave real world

Milena Dobreva, Andy O'Dwyer and Pierluigi Feliciati

Introduction

After looking at all the methods and examples presented in this book, one could feel overwhelmed by the multiplicity of options available, and also by the plethora of questions raised and with no definitive guidance provided. Having more questions than answers is definitely one of the challenges in the domain of user studies, but to explore and work in a domain that allows for initiative and discovery is a great opportunity. Looking at ongoing research one might also get an impression of fragmentation – for example, because various types of users are studied in different situations without building a coherent picture. It is indeed inevitable that particular studies are done and will continue to be done looking at specific cases and trying to answer very clearly defined questions within a limited context. Unfortunately, the project-driven culture in which most of us work does not accommodate work with users, at best. We have seen many projects, for example, where the definition of user requirements is done at the same time as the system architecture is being developed and, instead of informing the system architecture, becomes an activity that could actually contradict the technological solutions selected by developers, or that could be seen as simply 'ticking the user consultation box'. We hope that this book will start to help in fostering a change towards greater coherence and comparability in future user studies!

This final chapter aims to help readers to decide what type of a study could be of best help in a particular situation.

Designing a study

The first question to ask is 'What stage is my project at, and how exactly might user studies be helpful?'. We believe that there are several stages to go through.

Stage 1: Determine the type of user involvement

The various roles that users can play at different development stages are summarized in the following sections.

Front-end involvement

Front-end involvement of users is used to identify typical user groups, their needs and expectations and accessibility issues. User studies aim to define in detail what user needs and expectations should be accommodated in the digital library (DL). In addition to information gathered by doing research on similar solutions and technological capabilities, this stage needs to build a clear picture of the target users. The key points that such studies address are:

- Who are the target users of the DL?
- What accessibility issues need to be tackled (what specific user requirements and devices need to be addressed)?
- What are the user needs of the target user groups? (this informs functional requirements)
- What are the expectations of the target groups? (this could help to inform non-functional requirements)
- What users outside of these groups are most likely to visit the DL?
- What metrics could be used to measure user satisfaction in subsequent evaluations?
- Which functionality is needed for the users?
- Who exactly needs it? Could different users be addressed in the same way?
- Why is it needed?

Normative evaluation

Normative evaluation is done at the development stage using a prototype (or the current version of the DL in development). It helps to identify what works and what does not. The aim is to check how comfortable users feel with the product and whether or not it is infallible. At this stage, user studies take the form of iterative circles of design and evaluation. Most typically, such evaluations will focus on usability, but also could be used to identify radical changes in the product/service. Usability testing can be done without end-user involvement; however, if it is possible to apply some of the methods that involve users this is a good reality check. The typical questions for this stage are:

- What is the general look and feel of the product/service?
- Is the intended functionality working properly, without errors; does it meet user expectations?
- Are there any technical restrictions on the use of the product/service that hinder accessibility?
- Are there any stumbling blocks for the users, and what are their causes?
- What do users like and dislike?
- What definitely needs to be changed in order to appeal better to users, and what is not essential?

Summative evaluation

The key question here is 'Where does our product/service sit within the wider context?'. The focus is the final output and how it accords to the expectations and requirements of target communities/organizational structures/the wider disciplinary domain. At this stage, user involvement may help to valorize the digital resource and to establish its reputation after it has already been launched. Note that quite often users can be more critical in evaluating a final product; during the development stages they accept more readily that some features are not what they expect.

- Are the users satisfied with the product/service?
- Can users perform their tasks and are they happy with the results?
- How does the product/service compare with other similar offerings?
- What definitely needs to be changed in a next version?
- Are there any disadvantaged users? If yes, what developments can help to increase the accessibility of the product/service – expansion to other devices, interface refinements, introduction of special features?

Stage 2: Choose a user study method (or a combination of methods)

Probably one of the most confusing aspects of user studies is that there is no clear allocation of types of studies to specific purposes and the same methods can be used in different stages of a DL development. Here we apply a very pragmatic approach, looking not at stages but, rather, at the questions the study is trying to answer.

Table 24.1 *Methods for answering specific research questions*

Question	Stage Method F–front end N–normative S–summative	Method
Who are the potential users of a DL?	F	A *web questionnaire* can be used to address a potentially large community of future users. Their responses can be helpful in defining typical users. Depending on the available knowledge about these groups of users, a next step could be to use the *personas* method.
What are the needs and/or expectations of users of a DL that is still not developed?	F	*Focus groups* can help to gather ideas. *Ethnographic study* can help to identify current practices and gaps.
What accessibility issues need to be taken into account?	F	Best done through *expert evaluation*.
What makes the DL idea attractive to users?	F	*Focus groups* and *in-depth interviews* can help to gather ideas and inspiring statements.
How large is the potential user base for the DL?	F	To gather numerical data, one would rely on market research and existing data for *deep log analysis* of similar resources. For distribution across a particular community, web or traditional *questionnaires* are most suitable.
How to evaluate the usability of an existing DL?	N, S	This can be achieved through an *expert group study*. Direct user involvement can be accomplished through *focus groups* and *eye tracking*.
Is the design idea attractive to users?	F, N	*Focus groups* and *in-depth interviews* can help to identify likes and dislikes.

Table 24.1 *Methods for answering specific research questions (continued)*

Question	Stage Method F–front end N–normative S–summative	Method
How can we identify possible steps for extending the user community of an existing DL?	N, S	A *web questionnaire* and *deep log analysis* can help to build a picture of the current user community. For fine-tuning the measures that could be used to expand the user base, *expert evaluation* can be helpful. This may be connected to finding possible reuse scenarios.
What are the stumbling blocks for the users of an existing DL?	N, S	Best suited are methods with direct user involvement (*focus groups* or studies involving *eye tracking*); *deep log analysis* could also be of help in tracing how many times a user tries to execute a search, or what happens before a user leaves the resource.
How to improve the interface of a DL?	N, S	Use *eye tracking* to see what the individual users are doing and how, and use *deep log analysis* to define typical patterns of actions within the digital resource.
How does the DL compare with other similar DLs?	S	Comparison in this domain is still difficult because studies are too different; *expert evaluation* seems to be the best option here.

We will not comment on advantages and disadvantages of different methods, since these emerge from the chapters addressing specific case studies. However, we hope that the top excuses for not doing user studies (lack of time, resources, specialized facilities and knowledge of how to interpret the results) will gradually fade away.

Stage 3: Develop a methodology

This is the stage where necessary study protocols will be developed. It is very essential at this point to make sure that:

- various texts and questions are formulated in a non-ambiguous and unbiased manner
- there is a sufficient amount of background information
- unnecessary repetition is avoided
- there is clarity about the purpose of each of the questions
- it is clear what data will be gathered and how they will be processed.

It is a good idea to do a 'dry run' or to make a pilot study if you will be addressing a huge user community – this always helps in fine-tuning the design of the study.

Stage 4: Clear any ethical procedures

Different countries have various ethical regulations on studies involving human participants. Make sure that you are familiar with any regulations that would require preliminary approval of the study protocols, and also prepare necessary consent forms for participants (or the parents of children taking part in a study, for example).

Stage 5: Brief your staff

It is essential that studies are done in a coherent manner. It is essential that everyone involved in a study that has direct user involvement should follow a coherent procedure and try to establish the same depth of contribution by participants. There has been a trend in recent years of doing more international studies: assuring the comparability of results across different cultural settings might be a serious challenge!

Stage 6: Conduct the study

This book has presented methods and case studies in detail.

Stage 7: Document the study outcomes

This stage is sometimes neglected. User studies are done and, in ideal cases, they help with some of the decision making, but the fast pace of project work means that the rationale and outcomes are not always well documented. However, good documentation is essential and, since DLs are very often developed in stages, it is essential to record clear guidance as to why certain choices were made. Another role of documentation is to provide evidence that the methodology was sound and procedures were followed thoroughly.

Last but not least, we would like to encourage readers who do user studies to share their findings – and to identify clearly to which of the three complementary domains – information behaviour research, user-centric studies and evaluation of DLs – their work contributes most.

The best teacher in this domain is the real world of experience, and we hope you will have a great time and gain many insights from your future work.

Good luck!
Milena, Andy and Pierluigi

Index